PROJECT EMILY
THOR IRBM AND THE RAF

PROJECT EMILY
THOR IRBM AND THE RAF

JOHN BOYES

The History Press

To Sylvia

First published 2008

The History Press
The Mill, Brimscombe Port,
Stroud, Gloucestershire, GL5 2QG
www.thehistorypress.co.uk

Reprinted 2009 , 2013

© John Boyes, 2008

The right of John Boyes to be identified as the Author
of this work has been asserted in accordance with the
Copyrights, Designs and Patents Act 1988.

All rights reserved. No part of this book may be reprinted
or reproduced or utilised in any form or by any electronic,
mechanical or other means, now known or hereafter invented,
including photocopying and recording, or in any information
storage or retrieval system, without the permission in writing
from the Publishers.

British Library Cataloguing in Publication Data.
A catalogue record for this book is available from the British Library.

ISBN 978 0 7524 4611 0

Typesetting and origination by The History Press
Printed and bound in Great Britain

CONTENTS

Foreword	6
Acknowledgements	7
Introduction	8
Glossary of Terms	9
Missiles	12
The Birth of Ballistic Missiles	13
Early Disappointments and Successes	39
The Thor Agreement – Finding the Bases	45
Building The Infrastructure	73
The First Thor Arrives	87
Training and Squadron Operations	99
The Cuban Crisis and the End of Project Emily	129
Appendix 1	146
Appendix 2	146
Appendix 3	148
Appendix 4	149
Appendix 5	150
Appendix 6	150
Appendix 7	152
Appendix 8	153
Appendix 9	155
Bibliography	157
Index	158

FOREWORD

Marshal of the Royal Air Force
Sir Michael Beetham GCB CBE DFC AFC

Thor was the first venture by the Royal Air Force into the IRBM sphere of operations. At the time, the late 1950s, Bomber Command was responsible for Britain's strategic nuclear deterrent, independent but working closely with Strategic Air Command of the United States.

Our deterrent centred around the V-Bomber Force, highly efficient and kept at a high state of readiness. The American deterrent centred on the B-47 and B-52 bombers of Strategic Air Command, but they saw, as Britain did, that Soviet air defences were increasing in capability and that more might be required in the future to keep the Western deterrent fully effective. The Cold War was at its height and the Soviets, using German expertise from the Second World War, were making more major advances in rocketry.

Not to be outdone, the Americans poured enormous resources into the development of an ICBM programme to enable them to be secure, in their eyes, within 'Fortress America'. At the same time they went ahead with a less ambitious and quicker development of IRBMs for deployment foward in Europe within NATO. These missiles would have the advantage of being nearer to the Soviet Union and thus quicker to react to a threat. Thus was born the Thor Programme. The general public knew little about the plans for Thor deployment. The British Government had enough on their hands dealing with CND and other factions protesting against nuclear weapons and, to aggravate the situation in the public mind, Thor had American nuclear warheads, although the British insisted on maintaining control and a veto over their use. Thus the Government, whilst unable to conceal the deployment within the UK, certainly gave Thor minimum publicity.

Thor was in service with the RAF for five years from the late 1950s. John Boyes has done a great service in writing this book, detailing the protracted negotiations over deployment and control and the many problems of the development programme which, in their usual way, the Americans tackled energetically and successfully. In service with the RAF, Thor made a significant contribution to our strategic nuclear deterrent, nowhere more so than during the Cuban Missile Crisis of October 1962 where it maintained a very high rate of readiness and reliability. Thor fulfilled an important and unique role in RAF history and at a crucial period in the Cold War. The story needed to be told, and this John Boyes has done, covering comprehensively all aspects in great detail.

ACKNOWLEDGEMENTS

There are very many people who deserve recognition for the help they have given me in writing this history of the RAF's only foray into the world of surface-launched ballistic missiles. Many are credited in the text for their contributions, but there are others who are not quoted yet have nevertheless given me much assistance. They are: Wayne Cocroft (English Heritage), Dr Jack Dunham, Dr Jack Neufeld, Roy Dommett, Dave Wright, Nicholas Hill, Roger Tutt (for photographic assistance), Jim Wilson, former LCOs Doug Browne, Peter Rogers and Peter Vangucci, Dick Parker, Ted Gragg, John Atkison, Col. (Retd) Nick Gaynos, Hal Leonard, Col. (Retd) Orville Doughty, Roger Bradshaw, Col. (Retd) Charlie Simpson (Association of Air Force Missileers), Torri Ingalsbe and Kristopher Levasseur (Public Affairs, RAF Lakenheath), Jeff Goodwin (RAF Hemswell Association), Roy Clarke and Roy Tebbutt (Carpetbaggers Museum at RAF Harrington), Brett Stolle (National Museum of the United States Air Force), Amy Rigg and Jack Fulford at Tempus, and the many helpful staff at The National Archives, The Royal Air Force Museum at Hendon and Cosford and English Heritage at Swindon, Captains Nick Serle and Mark Graham (1KORBR), Brynley Heaven, Linda Ball (Feltwell Golf Club), Clive Brown, Mrs Eileen Dorr, R.P. Treadgold, Vernita Laws and Fran Thomas. My particular thanks go to Jeff Jefford for his help and guidance, and for helping me through the complexities of RAF records and terminology. If I have omitted anyone, please accept my apologies. Responsibility for any errors of fact or interpretation is, of course, entirely mine. I would welcome any comments by email at: Thor64IRBM@aol.com

John Boyes
West Wickham, September 2009

INTRODUCTION

I first saw a Thor site during an Easter holiday break with my family in 1959. Fascinated by all things aeronautical, my knowledge reinforced by *RAF Flying Review* (the arrival of which was a keenly anticipated highlight of every month!), I was well aware of what we were driving past. The site was close to the main road and one of the missiles was erect on its launch emplacement. Entreaties to stop to take a photograph with my Kodak Brownie 127, were, no doubt wisely, overruled by my father. However, later on in the day we passed a more distant site and I sneaked a quick photograph which showed little more than a few elements of the site on the far horizon but could nonetheless be identified as a Thor location.

My interest was rekindled in the mid-1990s when my job took me to the areas of the country where Thor had been located. I found some remains, mainly blast walls but a few other remains as well. Of other sites there was nothing left to indicate that at one time ballistic missiles trained on the Soviet Union were stationed there. Most sites are on private land and this should be borne in mind should any 'site visits' be planned. But apart from two chapters in Humphrey Wynn's book on *RAF Nuclear Deterrent Forces*, there seemed to be little authoritative history published on Thor and its period in RAF service.

Under the unassuming codename, Project Emily, the operation to deploy Thor began in March 1958. It generated a wide range of feelings, both political and military. Even within the operational RAF, knowledge of Thor was often very limited. However, along with the Jupiter IRBMs stationed in Italy and Turkey, these missiles were the first strategic ballistic missiles aimed at targets on the other side of the Iron Curtain. It was, of course, the Jupiters based in Turkey under the codename IBRAHIM II (supposedly because the word contained the letters IRBM) rather than the Thors that secretly defused the Cuban Missile Crisis. In reality, the Jupiters were of little or no military value and the integrity of the command and control of the Turkish missiles was a major concern to the Americans, a concern which reached its height during the crisis. The Soviet Union's military planners had been significantly upset by the placing of the Jupiters in Turkey, which gave them the unwelcome and unwanted requirement to provide countermeasures for a possible missile attack through their 'back door'. Was it entirely surprising, therefore, that the Soviets retaliated by placing missiles in Cuba? There was a clear parallel here that the Americans seemed unable or unwilling to accept. Nonetheless, the Thors were on full readiness and were used 'politically' by Macmillan as a further way of defusing the slippage towards real conflict. For this fact alone, they need to be remembered.

GLOSSARY OF TERMS

ABMA	Army Ballistic Missile Agency
ACAS	Assistant Chief of the Air Staff
AD	Air Division
ADD	Air Defence Division
AEC	Atomic Energy Commission
AFB	Air Force Base (USAF)
AFBMC	Air Force Ballistic Missile Centre
AFBMD	Air Force Ballistic Missile Division
AFETR	Air Force Eastern Test Range (Patrick AFB)
AFWTR	Air Force Western Test Range (Vandenberg AFB)
ALBM	Air Launched Ballistic Missile
ALERT CONDITION	Level of UK preparedness for war
AMR	Atlantic Missile Range
AMSO	Air Member for Supply and Organisation
APU	Auxiliary Power Unit
ARDC	Air Research and Development Command
AUW	All Up Weight
CAS	Chief of the Air Staff
CEA	Control Electronic Assembly
CEP	Circular Error Probable
CND	Campaign for Nuclear Disarmament
CTL	Combat Training Launch
DAC	Douglas Aircraft Company
DCAS	Deputy Chief of the Air Staff
DEFCON	Defense Condition (level of US preparedness for war)
EPPO	Electrical Power Production Operator

FDR	Functional Demonstration of Reliability
GSA	Guidance Systems Analyst
GSE	Ground Support Equipment
ICBM	Intercontinental Ballistic Missile
IOC	Initial Operational Configuration
IRBM	Intermediate Range Ballistic Missile
IWST	Integrated Weapons System Training
JAN-BMC	Joint Army Navy Ballistic Missile Committee
LASL	Los Alamos Scientific Laboratory
LCA	Launch Control Area
LCCO	Launch Control Console Operator
LCO	Launch Control Officer
LCT	Launch Control Trailer
LE	Launch Emplacement
LMCO	Launch Monitor Console Operator
LN	Liquid Nitrogen
LOX	Liquid Oxygen
MATS	Military Air Transport Service
MDE	Maintenance Dry Exercise
MOD	Ministry of Defence
MRBM	Medium Range Ballistic Missile
MSAT	Missile System Analyst Technician
MSC	Missile Servicing Chief
MT	Motor Transport
MT	Megaton
NSC	National Security Council
nm	Nautical Miles
OC	Officer Commanding
ORB	Operations Record Book
ORBAT	Order of Battle (the disposition and nature of friendly and enemy forces)
OSD-BMC	Office of the Secretary for Defense Ballistic Missile Committee
POL	Petrol, Oil, Lubricants
PPO	Unofficial abbreviation of EPPO
PTS	Propellant Transfer System

RIM	Receipt, Inspection and Maintenance (Building)
RP-1	Rocket Propellant (Fuel)
RSO	Range Safety Officer
S & I	Surveillance and Inspection (Building)
SAC	Strategic Air Command
SAC MIKE	Strategic Air Command (Missile Division)
SACEUR	Supreme Allied Commander Europe
SAGW	Surface-to-Air Guided Weapon
SAM	Surface-to-Air Missile
SLBM	Submarine Launched Ballistic Missile
sm	Statute Miles
SM	Strategic Missile
SMW	Strategic Missile Wing
SOP	Standard Operating Procedure
SoS(A)	Secretary of State for Air
SPOG	Special Projectile Operations Group
SSA	Special Storage Area
SSQ	Station Sick Quarters
SSM	Surface-to-Surface Missile
STL	Space Technology Laboratory Inc.
TAC	Tactical Air Command
TEW	Thor Electrical Worker
UOC	Ultimate Operational Configuration
USAF	United States Air Force
USAFE	United States Air Force in Europe
VCAS	Vice Chief of the Air Staff
WADC	Wright Air Development Center
WDD	Western Development Division (later BMD)

MISSILES

ATLAS	First US ICBM
BLOODHOUND	UK SAGW operated by RAF Fighter Command to defend the V-Force and the Thor sites
BLUE STREAK	Proposed silo-launched UK MRBM. Cancelled in 1960
JUPITER	IRBM originally developed by the US Army. Very similar to Thor
MINUTEMAN	Third US ICBM (silo-launched, solid fuel)
SKYBOLT	US air-launched ballistic missile. Ordered for the RAF but subsequently cancelled by the US
TITAN	Second US ICBM (silo-launched)

Our task ... is to hold our 'Thor' missiles in immediate readiness – by day or night – throughout the year. These weapons are the first of a new generation; they take their place beside those which the Royal Air Force has already proved. Their very novelty offers a challenge which our Service gladly accepts. At the same time we should remember the responsibility which has been entrusted to us to operate the latest and most powerful part of the deterrent force. I ask you to do your best.

(The Commanding Officer's foreword in the 'Feltwell Information' booklet issued to RAF personnel stationed at RAF Feltwell.)

CHAPTER ONE
THE BIRTH OF THE BALLISTIC MISSILE

At 7.28a.m. on 8 September 1944, a German Army V-2[1] missile was launched from the sanctuary of a mobile site in the Ardennes Forest, near to St Vith. Its target was Paris. Despite a successful lift-off, the missile never reached its target, apparently disintegrating on re-entering the atmosphere. This was not an unknown problem, one which was never fully resolved during the war. However, a second missile, launched some three hours later, landed in the Parisian suburb of Maisons-Alfort killing or injuring around thirty people. Without any warning, the age of the ballistic missile had arrived. That evening the first V-2 to reach London landed on Staveley Road in Chiswick.[2] Again, there was to be no warning of the missile's arrival and there were no countermeasures against it, its supersonic arrival speed assured its invulnerability. Even if the mobile launch points could be identified, the launch crews would have already moved onto another launch site by the time any aircraft arrived in retaliation.

The V-2 Programme was masterminded by Army General Walter R. Dornberger with the technical side led by his able protégé, Wernher von Braun. The V-2 was a complex and temperamental weapon. It had taken five years to develop to operational status and was still prone to launch failures. The first two attempts at an operational launch both ended up with the missiles failing to leave the launch pad because insufficient thrust was developed when the rocket motor was ignited. The V-2 carried a relatively meagre 1,650lb warhead and, in simple terms, it did not do well in a basic 'bangs for bucks' evaluation, although the effect of the relatively small warhead was magnified by the fact that it arrived on its target at supersonic speed. In a final analysis, the main effect of the weapon proved to be psychological rather than military. The V-2 was unreliable, erratic and it could not be produced in sufficient quantities to provide a sustained bombardment. The original plan to launch the V-2s from secure bunkers in the Pas-de-Calais and the Cherbourg peninsula had fallen prey firstly to the Allied bombing offensive, and secondly to the advancing Allied Armies following D-Day. Hence, the decision was taken to launch from mobile sites in the hope that these would outwit the reconnaissance efforts of the Allied 2nd Tactical Air Force. The decision was completely vindicated as no V-2 launch site was ever discovered with the launch crews or missile *in situ*. In his testimony to the US Senate on

17 December 1957, von Braun confirmed that 'not a single V-2 was ever lost at a mobile launching site – and this despite the fact there was a 30-to-1 air superiority by the United States Air Force, along, of course, with the Royal Air Force, in that area'. However, von Braun had not originally been a supporter of mobility. Along with his technical associates he was 'utterly sceptical that the V-2 was sufficiently advanced for mobile deployment'.[3]

The V-2 had been developed at the remote research facility at Peenemünde on the Baltic Coast. Peenemünde was shared by the German Army and the Luftwaffe.[4] Whilst the Army was developing its V-2 rocket, the Luftwaffe was concentrating on a much more simple pilotless flying bomb, the Fiesler Fi-103, which was to become the V-1. However, on the night of 17–18 August 1943, 597 Lancasters, Stirlings and Halifaxes of RAF Bomber Command attacked the location, their targets being marked for them by sixty-five Pathfinder aircraft. Forty aircraft failed to return but considerable damage was inflicted.[5] It was clear that Peenemünde was too vulnerable and so production of the missiles was moved to a near invulnerable underground factory at Nordhausen, deep inside the Harz Mountains in Southern Germany.[6] Here a plentiful supply of slave labour was provided from the nearby Dora-Mittelbau concentration camp. Sixty thousand workers brought the missiles to mass production. It is estimated that a third of their number died in the process, victims of the appalling conditions within the underground factory.

The advance of the Allied Armies pushed the launch sites further towards the German border, but it was not until 27 March 1945 that the retreating Germans launched the last of 1,115 V-2s against London, although less than half that number actually fell on the city. Allied commanders had been greatly concerned at the possibility of the missiles being used against the Dutch and Belgian ports, which were so vital to the logistic train of the advancing armies. Although it is widely believed that the majority of V-2s were directed at London, more in fact landed on Antwerp than on the British capital. Very significant resources and *matériel* which could otherwise have been used directly in prosecuting the war effort had to be diverted to seeking out and attacking whatever evidence of the missiles could be found.

As the Allied Armies advanced from east and west on a ruptured and disintegrating Germany, where only sporadic but still fanatically loyal elements of the SS seemed to hold any control, they sought not only victory but also the victor's spoils of war. German industrial capability was carefully examined, but the main areas of interest were the aeronautical industries and the rocket research centres. Many post-war aircraft designs in both the West and the Soviet Union used design features which had originated on the drawing boards of Junkers, Heinkel, Messerschmitt, Horten and others. But rockets were, if anything, even more important. The legacy of Peenemünde in both post-war East and West can be found to this day in every significant civilian launch vehicle or ballistic missile.

Combat Command B of the 3rd US Armored Division entered Nordhausen on 11 April 1945 and found to their amazement that the plant was still largely intact. The whole area was to fall into the Soviet sector of influence on 1 June, so time was short. However, when the Soviets occupied the area and entered the underground complex, they discovered, as Colonel Yuri A. Pobedonostsev later admitted, that the Americans had 'cleaned the place out'.[7] The Soviets fared better in Peenemünde, which had fallen into their hands on 6 May 1945 when the 2nd White Russian Army, commanded by General Konstantin Rokossovskii, reached the peninsular. Two hundred rocket scientists were transported to the Soviet Union. Their experience was to be somewhat different to those who sought their future in the West.

The Birth of the Ballistic Missile

Following Hitler's suicide on 30 April 1945, Dornberger and von Braun, displaying perhaps a certain prescience, had determined to make contact with the American forces in the area. They therefore sent von Braun's English-speaking brother, Magnus, to find the advancing US 7th Army. He located the US 44th Infantry Division at the small Austrian town of Reutte, which nestled at the foot of the Adolf Hitler Pass, and surrendered to them. Other members of the rocket team willing to cast their lot with the Americans followed soon afterwards. The whole group was taken to Garmisch-Partenkirchen for interrogation. Deprived of their files, many of the statements made appeared to conflict, but gradually a complete picture emerged of the development of the A-4 (V-2) as well as other rockets, notably the A-9/A-10 two-stage intercontinental rocket, designed to be used against New York.[8] During his interrogation, von Braun stated that he considered 'the A-4 rocket developed by us as an intermediate solution conditioned by this war, a solution which still has certain inherent shortcomings and which compares with the future possibilities of the art in about the same way as a bomber plane of the last war compares with a modern bomber'.

The highly secret program to exploit the V-2 knowledge, inaugurated on 19 July 1945, was known as Operation Overcast, later known as Operation Paperclip. It was established under the Chief Military Intelligence Service on an island in Boston Harbor at a camp known as Fort Standish. A certain degree of discretion had to be exercised as the British, who had suffered the effects of the V-2 bombardment which had taken over 2,750 lives and seriously injured a further 6,000, were more disposed to classing the rocket personnel as war criminals rather than valuable war booty. The existence and horrors of the Dora-Mittelbau and Nordhausen concentration camps were conveniently suppressed,[9] as was von Braun's membership of the NSDAP from 1937 and his subsequent commission in the SS.[10] However, rocket development was now a vital area of research, particularly since the Soviets had their own interest in the subject through their own captured rockets and engineers. The German scientists were seen as vital to America's interests in this field but both Dornberger and von Braun were still under interrogation in Great Britain. Von Braun was to travel onwards to the United States, but Dornberger was held until 1947 until the possibility of war crime proceedings was dropped.

Neither Great Britain, the United States, nor the Soviet Union had any serious experience of missile technology, although in the US the rocket scientist Dr Robert H. Goddard had tried unsuccessfully to interest the Army in developing rockets. Whilst a considerable fund of knowledge about A-4 logistics had been assembled, little was known about the actual practical aspects of preparing and launching the rockets in the field. To enhance the overall security of the A-4 programme, full technical manuals for the troops undertaking the actual firing of the rockets had never been prepared. Each soldier knew only his particular part of the operation so that, if captured, little of the overall scenario could be determined. The Allied Air Defence Division (ADD) was under the command of a former Royal Engineer, Major General Alexander Morris Cameron. It was his Personal Aide, Junior Commander Joan C.C. Bernard ATS, who suggested that the captured rocket troops together with some of the A-4s taken from Nordhausen be used to undertake launches of the rocket, so that the complex launch procedures could be fully documented and the technical problems analysed. The British section of the ADD became the Special Projectile Operations Group (SPOG) and, still under Cameron's command, was given responsibility for the project which was codenamed Operation Backfire. Colonel W.S.J. Carter, Assistant

Chief of the ADD, was appointed Colonel, General Staff, SPOG, and was given special responsibility for the project.

The site chosen for the test firings was the Krupps naval artillery range at Altenwalde near to Cuxhaven. Facilities existed there to track projectiles fired out to sea. Some 2,000 Royal Canadian Army sappers constructed a launch site complex with a 300ft-long assembly shed, roads, a concrete launch bunker and a vertical inspection building, which was constructed from Bailey bridge components. Both Dornberger and von Braun were brought to Cuxhaven and, although not taken to the launch site, were nevertheless co-operative along with a specialist German team in advising on aspects of the launch procedures and potential associated hazards.[11] A successful launch took place on 4 October 1945.[12] Eventually, only eight missiles could be assembled from the components available. The Germans had determined there was little need for a comprehensive inventory of spares for missiles that essentially went straight from factory to launch pad. All eight missiles were, however, launched and in January 1947 a five-volume technical manual and an accompanying film on all aspects of A-4 handling and launching had been completed and lodged with the War Office. It was to be quite some time before the UK was again to launch a missile of any size.

With von Braun now in the United States, an 'advance guard' of 118[13] German rocket scientists was taken to El Paso in Texas to start work on the US Army's nascent rocket programme. Their main function was to advise the Army and General Electric (GE), who had been appointed supporting contractor for the programme, about the launch procedures for the rockets. Salvaged components for about 100 A-4s had been stored at Las Cruces, New Mexico, while the open desert of the White Sands Proving Ground had been chosen as the main test area, with the overall headquarters for the programme at Fort Bliss, Texas, designated the Ordnance Research and Development Division, Sub-Office (Rocket). Von Braun now awaited the arrival of the rest of the German team once they had been paid off from Operation Backfire. Although the Americans were entitled to full details of the Backfire reports, their series of A-4 test launches, which started on 16 April 1946 after a static test firing on 14 March, initially at least, merely duplicated what the British programme had already achieved. The Americans, perhaps a little disingenuously, claimed that they had learnt little from the earlier project, stating that the major purpose of their programme was high altitude research.[14] The lack of components which had proved to be a limiting factor for Operation Backfire similarly caused problems for the Americans. Their rockets were now many months old and required a significant amount of maintenance. The Germans were soon to discover that the US Army appeared to have only limited funds available and even the most basic equipment seemed to be lacking. They passed the time with further theoretical studies of the rockets' potential or, by way of interviews, confirmed what they had already achieved and its ongoing significance.

In the same way that the German Army had seen the missile as a natural extension to its artillery capability, the US Army was to use this argument to claim the authority to operate any missile system launched from the land. However, the newly formed US Air Force was to claim that the missile was a derivative of the aircraft and should therefore come under their control. Neither supposition was really completely true, although of course the missile did reflect elements of both arguments. If an atomic warhead could be mated with a missile, the Army also saw this as a way of wresting from the Air Force its monopoly on delivery of atomic weapons, although this capability was, from a technical point of view, still some time away.[15] Thus the work of von Braun and his team, whilst partly exploratory, could also have a practical side in extending the Army's firepower. Increasingly, however, the other services were taking an interest in what the Army was doing and the resulting, if inevitable, inter-service rivalry underscored by the emotive question of 'roles and missions' was to delay the development of a properly organised US missile programme for some years to come.[16]

As well as the V-2s, the US Army had also experimented with JB-2 Loons (LTV-A-1), a US-built copy of the V-1. The US Navy had done likewise and to further its interest in missiles it had obtained two of the A-4s to assess the practicality of launching the missile from a warship. The aircraft carrier USS *Midway* (CVB 41) was chosen and on 6 September 1947 the missile was launched from the deck.[17] Whilst the concept could have had a valid use in extending the stand-off range of naval gunnery, and the Navy did not want to lose out in adopting this new technology, concerns remained about the practical difficulties of handling volatile liquid fuels on a pitching warship, and although the Navy by no means gave up its interest in missiles, it was not until the development of reliable solid fuels that missiles were willingly accepted onboard.

During the Second World War sixteen US Army Air Forces had been deployed to the various theatres of war. The strategic significance of the bombing campaign had led to them becoming increasingly autonomous and in recognition of this Strategic Air Command (SAC) was formed on 21 March 1946 under the command of General George C. Kenney. The role of the air arm in future warfare was further consolidated with the formation of a separated US Air Force on 18 September 1947. The Air Force, however, found itself presented with a dichotomy. On the one hand, it already had, with its bombers, the sole capability to deliver the atom bomb, the most awesome weapon known to man, whilst on the other hand it recognised the significance of the missile and did not intend to let either the Army or the Navy steal a lead in the development of the new technology. In the absence of any coordinated approach between the three services (or 'three and a half' if the Marines were included) towards the development of missiles, the assumption was made that the 'first past the finishing post' would earn the right to become the custodians of these weapons. Ideally, from an Air Force point of view, airborne capability and missiles should be combined, but the weight of the atom bomb precluded, at least for the time being, the thoughts of using missiles as carriers of these weapons or the even more awesome weapon then being developed – the thermonuclear bomb. In October 1948 the charismatic General Curtis E. LeMay was appointed head of SAC.[18] LeMay transformed SAC, which had been forged out of a collection of left-overs from the Second World War, into the world's most powerful military 'force in being', which successfully projected the post-war nuclear threat with its squadrons of Boeing B-47 Stratojets, Convair B-36 Peacemakers and later the supersonic B-58 Hustlers and the awesome Boeing B-52 Stratofortress long-range bombers. Atomic bombs, and there were still not too many of them, were too large to be carried by anything but manned bombers. The implosion weapons were easier to produce than the gun-type but were bigger and heavier. Furthermore, the US Atomic Energy Commission had not proved particularly cooperative in discussions about warheads for ballistic missile use. SAC and its bomber squadrons had unique supremacy – at least for the time being.

By early 1950, von Braun's contribution to the White Sands launches was largely complete – although the last of the sixty-four missiles that could be assembled from the salvaged components was not launched until 19 September 1952.[19] The A-4 design had been taken to the limits of its capability and the Army was now keen to use the Germans' talents on a new generation of rockets. Beginning on 15 April 1950, von Braun and around 130 other German scientists were transferred to the Ordnance Guided Missile Center which had been set up at the Redstone Arsenal in Huntsville, Alabama, under the command of Major James P. Hamill. Hamill had organised the removal of the A-4s from Nordhausen and had already been involved with the Germans at Fort Bliss. Huntsville was to be a location with which von Braun was to remain closely linked for the rest of his life. The centre received an instruction in July 1950 from the Office of the Chief of Ordnance to develop a surface-to-surface missile (SSM) with a range of 500 miles. The post-war fracturing and realignment of the wartime Allies and the descent of Churchill's 'Iron Curtain', dividing East and West Germany, had called for a full appraisal of the West's political and military aims. The Soviets had demonstrated, by their rapid acquisition of nuclear technology, that they were not as backward as had been assumed in the days following the Second World War. However, the information provided by a group of atomic spies including Klaus Fuchs,[20] a member of the British team working on the Manhattan Engineering District programme at Los Alamos, would appear to have helped to some degree. The first Russian atom bomb, RDS-1, codenamed 'Joe-1', was in design and appearance very similar to the US Mk III 'Fat Man' used against Nagasaki. Their first test was on 29 August 1949 and took the West by surprise, as did their first test of a hydrogen-type nuclear device, the RDS-6 'Joe-4', on 12 August 1953. Worryingly, this latter test was of a design which was close to being an actual weapon as opposed to being merely an experimental prototype and this was confirmed on 22 November 1955 when the Soviets conducted the world's first air-dropped fusion weapon test, the 1.6MT RDS-37. A somewhat alarming US Intelligence Estimate of the same year predicted that the Soviets would have 1,250 bombs by 1958. They were known to be developing a missile technology based, it was presumed, though wrongly so, on their continuing use of the German rocket scientists who had been enticed into the Soviet net.[21]

The depth of front line military operations that would have been represented in any future war had increased as weapons capability increased. An intermediate range missile was therefore an attractive option as such a weapon would be able to reach a number of Soviet targets. Furthermore, the scientists at the Los Alamos Scientific Laboratory (LASL), who were developing the next generation of nuclear weapons, were also promising a reduction in the weight of the weapons such that it was now realistic to design a missile with a nuclear capability.[22] However, the Army had to address a number of problems which would significantly affect its future path in missile development. As part of the consequences of the separation of the Air Force from the Army, the roles of the US services had been outlined in the 1948 Key West Agreement. The Army had suffered badly in this protocol. Responsibility for its airlift and airborne logistic support was now the responsibility of the Air Force, but the Army had no control over the Air Force budget and the latter was clearly favouring SAC and Continental Air Defense as its priorities, thereby sacrificing the Army's needs. Strictly speaking the Army was not totally deprived of its own organic air capability but this was restricted to aircraft with a wing loading of less than 5,000lb.[23] The Korean War was further to emphasise the difference in Army and Air Force doctrine to the detriment of the Army's operations where it depended on Air Force support.

But the Army had von Braun and there were few who would dispute that his Huntsville Arsenal Team represented the pre-eminent group of rocket engineers in the US. In September 1950, GE transferred to Redstone a missile project known as Hermes C1, on which the company had been working since 1946 under a contract initiated in 1944 by the Ordnance Department of the Army Services Forces (ASF). In overall terms it was very similar to what the Army was now seeking. The project was known for the next two years under different code names, including Ursa, Major, XSSM-G-14 and XSSM-A-14, before the missile was officially named Redstone in April 1952. In March 1951 the specification of the missile was changed to accommodate a heavier payload. Payload weight is inversely proportional to range so the only way of achieving this was to reduce the latter and Redstone therefore ended up with a range of only around 250 miles. This was hardly better than the A-4 and in many ways the Redstone could only be considered as an 'improved A-4' and was acknowledged as such by von Braun.

In one respect, however, Redstone was significantly different from the A-4 employing, as it did, an idea which had already been thought out at Peenemünde. In the German rocket's design the entire missile returned to earth. This had necessitated a robust enough construction to ensure that the body of the rocket did not break up in flight, the very problem in fact that was thought to have affected the first combat launch and was never really solved or fully understood during the V-2's operational career. But it was, of course, only the warhead that needed to complete the whole path of the trajectory. In the Redstone therefore, a re-entry section, comprising the warhead and an associated inertial guidance unit, separated from the main body, or thrust unit, which would thereafter burn up in the heat of re-entry caused by the friction of the atmosphere. Steel fabrication was kept to a minimum and used only in the re-entry section with the thrust unit made from aluminium. Furthermore, whereas the fuel and oxidant tanks in the A-4 design had been separate containers within the outer aerodynamic shell of the rocket, the Redstone design used the shell of the rocket for the tanks which were separated by an internal bulkhead. This monocoque construction led to a considerable saving in overall weight; a greater percentage of this overall weight was represented by fuel and therefore a greater payload capacity resulted.[24]

The 69ft-long missile weighed 62,000lb, had a range of some 250 miles and, like the A-4, could be launched from mobile sites. The Chrysler Corporation was nominated the prime contractor in October 1952 and a full contract signed on 19 June 1953.[25] The missile was powered by a version of the rocket motor developed by North American Aviation to power the USAF's Navaho cruise missile[26] and used ethyl alcohol and liquid oxygen. The inertial guidance unit which controlled the path of the re-entry section as it headed towards its target was essentially the product of Peenemünde research, although only preliminary testing had been achieved during the war. The re-entry section, over 26ft long and, like the thrust unit, 70in in diameter, had an all up weight of 7,900lb including the nuclear warhead. The nuclear capability of the missile was eventually to be determined by the Joint Committee of the US Army-AEC when, on 1 August 1956, they instructed that the Mk 39 low yield nuclear bomb, itself a derivative of the Mk 15, be modified to become the operational W-39 warhead for Redstone. The first Redstone was launched on 20 August 1953. Thirty-six further test firings followed culminating in two high-altitude nuclear test explosions to prove the W-39 warhead. These two explosions, codenamed Teak and Orange, were part of the Hardtack series of nuclear tests. Both launches took place from Johnston Island in the Pacific, south west of Hawaii. Soldiers from the 40th Field Artillery Missile Group fired the Army's first operationally configured Redstone on 16 May 1958 and the missile entered service in Germany the following month. The W-39/YMod1 warhead was released for Army use on 8 July 1959. Overall, some sixty W-39/YMod1 and /YMod2 warheads, each with a yield of 2-2.5MTs, were manufactured. The Redstone missile was also to see service in modified form as the launch vehicle for both the first US satellite and the first two manned launches in the Mercury Programme series.[27]

In July 1955 the eminent rocket scientist Dr Hermann Oberth joined the Redstone Project Team. He had accepted an invitation from von Braun to leave Germany, where he was finding little productive use for his prodigious talents. During the same month, proposals were put forward for a follow-on missile to succeed Redstone. This follow-on missile was to be called Jupiter – the king of the Olympian Gods and the largest planet in the solar system.[28] Jupiter was an Intermediate Range Ballistic Missile (IRBM) of 1,500nm range and was a step nearer to von Braun's long-cherished ambition to achieve earth orbit as a necessary step towards even greater things. There was still a feeling that the 'first past the finishing post' would inherit the missile role and the Army did not intend to finish in second place.

Efforts to make economies in national defence budgets have repeatedly attracted politicians to pursue the development of weapons which could be used by more than one service or which could perform widely differing mission profiles. Such a policy has not always proved successful; however, such an economy was but one factor in the thinking behind the contents of a report prepared by a secret committee chaired by President Eisenhower's special adviser on science and technology, James R. Killian Jr from the Massachusetts Institute of Technology (MIT). Killian had been asked to evaluate the degree of the threat, existing and projected, from Soviet developments in missile technology. The report of the committee tasked with this request, the Technological Capabilities Panel of the Science Advisory Committee, Office of Defense Management, dated 14 February 1955, was considered by the President and the National Security Council (NSC). One of its recommendations was the collaboration between the Army and the Navy in the development of an IRBM with a range of 1,500 miles. The NSC approved and accepted the committee's report and, on 8 November 1955, the Secretary of Defense (SecDef), Charles E. Wilson,[29] sanctioned the formation of the Joint Army Navy Ballistic Missile Committee (JAN-BMC). The two services set up their own internal organisations to direct the progress of their respective sides of the development. The Navy created the Special Projects Office (SPO) on 17 November 1955 under the command of Rear Admiral William F. 'Red' Raborn Jr who took up his post as Director, Special Projects, on 5 December. Raborn had been appointed by Admiral Arleigh A. Burke, Chief of Naval Operations, and his position was conferred with considerable authority. He reported directly to the Secretary of the Navy (SecNav). Alongside the SPO was formed the Navy Ballistic Missile Committee. This committee comprised the Secretary of the Navy, the Assistant Secretary of the Navy for Air, the Deputy Chief of Naval Operations for Readiness, the Director of Guided Missiles and the Assistant Secretary of the Navy for Financial Management, and was tasked with dictating the Navy's policy towards the missile as a seaborne IRBM. The inclusion of the Assistant Secretary of the Navy for Air was an interesting and significant appointment if taken alongside Raborn's own appointment, for Raborn had spent much of the war with the Pacific Fleet's carrier forces. The knowledge of a naval aviator was deemed to be important to provide a liaison facility with the Air Force. The Navy were wary of SAC, and rightly so. LeMay was determined to ensure that SAC remained dominant in its ability to deliver its ever-increasing stockpiles of nuclear weapons right to the heart of the Soviet Union. His plans, effectively encompassing the United States' nuclear war capability, were drawn up with little or no reference either to the Joint Chiefs of Staff (JCS) or indeed to the President himself. Co-operation with the USAF and an understanding of its needs was considered to be important. The Navy had therefore charted a course which sought to use atomic weapons only to 'reduce and neutralise the airfields from which enemy aircraft may be sortying to attack the fleet'.[30] They were careful not to suggest that they wanted their own Naval SAC and, therefore unthreatened, the Air Force left them largely to their own devices. Nor did any jealousy exist in the Navy's relationship with the Army, who saw a naval IRBM as no competitor to its own requirements.

Raborn set up his office in early December. On 20 December, the Office of the Secretary of Defense Ballistic Missile Committee (OSD-BMC), an organisation combining the missile interests of all the services, authorised JAN-BMC to proceed with the development of the missile. Raborn then began to form a team under his command. As his deputy, he appointed Captain John B. Colwell, an authority on naval ordnance. Commander William Haslar was appointed to take charge of the naval team that was to be working on site with the Army.

For its part, the Army delegated control of its interest to the Redstone Arsenal where internal reorganisation of the Arsenal's Missile Division saw the formation, on 1 February 1956, of the Army Ballistic Missile Agency (ABMA) under the command of Major General John B. Medaris. He was an engineer officer with a reputation for achieving results.

The Army/Navy Jupiter was little different in concept to von Braun's initial proposals for a successor to Redstone, using many of its components, and, with its existing experience, the Army was appointed project manager. The desired range of the missile dictated a length of around 60ft to accommodate the required fuel load, and it was decided that the design would incorporate a new type of nose cone which would be covered in an ablative material to absorb the frictional heat of re-entry. The ABMA received increasing pressure from within the Army's ranks to proceed with the development of Jupiter with utmost speed, with the aim of having it operational by 1958, before the most optimistic in-service date of the 5,000nm range Intercontinental Ballistic Missile (ICBM)[31] that the Air Force was developing. This, it was hoped, might secure further funding for a development programme to increase Jupiter's range. As speed was of the essence, and with substantial funding already confirmed, von Braun and his Army team can perhaps be forgiven for being less than enthusiastic about some of the changes which Haslar's team, newly arrived at Huntsville, sought.

Handling the missile on board ship was still considered to be a major problem, and thus the Navy hoped to limit the overall length of the missile to 55ft. The eventual length of 58ft was therefore a compromise which did, however, require that the diameter be increased. The eventual diameter was 8.7ft and the overall weight was some 110,000lb. In view of the Navy's wish to launch the Jupiter from tubes, there could be no external fins. Without these, however, the missile would be unstable and this problem could only be overcome by fitting gimballing exhaust nozzles to the rocket motors. The Navy correctly pointed out that fins were only effective during the limited time when the missile was still in the Earth's atmosphere. Guidance would be by an inertial guidance system developed from that used in Redstone. Two updated versions of Redstone called Jupiter-A and Jupiter-C, an abbreviation of its full title, Jupiter Composite Re-entry Test Vehicle, were used to test various components of the projected missile. It was first flown on 20 September 1956 and reached a record altitude of 684sm and a range of 3,335sm. Had the fourth stage not been inactive and ballasted with sand, this launch could have reached orbit. The Army was in fact 'confident that [it] could orbit a satellite and it proposed to the Department of Defense that [it] be allowed to do so. This was refused. Specifically the Redstone and Jupiter would *not* be used to launch a satellite'.[32] This task had been allocated to the US Navy's Vanguard launcher programme. Subsequent flights tested the ablative materials, layers of fibreglass, plastic and asbestos, which were to be used on the nose cone of the IRBM.

The Navy, meanwhile, had been giving very full consideration to its involvement in the Jupiter programme. On 12 March 1956 the JAN-BMC had been authorised to consider the development of both naval surface and undersea launching platforms and Rayborn's SPO was responsible for proposals for these. On the 20th of that month, the OSD-BMC had given approval to a programme to investigate the practicality of solid fuel as a missile propellant.[33] This was as a result of significant advances made in the specific impulse of solid propellants by Keith Rumbel and Charles Henderson at the Atlantic Research Corporation. This gave the Navy the breakthrough that they had wanted and they worked fast. By 14 April, SecDef Wilson had approved the development of what was to become the Polaris SLBM, a missile to be launched from submerged and essentially invulnerable submarines. By the end of the year progress was such that it was clear that Jupiter-S, an interim missile now being considered by the Navy, was no longer required and on 8 December the Navy was instructed to cease all work on its Jupiter programme. But whilst this would allow the Army to concentrate on a land-based missile without the complications of a naval version, it did not by any means ensure that its role would be confirmed because by then the Air Force had started work on its own IRBM under a General Operation Requirement (GOR-50) issued on 2 December 1954.[34] The USAF IRBM was to be called Thor, the Norse god of Thunder.

The 20 September Jupiter launch had been a spectacular success and the Army was less than pleased when public knowledge of this test was suppressed. This can be seen as evidence of the increasing isolation of the Army within the JCS. This was the last thing the Army needed, as intense inter-service rivalry developed between the two services over the IRBM roles and missions. Either the Army's or the Air Force's IRBM would be chosen and with it, it was still presumed, the right to operate the missile. But both missiles were fast reaching a stage of development when long-lead items, mainly consisting of the Ground Support Equipment, would need to be ordered. This pot could not be allowed to simmer for much longer. Wilson needed to make a decision. Even the President was making uncomforting remarks about the Army's role. He saw the Jupiter's mission compromised by the Army's inability, through lack of deep aerial reconnaissance capability, to complete an effective battle damage assessment after a strike.

The origins of the Air Force's IRBM programme can be found in a January 1955 meeting of the Scientific Advisory Committee. Their recommendation to develop a Tactical Ballistic Missile (TBM) to replace the Martin TM-61 Matador was largely in response to the awareness of intelligence reports of an emergent Soviet IRBM programme. The US Air Force's missile programmes fell under the jurisdiction of the Wright Air Development Center (WADC), formed in 1951 to determine the direction of missile development, and it therefore took on the proposal for the TBM. As a tactical weapon it would theoretically fall to Tactical Air Command (TAC) rather than SAC to sanction the proposal, as TAC was responsible for battlefield level air support. The Air Research and Development Command (ARDC) was instructed to report by 1 June 1955 on how the proposal could best be fulfilled.

The Air Force's main effort at that time was being directed towards their ICBM programme and this definitely fell into SAC's theatre of operations. The ICBM would allow the launch of missiles against the Soviet Union from the sanctuary and safety of mainland United States. Initiated in 1951, the USAF programme to do this was Project MX-1593, later to be called Atlas (WS-107A), apparently as a reference to prime contractor Convair's parent company, The Atlas Corporation. The program had been publicly announced on 16 December 1954. It was not going to be an easy project as it required considerable advances in state-of-the-art technology of the time and it was estimated that the missile would take ten years to bring to operational use, a time period reflecting the complexity of the project. A combat aircraft could typically be expected to require seven years to be brought into operation. Von Braun's A-4 had taken five years but this was under wartime conditions and, although brought to mass production, it had still suffered reliability problems. The ICBM warhead would need to survive the heat of re-entry – re-entry velocity and hence temperature would be higher than for the IRBM – and then land with a fairly high degree of accuracy on its target, because the weight constraints determined by the limitations of the rocket meant its yield would be limited. Von Braun was sceptical about the design for Atlas, which took a very different approach to that taken by the Army Team for Jupiter. Atlas was a thin-skinned, pressurised missile and von Braun did not believe that it was strong enough to withstand the windsheer in the upper atmosphere, let alone the frictional heat of re-entry. Indeed, recognising the potential problems that might be encountered, the USAF's Scientific Advisory Board, chaired by Dr Clark B. Millikan of the California Institute of Technology, had proposed a stepped approach to the missile's development using flight testing with first one, then two and eventually three engines (after the Atlas design was modified from its original five-engine configuration).[35] This would take time; however, there were increasingly disturbing rumours from the intelligence community about the Soviet IRBM program that threatened to put the Soviets significantly ahead of the US by the late 1950s. It was believed that the Soviets had developed an engine with a thrust of 265,000lb. Such an engine incorporated into a missile would give the Soviets the capability of reaching significant targets in Western Europe. Unencumbered by the layers of bureaucracy which slowed down the US decision-making process and with a ruthless policy against failure, the Soviets, it was feared, could well have operational missiles targeting Western Europe before the US, or any of the other Allies for that matter, could respond.

Just as an IRBM would do the job for the Soviets, then equally so would an IRBM give NATO the ability to retaliate from its bases in Europe. A further consideration was that missiles based in Europe would reach their targets before either the manned bombers or US-based ICBMs. Although placing US weapons in host nations was never the perfect solution from a political point of view, it could be argued that it was, in this case, a necessary stopgap. The missiles could be deployed in Europe on behalf of the US and the technical problems in developing such an IRBM, though not insignificant, were considerably less than the potential problems that faced Atlas. The USAF argued the need for an IRBM, rather than the less capable TBM, to act as an insurance policy until Atlas was fully operational.

On 1 July 1954 the ARDC had established, under the deliberately non-specific title of the Western Development Division (WDD), an agency to oversee the Atlas programme. It now took on the IRBM project as well. The WDD was located in Inglewood near to Los Angeles International Airport. Its first Commander was Brigadier General Bernard A. Schriever.[36] With extraordinary and remarkable tenacity Schriever was to bring to operational status the USAF's big three ICBM programmes, Atlas, Titan and Minuteman, and also the Thor IRBM.

However, the Air Force was by no means unanimous in its support for an IRBM, which was not the solution it wanted if it was to retain supremacy in delivery of nuclear weapons. This could only be done properly by an ICBM, the only missile with sufficient range to allow it to be deployed from the sanctuary of the continental United States. Meanwhile SAC's fleet of heavy bombers would take the nuclear weapons to their targets. However, the decision to develop Atlas was in response to the realisation that in due course the bombers would be too vulnerable to Soviet air defence surface-to-air missiles (SAMs). With its limited range, an IRBM force would have to be hosted by another country or countries. Furthermore the Air Force did not want to dilute the considerable scientific resource allocated to developing Atlas by diversifying into an additional programme with a potentially limited lifespan. On the other hand, if the Atlas programme did fall seriously behind, and the Air Force was aware that von Braun and his team thought that the required technology of Atlas was too far advanced, there was a risk that the Army and the Navy may steal a lead in deploying missiles. Inter-service rivalry still played a significant role in the decision-making process.

The Air Force did, however, have on its side the 'New Look' defence doctrine. This had been proposed in a secret document titled 'Basic National Security Policy'[37] in July 1953, approved by Eisenhower on 30 October 1953. Wilson was in charge of its formulation. Eisenhower had criticised the previous Truman administration for being too passive on defense issues and the New Look was his administration's response to this. The new doctrine sought to make the US proactive in its approach to the Soviet threat whilst also recognising the need to be able to respond to threats of a conventional or limited nature. Despite the shortcomings disclosed by the Korean War and the keenness with which some of the US commanders had considered using tactical nuclear weapons, the New Look placed considerable emphasis on the projection of a nuclear presence through strategic air power deployed by a modern air force. There was the recognition that this demonstration of power would have to be backed up by the continental deployment of US troops, predominantly in the support of NATO, but overall there was a target of significant budgetary cuts achievable by reductions of regular ground forces but with an increase in the reserves – seen as a more cost-effective option. The prospects for the Army were not good. It saw an important role for battlefield tactical nuclear weapons which could produce high levels of attrition but in relatively confined areas. Success on the battlefield was linked to the ability to bring unrelenting firepower onto the enemy positions. It was keen to develop its range of weapons to embrace nuclear weapons of differing capabilities to fulfil a variety of scenarios.

The ICBM had only become a realistic possibility after the 'thermonuclear breakthrough' was announced by Dr John von Neumann, chairman of the Scientific Advisory Board, in October 1953. This breakthrough had originated in the series of nuclear tests, codenamed Operation Ivy, that had taken place at Eniwetok in the Marshall Islands in the Pacific Ocean. On 1 November 1952 the first thermonuclear bomb had was successfully detonated. Shot Mike had been purely an experimental device, not a practical weapon, but it gave assurance of what could now be developed. The greatly increased yield of these second-generation weapons was such that the accuracy required for the original atom bombs was no longer so important and this resolved one of the problems inherent in the development of long-range missiles. Von Neumann had chaired a number of Air Force Advisory Groups and had taken a specific look at nuclear capability, although it was not nuclear capability as such that was to drive the ICBM programme. He first considered and confirmed the practicality of a 20MT weapon that could be carried by the B-52, expected to enter service in early 1955. The destructive power of such a weapon meant that pinpoint accuracy was not a requirement.[38] He then turned to the question of a warhead for Atlas and confirmed that a 1MT warhead was a practical possibility. This meant that the original Atlas design for a five-engine, one-and-a-half-stage missile could now be considerably reduced in size to a three-engine missile. Von Neumann was then to go on to chair an even more important committee. Its official name was the Strategic Missiles Evaluation Committee but it became better known as the 'Teapot Committee'. He was appointed to this committee by Trevor Gardner.[39] Gardner was prescient in understanding the ICBM issues and knew that von Neumann would arrive at the correct answer. Conversion of the Air Force to a pro-missile policy can be largely attributed to Gardner. But he was, at the age of thirty-seven, considerably younger than those he would order, and his sharp, cold style did not enhance his popularity amongst senior Air Force officers. The eleven members of the Teapot Committee were all found from outside the military.[40] The committee's brief was to evaluate and advise the administration on the way forward in the field of missile technology. The committee met three times and delivered its report on 10 February 1954. It endorsed Atlas and, though recognising the complexity of the programme, took note of the reports on Soviet ICBM developments and predicted that with the correct management and priority status and accepting the design advantages inherent in the promise of smaller warheads, the Atlas operational capability 'could be achieved by the 1960-62 time period'. Initially, the view had been taken to cancel the Snark cruise missile, but this was later revoked. Yet the committee did recommend cessation of work on the Navaho because of the limitations of its ramjet technology. This missile was nonetheless to provide valuable technology to both Thor and Atlas. A parallel study had meanwhile been undertaken by the RAND Corporation, and in fact the Teapot Committee had placed much reliance on this. RAND reported two days prior to the Teapot Committee and the findings of the two were mutually supportive.

Despite these authoritative recommendations, however, the according of priority status was by no means immediate, although an acceleration of the program was confirmed in March 1954. It was not until September 1955 that Atlas was to be accorded top priority by Eisenhower, whose administration was characterised by policies of fiscal restraint. This was only possible by the concerted and continuing efforts of Gardner, von Neumann and General Schriever. All three had a mutual trust in each other and were all totally committed to the ICBM Programme.

Meanwhile, further nuclear tests from March to May 1954, under the codename Operation Castle, had confirmed that a small, lightweight, yet high yield warhead was now a practical possibility.

The WDD was now advancing initial considerations on the Thor project. The missile would have a range of between 1,000 and 2,000nm, but the Air Force preferred to see this as a strategic rather than a tactical missile, changing the eventual designation to IRBM and thereby transferring the responsibility for operating it from TAC to SAC. Schriever was initially unenthusiastic about the proposal, believing that it would dilute necessary attention and resources to the Atlas programme, the success of which would essentially make the IRBM obsolete. However, he was wary of the Army's Jupiter programme and the risk it presented to the Air Force's roles and missions. The following month the Air Force was made aware of latent interest from the United Kingdom in a joint IRBM project. The ongoing problem restricting the exchange of atomic information, however, presented a stumbling block and was a factor that would continue to frustrate Anglo-American co-operation. Although Gardner made representation to modify the restrictions, nothing concrete resulted. However, Gardner was attracted by the idea of assisting the UK to develop its own missile. Whilst a US IRBM would only represent an interim measure and would become redundant once the ICBM was operational, Britain, because of its proximity to Russia, would never require a longer range weapon than an IRBM. Perceiving that the proposal would relieve the US budget and ultimately would be more cost effective, Gardner had already instituted an assessment in late 1954 of the UK's capability to undertake such a missile programme. This assessment had been undertaken by the Aircraft Industries Association, but their report identified many weaknesses including a lack of sufficient computer capability within the UK aircraft industry. Given the speed with which the project was likely to proceed, the UK was deemed unable to match the requirements of the programme. The US assessment concluded that the UK was five years behind the US, although this could be reduced to three with US assistance.[41] The interest was nonetheless noted. In that same month, the Killian Committee[42] underscored the US need to take a lead in IRBM development to counter the increasing vulnerability of the US to surprise Soviet attack. The IRBM project was given independent status in July when the Deputy Secretary for Defense, Reuben B. Robertson, who was also chairman of the OSD-BMC, declared that the IRBM was not to be a derivative of the Atlas programme but a separate missile, although it could use components developed for the ICBM. This was in case problems with Atlas would merely be reflected in the IRBM, leading to unacceptable delay. In this context the preferred solution would be to use components from the alternate ICBM, which became Titan, a project also taken on by the Air Force as an insurance policy.[43] The technical demands of the IRBM were much less than for the ICBM, so ICBM systems could be incorporated into the IRBM without anticipated problems.

Yet why develop another IRBM when von Braun's team was already engaged in Jupiter? The crucial decision remained the question of roles and missions. These were still broadly based. The military world was changing and the Air Force, conscious that it was only a few years old and therefore very much the junior service, knew that eventually its conventional bombers would become obsolete in the face of inevitable advances in Soviet air defence capability, and it needed to add strength to its arsenal otherwise it risked becoming second string to the Army. Whilst it was certain of the power that the ICBM would give it, it recognised this as a complex programme and therefore accepted the need for the IRBM as a short to medium-term insurance to counter the Army's ambitions. Eisenhower had reorganised the US politico-military structure in 1953. The new system was still finding its feet and this factor, allied to the inter-service rivalry inherent in the JCS, made the decision of which missile to back simply too complex to resolve. This rivalry could be counter productive. Chairman of the JCS, Admiral Arthur Radford, had warned that 'the more [the Chiefs of Staff] disagree, the more power they hand to the chairman'.[44] So the somewhat surprising decision was made to develop both missiles. The Air Force was instructed to proceed with IRBM Number 1, a land-based missile, whilst the Army/Navy team would continue their programme to develop IRBM Number 2 – Jupiter, seen basically as a sea-based missile, but with a land capability should the Air Force effort flounder, although Jupiter was to become a fully-fledged, land-based missile once the Navy withdrew from the project. There were those who believed that this competitive element was a good discipline, and that in any case at some stage a decision on one of the missiles would have to be made; but would the winner thereby also win the sole right to IRBM operations? The answer was 'not necessarily'. SecDef Wilson maintained an atmosphere of ambiguity. He had indicated in a press conference in May 1956 that the missiles would first be developed and then 'let's see how we ought to use them and who ought to be responsible for them'.[45]

It was apparent that to some contractors the nascent IRBM project had more appeal than the ICBM. It was almost certainly going to be an easier project to bring to Initial Operational Capability (IOC)[46] and therefore the payback to industry would be quicker and more attractive.[47] Yet contractors had to consider carefully where they already had lucrative contracts with all the services. Many of the Army contractors needed to maintain a neutrality.[48] It was with the Air Force contractors that the big defence budgets were spent. By contrast, Chrysler, responsible for the Jupiter, was ninety-fourth in the league.[49] The Douglas Aircraft Company, along with Bell Telephone Laboratories – both companies had collaborated successfully on the Nike SAM programme – had been invited by Schriever to submit a proposal for the alternate ICBM and, whilst they did so, Douglas in particular was expressing a greater interest in the IRBM programme. However, Atlas now enjoyed highest priority status, and at that time there was no indication that the IRBM would necessarily be accorded similar status and the whole project could still be compromised by the success of the Atlas Programme. Schriever, meanwhile, continued to make representation to General Thomas S. Power, commanding the ARDC, that the TBM/IRBM Programme must not be allowed to compromise the ICBM Programme.

On 30 November three aircraft companies were invited to present proposals for the missile: North American Aviation, the Lockheed Aircraft Company and the Douglas Aircraft Company[50] – Glenn L. Martin and Convair were excluded as they were already fully committed to the ICBM Programme. Simplicity and flexibility in operations were seen as basic requirements and a range of between 600 and 1,000 miles confirming the missile as an IRBM.[51] The decision on which proposal to select was made by the same Air Force Source Selection Board that had decided on the Titan ICBM.[52] Resulting from this, on 24 December 1955, the Douglas Aircraft Company Inc. (DAC) was awarded a contract to start work on designing an IRBM under contract WS-315A (Weapon System 315A). This was to become a missile designated SM-75/PGM-17 and was to be called Thor. The origin of the name arose from a misunderstanding by DAC who had not given their proposal a name. Joe Rowland, Director of Public Relations for the Glenn L. Martin Company, had been given the task of suggesting names for Martin's ICBM proposal. From his list of suggestions the name Titan was selected, with Thor as a second suggestion. In the event Titan was the agreed name for Martin's missile and Rowland therefore suggested to Donald Douglas Jr that he may like to use Thor for DAC's IRBM. Douglas agreed and proposed the name to the ARDC who confirmed the choice.

Douglas was to be prime contractor and responsible for the airframe. The company did have missile experience with the Honest John, Sparrow, Nike-Ajax and Hercules, not that any of these was as large as the proposed IRBM. The decision was communicated to Douglas Management as they enjoyed a Christmas Eve celebration.[53] Barely allowing time for the Christmas celebrations, the necessary contracts were signed in the BMD's offices on 28 December. Donald Douglas Jr signed on behalf of DAC, whilst Lt Col. W.D. Smith from Air Matériel Command signed on behalf of the Air Force. Separate 'prime' contracts would be negotiated with other suppliers to cover the major sub-systems – propulsion, guidance, computers and electronics and nose cones. This was in parallel to the way that the Atlas contracts had been agreed, although it was not the way that the major aircraft manufacturers preferred as it led to a slicing up of the contract cake.[54] It did, however, provide protection against any problems within a prime contractor. Yet it only exacerbated the Thor-Jupiter controversy. The missiles were so similar, apart from their differing approaches to re-entry. Indeed some regretted missing the opportunity to instruct the contractors to take different approaches to the fundamentals of missile design. This was in part justified when turbopump problems, which required a redesign, threatened both projects which used only slightly different versions of the same engine. Therefore, perhaps technological advances may have been more significant. Nonetheless, Wilson remained very much in charge of the decision-making process. He was an autocratic leader whose opinion was rarely shifted once he had made up his own mind, based largely on his own criteria. One of his Chiefs of Staff characterised him as 'the most uninformed man, and the most determined to remain so, that has ever been Secretary'. The JCS ratified his decisions. These decisions were often on a two against one basis but they still had to maintain a united front in the face of Congress, and therefore the opportunity to present a specific case by an individual service was severely curtailed. However, Wilson seemed reluctant or unable to draw the matter to a conclusion, until on 26 November 1956 he took action not to select one of the missiles but to take the Army out of the running for the right to deploy their missile. In his 'Rôles and Missions Directive' he limited the Army to the development and use of SSMs to ranges not exceeding 200 miles.[55] The Navy and the Air Force would hold joint responsibility for missiles of greater range. Wilson had not cancelled Jupiter, which the Army could continue to develop, but would the Air Force purchase Jupiter in preference to their own home-bred Thor?

Douglas had put Jack L. Bromberg in charge of the project. He was backed up by Hal M. Thomas. The contract required the assembly and testing of missiles leading to a production run of 120 missiles, to be operational by January 1960. They took an early decision to adopt a 'concurrency concept' in the missile's development. This was an 'all or nothing' approach. It was a brave decision but would save valuable time in bringing the missile to IOC – if it worked. The great advantage of the concept was that the missile was designed from the start for production and its design and manufacture were in the same hands. Jupiter, on the other hand, designed in a more conventional manner, could expect inevitable delays when it was transferred from the design stage to a separate contractor for production. Concurrency bore a resemblance to the 'parallel' approach being used for Atlas, which in turn had been imposed because it was believed that the Soviets had developed the capability of reducing the lead time on new weapons. It countered the traditional policy in acquiring air weapons of 'fly before you buy'. All parts of the programme would be run concurrently – design, development, launch facilities, technical data and initial crew training would all be going on simultaneously. There would be no 'prototypes' in the conventional way that aircraft were developed. The missiles would be built from the start to a semi-operational standard. Problems would be addressed, resolved and incorporated into the necessary programme as they arose and were solved. The risk was that something serious would go wrong and thereby affect the entire programme if a fundamental design change was needed. Time was of the essence and it was deemed to be a risk worth taking.

To act as a further proof of design, Douglas was given the outline design parameters of the missile by the BMD-STL. Unknown to them, Schriever had already set up his own IRBM assessment. He had seconded Robert Truax from the Navy and Dr Adolph K. 'Dolph' Thiel, formerly part of von Braun's team, from the Ramo-Wooldridge Corporation. They had come up with their criteria for an IRBM but these more detailed conclusions were deliberately not given to Douglas. It was, therefore, with a certain relief that the Douglas design came within less than 1 per cent variation of the BMD-STL design. What Douglas did not know was that the Truax-Thiel design had itself a margin of error built in as an insurance policy.

Now fully committed to the IRBM programme, the Air Force was keen to have the first test flight by the end of 1956, an amazingly short period of time. The development of new systems for the missile was essentially out of the question. Existing technology would have to be used wherever possible. This was not the problem it may have seemed, as many 'off-the-shelf' systems were readily available. Thus the main rocket engine came from Rocketdyne as a derivate of the Atlas booster engine, which in itself had come from the Navaho Project. Guidance systems and the Re-entry Vehicle (RV) were derived from Atlas components. The dimensions of the missile were determined by the Air Force. As it would not be operated from the continental United States it would need to be easily transportable, so it was decreed that it would have to fit inside a C-124 Globemaster II and the later, bigger C-133 Cargomaster, both aircraft, perhaps fortuitously, also made by Douglas. Here, Thor had an advantage over Jupiter where this need had not been foreseen. It was too big to fit inside an aircraft.

The final design was for a missile with a lightweight airframe 64ft 10in long and 8ft wide. The basic construction was formed from three aluminium alloy panels each forming a 120 degree arc with double plane curvature. The US Chemical Milling Corporation then etched the interior of these panels into a waffle pattern to provide maximum strength to the airframe. In the nose of the missile was the W-49 warhead inside a Mk 2 RV. The RV was secured to the main missile body by three payload latches.

Behind this was the Guidance Section which comprised Control Group and Platform Group equipments, with three fluorolube coated gyros set at right angles to each other, for which the AC Spark Plug Division of General Motors based at Milwaukee was the prime contractor. The system chosen was the AChiever inertial system, already proved in use in the Mace and Regulus II cruise missiles. Between the aft bulkhead of the Guidance Section and the forward edge of the Centre Body Section lay the fuel tank. The fuel was RP-1 kerosene – light-cut petroleum consisting primarily of aliphatic hydrocarbons, to military specification MIL-F-25576A. The Centre Body section formed the union between the bulkheads which separated the fuel tank from the larger Liquid Oxygen Tank, but the Centre Body section also had attached externally two retrorockets which slowed the spent missile body to allow a clean warhead separation to be achieved. The tankage accounted for approximately two-thirds of the missile's total length. Fuel was fed from the fuel tank, which was pressurised with nitrogen, to the engine via a lagged and heated pipe which passed through the LOX Tank. Below the LOX Tank lay the Main Engine and its associated Accessories Pack, including the Pneumatics Systems, Gas Generator and APU. An exterior tunnel made of curved fibreglass protected the electrical cabling, destructor lead and the pneumatic plumbing between the various sections of the missile. External to the aft bulkhead of the missile were the open end of the Thrust Chamber, the Turbine Exhaust Duct on which were mounted bottles containing high-pressure nitrogen for pressurising the fuel tank, and a heat exchanger used for generating gaseous oxygen for pressurising the LOX tank. There were also two vernier engines placed at 180 degrees to each other and mounted inside protective fairings. These vernier rockets provided fine adjustment to the trajectory to place the missile onto its final ballistic path. On the aft bulkhead were located six sockets into which fitted worm-driven pins to hold the missile on the launcher. Each socket was stressed to exceed one-sixth of the weight of the missile to allow for the effects of windsheer in the vertical position. The missile was originally configured with four small triangular fins around the base, and these can be seen on photographs of the early launches. They were designed to provide stability in the initial part of the trajectory, but were later deemed unnecessary and were deleted, thereby saving much-needed weight. At launch the missile weighed 110,000lb and it subsequently reached a speed of 10,250mph. Although from the start Thor and all its support equipment was designed to be moveable, mainly because it would have to be air-transportable, it would nonetheless be launched from fixed sites as an expedient measure to allow it to become operational as quickly as possible. This was accepted even though the shortcomings of fixed sites were known from the German experience of their massive launch bunkers, which never in the end fired a single operational V-2. Some consideration was given to having dispersal sites to which the missiles could be moved in times of heightened tension, much along the lines of the V-Bomber dispersal plans, but it was not taken further and would in any case have added considerably to the costs. Meanwhile, Jupiter was designed to be mobile, but in reality was only really moveable, a fact that von Braun acknowledged with some reluctance. The concept of total mobility was unrealistic for a missile that weighed 50 tons at launch: 'If you set up a hundred thousand pound missile, we have the idea that maybe you ought to lay out a little piece of concrete about twenty feet square to put it on.'[56]

However, the confirmation of Thor did nothing to move the decision between Thor and Jupiter any further forward. A decision had to be made and everyone knew it, but Wilson remained indecisive. The catalyst to the final decision came, perversely, from the very nation against which the missile would be targeted.

On 4 October 1957, the Soviet Union took the world by surprise when an R-7 booster was launched from the Tyuratam Cosmodrome[57] and took the first artificial satellite, Sputnik-1,[58] into space. It was no longer necessary to speculate about Soviet missile capability. The launch booster for Sputnik was correctly interpreted as a derivative of a military ballistic missile. The Soviets had demonstrated that they were significantly ahead of the Americans – what became known as the Missile Gap.[59] Although there were efforts to play down the significance of the Soviet satellite, 'they captured better Germans than we did' was a disingenuous excuse and it was true that Sputnik did nothing except transmit a radio signal. It was plain to see that the Soviets were well into the ascent of the military high ground of space. Unknown at the time was the fact that the Soviets had not attempted to make bigger and therefore more complex rocket engines. Under the guidance of the unidentified Chief Designer Korolev[60] they had opted for clusters of smaller rocket engines, the major technological challenge being the co-ordination of these clusters working in unison. The Sputnik launch vehicle, developed from the R-7 ballistic missile, employed a central core of four RD-107 engines with four strap-on boosters each with four similar RD-108 engines.

The US population was concerned, even frightened by the Soviet success. A chill wind coursed through the corridors of the Pentagon. It swept aside those who may have harboured doubts about the wisdom of developing either or both of the IRBMs. Politically this was not the time to be seen to cut back on strategic capability. Sputnik justified the continuation of both programmes. Secretary to the Air Force (SecAF) Donald A. Quarles, testifying to the Mahon Subcommittee on 20 November, indicated that production of both missiles was increasingly likely. On the 27th Defense Secretary Neil H. McElroy[61] advised the Senate Armed Services Committee that both missiles would be produced. The two missiles had still to prove themselves although the Jupiter development appeared to be ahead of Thor. In part this was suggested by the fact that the Jupiter-As and -Cs that had been launched were essentially Redstone 200nm-range vehicles modified by the addition of upper stages. The true position was that Thor possibly had a slight lead in terms of the final operational missile. However, the Jupiter tests had successfully explored a number of the problems that were anticipated with nose cone temperatures at re-entry speeds. A launch on 20 September 1956 had achieved a range of 2,960nm with a re-entry speed of Mach 20. In August 1957 a Jupiter-C tested the Re-entry Vehicle which would house the warhead. Coming back into the atmosphere at Mach 14, the glass fibre, melamine-impregnated nose cone displayed much less than the anticipated levels of ablation. Because of unknowns such as the performance of the RV and given the new urgency in the programme, to choose only one missile which might then experience technical problems was too great a risk to take. The chairman of the Senate's Permanent Defense Investigating Subcommittee, Lyndon B. Johnson, voiced the committee's relief when he told McElroy, 'Without passing judgement on the wisdom of the decision, I congratulate you on the fact that a decision has been made'.[62]

The question of where to base the missiles was not considered to be a problem. In this respect the US failed to understand that there were now great doubts in Europe about where the Americans stood in terms of their relationship with the other

NATO countries. The Soviets had demonstrated their technological superiority over the much-vaunted US military, and doubts were being raised about the uncertain political direction of the US. Europe was wary, and even if largely unaware of or disinterested in the vacillations over the two IRBMs, NATO countries were to express this wariness in negotiations over the basing of the missiles. What was unknown to the West was that, as the US planned its deployment of its IRBMs in Europe, the Soviet Army, under Directive 589-365SS issued by Khrushchev in 1955, was also planning its deployment in 1958 of R5M SSMs (known by NATO as the SS-3 Shyster) to the north of Berlin at Fürstenberg and to the south east at Vogelsang near the Polish border. So secret was this deployment that even the East German hosts were unaware of their presence.[63] Keen to advance the operational date, the Teapot Committee met again in the somewhat surprising surroundings of the Walter Reed Army Hospital, where von Neumann was being treated for the cancer that would shortly take his life. They set a revised timescale. The first launch would be by the end of 1956, the first full-range R&D flight by July 1957 and operational deployment by July 1959. It was to be a demanding schedule.

Notes:
1 The missile was technically an A-4 but was better known as the V-2 – Vergeltungswaffe 2 (Vengeance Weapon 2).
2 Two separate units had been formed from Batterie 444 to launch the attacks, codenamed Operation Pinguin. Group Sud, which achieved the first combat launch, encompassed targets mainly in France, while Group Nord launched predominantly against London. As the Allied advance progressed and the two units were forced to retreat, targets within the Low Countries increasingly became the priority.
3 Gavin, Lt-Gen. James M., *War and Peace in the Space Age*, p.82.
4 Peenemünde had been chosen both for its remoteness and its location on the Baltic coast where tracking facilities could be set up. The Army had the major share of the site covering Peenemünde Öst and operated under the title of Heeresversuchsanstalt Peenemünde. The Luftwaffe occupied Peenemünde West.
5 Operation Hydra. 735 people were killed, including a number of foreign workers who were billeted in the Trassenheide Barracks to the south east of Peenemünde. Also amongst the dead were a number of scientists including Dr Walter Thiel, who was in charge of rocket motor development. Despite the tonnage of bombs that had been dropped, some of which missed their target and landed in woodland, overall damage was significant but not disastrous. By repairing only essential buildings, the Germans gave the impression that much of the site had been abandoned and thereby escaped the further attentions of the RAF for some nine months.
6 Mittelwerke GmbH, which operated the Harz facility, had manufactured 5,789 rockets by the time that it was evacuated on 18 March 1945. The site in the Kohnstein Mountain had been owned since 1934 by Wirtschaft Forschungs GmbH and had been used primarily for the storage of strategic raw materials, its remote location providing reasonable protection from air attack. Under the overall command of SS Brigadeführer Hans Kammler, prisoners from Buchenwald concentration camp were used to extend the deep underground tunnels. Working in freezing conditions, many of these prisoners died, their bodies being returned to Buchenwald for cremation. An additional concentration camp was developed nearer to the site at Dora-Mittelbau. This also had its own

crematorium, capable of handling 100 bodies per day. A sub-camp of Dora-Mittelbau was built at Nordhausen. This was classed by the SS as a Vernichtungslager, a special camp for sick prisoners where no sanitation or medical care existed. Incarcerated in concrete detention blocks, prisoners unable to work productively at the Mittelwerke complex simply starved to death, their bodies being left to decompose.

7 Aware that an underground production facility existed near to Nordhausen, the Rocket Branch of the US Army Ordnance Corps instructed Colonel Holger N. Toftoy to move from his Headquarters at the Ordnance Technical Intelligence in Paris to locate and salvage whatever could be found at the site as soon as it was captured.

8 The Soviets did manage to recover the plans for the two stage A-9/A-10 missile. They also found Helmutt Gröttrup, the chief electronics engineer.

9 It was only after the re-unification of East and West Germany that the use of slave labour in the production of the A-4 became widely acknowledged.

10 Reichsführer SS Himmler, in seeking his own involvement in the rocket programme, gave von Braun the rank of SS Untersturmführer on 1 May 1940. By their very activities in developing the A-4, most of the personnel would have been classed by the Allies as Category 1 offenders and could have expected to have spent up to ten years in labour camps if found guilty.

11 Oberstleutnant Wolfgang Weber, who had commanded Gruppe Sud, was now appointed Commanding Officer of Altenwalde Versuchs-Kommando (AVKO) with overall responsibility for the 591 Germans assisting with Operation Backfire.

12 The first launch attempt was made on 1 October 1945 but a faulty igniter caused the rocket to remain on the pad. The Germans philosophically accepted this as being a normal launch problem, but the British were apprehensive that it was some form of sabotage. They were more responsive to the German explanation when the same problem occurred during a second launch attempt. This rocket was, however, the one successfully launched on 4 October. A second was readied for launching on 15 October. Was it not for the fact that this launch had a high-ranking audience, and that the press too had been invited, it is probable that it would have been postponed owing to the appalling weather conditions. However, the launch was conducted successfully at 3.06p.m. although the rocket fell some eleven miles short of the designated target and slightly to the right of the intended track. This launch was generally more interesting from the point of view of an examination of the 'guest list', particularly in respect of the Americans and Soviets who had been invited as observers. The Soviet delegation included Colonel Probedonostsev and Colonel Valentin Petrovich Glushko, an authority on rocket propulsion, who was supervising test firings of A-4 engines captured from Peenemünde as part of the Soviet's research programme. Two unexpected Soviet officers arrived and were forced, despite much protest, to observe the launch from outside the official compound. General Gaidukov was at that time based at Nordhausen investigating what could be salvaged from the Mittelwerke plant, and a captain who accompanied him was in fact Colonel Sergei Korolev. Korolev was to become the shadowy Chief Spacecraft Designer who, only after his death, was publicly acknowledged to have masterminded the Soviet manned space programme. Appointed by Joseph Stalin as Chief Designer in charge of developing targetable rockets on 9 August 1946, Korolev studied the A-4 design as part of his brief but was later to claim that 'a study of the German A-4 liquid propellant rocket yielded no revelations. These combat missiles were largely based on Tsiolkovskii's ideas. Our own construction methods had to be evolved in order to build powerful and reliable rockets'.

13 The actual number of Germans is difficult to identify and varies from source to source. Armacost quotes 127.
14 It was not only the Soviets who had sent observers to Backfire who were not all they might have seemed to be. Sporting the uniform of a colonel was Dr Theodor von Kármán, Director of the Jet Propulsion Laboratory (JPL) at the California Institute of Technology (Caltech). Also from Caltech was Dr William Pickering, a future Director of JPL, and Dr Howard S. Seifert from JPL's Liquid Propulsion Section, who was at that time on secondment as Technical Adviser to the Military Attaché at the US Embassy in London. Lieutenant Commander Grayson P. Merrill, a US Navy officer who was compiling a report on US observations of the Backfire tests, accompanied these scientists. Merrill had already been involved in research into pilotless aircraft and was later to edit a ten-volume report entitled 'Principles of Guided Missiles', before becoming Technical Director of the Polaris SLBM programme.
15 The US Army Air Force (AAF) had similar ideas about atomic missiles and for two years discussed the matter with the Manhattan District, later to become the Atomic Energy Commission (AEC), but the technical complexities of the weight of the warhead and limitations on missile performance produced no meaningful results.
16 Inter-service rivalry in the field of missile research had existed, perhaps surprisingly, since 1944. The operational arrival of the V-1 and V-2 weapons had sparked interest in missile development from within the Army Air Force (AAF), Army Ground Forces (AGF) and Army Services Forces (ASF). Lines of demarcation initially evolved along whether the missile was an evolution of aircraft technology without a pilot – broadly-winged, jet-powered missiles – or an extension of artillery – rocket-powered missiles, the same generic distinction between the V-1 deployed by the Luftwaffe and the V-2 deployed by the German Army. At times esoteric arguments were used. When was a fin really a wing? Efforts were also made by the AAF to call guided missiles 'pilotless aircraft'. The policy was clarified by the McNarney Directive of October 1944. This gave responsibility to the AAF for all air-launched missiles and those ground-launched missiles dependent on aerodynamic lift. All other ground-launched missiles dependent on the momentum of their engine would come under the auspices of the ASF. The AGF could specify its needs and direct development to either the AAF or the ASF. Rivalry between the AAF and US Navy had traditionally been based on their individual roles and missions. The arrival of the atomic bomb had caused concern within the naval hierarchy that the AAF may usurp the Navy's strategic role and the development of missiles might follow the same course. These jealousies between the services, complex at the best of times, were not truly resolved until the mid-1950s. The basic outlines of this policy can be seen in the development of the North American SM-64 Navaho and Northrop SM-62 Snark, both air-breathing, winged cruise missiles by the AAF, later the USAF, whilst Army interests moved towards rocket-powered ballistic missiles.
17 This experimental launch, codenamed Operation Sandy, was under the command of Rear Admiral Daniel V. Gallery, Assistant Chief of Naval Operations (Guided Missiles). It was undertaken by Task Force 41.16, which put to sea on 2 September 1947. Accompanying the *Midway* were four destroyers from Destroyer Division (DesDiv) 142, which were to be used for tracking, six PB-1W aircraft from VX-4 Squadron and the SOFAR sound laboratory ship PCEr 852. The latter's task was to monitor the explosion of a SOFAR bomb placed in the missile. The *Midway* carried two live missiles and one dummy one which was to be used for handling purposes. The actual

launch equipment used was the original German equipment modified for use on deck. Launch operations were under the command of Commander P.G. Holt from the Bureau of Aeronautics. Ignition of the missile took place at 3.53p.m. (X Hour) and, watched by some 100 observers headed by Admiral W.H.P. Blandy, Commander in Chief of the US Atlantic Fleet (CinCLanFlt), the rocket rose somewhat erratically, passing quite close to the ship's superstructure, before heading upwards. The missile exploded when it reached 5,000ft. This unexpected explosion reinforced in the minds of many of the observers the very real dangers that rockets still presented. One hour thirteen minutes after the launch, all equipment had been removed from the deck and twelve minutes later the carrier was ready again to accept aircraft. To prove the point, six F4U aircraft were launched in rapid succession some eighty-eight minutes after the launch took place.

18 General Curtis Emerson LeMay (1906–1990) commanded SAC from 1948 until 1957. His first war plan for SAC, drawn up in 1949, involved delivering the entire US stockpile of atomic weapons in a 'single massive attack'.

19 The technical climax of the White Sands programme had been achieved with the Bumper WAC Series of launches, the first of which took place on 24 February 1949. This saw a WAC-Corporal rocket mounted on the warhead compartment of the A-4, thereby producing a two-stage rocket. Considerably smaller in size than the A-4, the WAC-Corporal had been developed at Caltech during the final stages of the war and used a self-igniting fuel combination of nitric acid and aniline. This two-stage rocket reached record altitudes of around 244 miles and reached a velocity of some 5,150mph.

20 Klaus Fuchs (1911–1988). German-born Fuchs had emigrated to France in 1933 and then came to Britain, being granted British citizenship in 1942. He accompanied Rudolf Peierls to the US in 1943 to work on the Manhattan Project and worked in the Theoretical Physics Division at Los Alamos from August 1944, working under Hans Bethe. In January 1950 Fuchs eventually confessed that he had passed on information on both the US atomic and thermonuclear designs and had also disclosed the US rate of production of U-235, which enabled the Soviets to calculate the rate of production of US weapons. Convicted of spying, his British citizenship was revoked and he spent nine years in prison. After his release he was allowed to leave the UK for Dresden, East Germany, where he spent the rest of his life.

21 A number of the German rocket scientists had elected to side with the Soviets on the promise of remaining in Germany. However, after an initial period in Nordhausen they were taken to the Soviet Union. They were used for a short period but within a year all had been returned to Germany. The Soviets then continued to develop their own programme independent of outside help. Such was their paranoia about utilising German know-how that even in their own A-4 derived programme the rockets were all built from scratch without using any 'German made' components. Their military version of the A-4, known by the West as the SS-1, was the first operational missile after the Second World War.

22 The Mk I atom bomb, nicknamed 'Little Boy', which had been dropped on Hiroshima, had weighed 8,890lb, whilst the Mk III 'Fat Man' allocated to Nagasaki had weighed 10,000lb. By comparison the A-4 had a warhead of only 1,650lb of amatol.

23 Armacost, Michael A., *The Politics of Weapons Innovation*, p.39.

24 In fact most of these improvements had already been incorporated in Project MX-774, an AAF contract awarded to Convair in 1946. Only three vehicles were launched and

none of the flights were wholly successful. Funding for the program ran out in 1949 but the missile verified the proof of concept and essentially formed the basis of the Atlas ICBM program.
25 The Redstone Arsenal was keen to set up a production facility within the Arsenal but this had been vetoed by the Office of the Chief of Ordnance in April 1952.
26 The significance of the Navaho Missile is often overlooked. It was one of a number of early post-war missile programmes and was principally designed to test the feasibility of the German A9/A10 intercontinental rocket design. Although plagued by problems (it was nicknamed the 'Never-go-Navaho') the missile achieved a number of 'firsts' and elements of current rocket technology can still trace its ancestry back to systems developed for the Navaho. It was cancelled in July 1957 partly because of the on-going problems but with the imminent arrival of the Atlas ICBM, it had simply become outdated.
27 After the US Navy had conspicuously failed to launch the first US satellite with their Vanguard rocket, von Braun was asked to step in to reclaim US credibility. This he did with a Jupiter-C derivative which launched Explorer 1 on 31 January 1958.
28 Von Braun's next rocket followed the planetary theme initiated by Jupiter, although by then he had left the ABMA to work for NASA at the Marshall Space Flight Center. It took its name from the second largest planet, Saturn, and as the Saturn V was the launch vehicle for the Apollo Moon Programme.
29 Charles E. Wilson (1890–1961). Wilson had been President of General Motors during the Second World War and was appointed Secretary of Defense by Eisenhower in 1953. He carried through Eisenhower's New Look defence concept. He retired from office in 1957.
30 Millis, Walter (editor), *The Forrestal Diaries*, p.392.
31 The original acronym was IBMS (Intercontinental Ballistic Missile System) but so as not to lead to confusion with the IBM Corporation it was changed to ICBM.
32 Gavin, *Ibid*, p.27.
33 The feasibility of constant pressure, solid fuel rockets can be traced back to the Army Air Corps Project GALCIT of 1940, although at that stage the role of solid fuel was for Jet Assisted Take-Off (JATO) augmentation units. The subsequent work done in the field of castable solid propellants paved the way for the development of practical solid fuels for ICBMs and SLBMs.
34 Gibson, James T., *Nuclear Weapons of the United States: An Illustrated History*, p.166.
35 Hartt, Julian, *The Mighty Thor*, p.27.
36 Bernard (Bennie) Adolph Schriever (1910–2005) was born in Bremen, Germany. He emigrated with his family to the US in 1917, becoming a naturalised US citizen in 1923. Commissioned into the US Army in 1932 he started flying and was awarded his US Army Air Corps Wings the following year. After graduating from the Air Corps Engineering School in 1941 he was awarded a Masters Degree in Aeronautical Engineering in 1942, and thereafter saw active service in the Pacific Theatre. After the war, promoted to Colonel, Schriever was appointed Chief of the Scientific Liaison Branch in the Office of the Deputy Chief of Staff for Matériel in the Pentagon. He was instrumental in emphasising to the Air Force Chiefs the importance of scientific research and development, a policy that was to assist greatly in the rapid development of the US missile arsenal.
37 NSC 162/2.
38 A side issue to this, but interesting nonetheless, is to be found in the question of bomb sights for the V-Bombers. Little development had been done on these as there was no perceived necessity for a highly accurate bomb sight to deliver nuclear weapons. The

same was not true when the V-Bombers reverted to conventional weapons and this may be considered in the context of the Black Buck Vulcan missions against Port Stanley airfield during the Falklands conflict.

39 The Honorable Trevor Gardner (1915–1963) was born in Cardiff and emigrated to the US in 1928, becoming a naturalised citizen in 1937. In the Second World War he worked at the California Institute of Technology on projects related to rocketry and atomic weapons. After the war he moved into the industrial private sector before being asked to join the Eisenhower administration as Special Assistant for Research and Development to Secretary of the Air Force, Harold E. Talbott. He was described by Lt Gen. James H. Doolittle as a 'sparkplug (who did) a tremendous job in expediting development of the missile, in directing funds and brain power into the missile program'.

40 The eleven members were, in addition to von Neumann, Simon Ramo and Dean Wooldridge, the founders of Ramo-Wooldridge; Clark B. Millikan, Charles C. Lauritsen and Louis G. Dunn (all from Caltech); Hendrick W. Bode (Bell Telephone Laboratories); Dr Allen E. Puckett (Hughes Aircraft Company); George B. Kistiakowski (Harvard); Jerome B. Wiesner (MIT); and Lawrence A. Hyland (Bendix Corporation).

41 Britain did embark on its own MRBM programme called Blue Streak. The programme was seriously affected by technical problems and delays and was eventually cancelled in 1960.

42 The Technological Capabilities Panel, better known as the Killian Committee after its Chairman James R. Killian Jr (1904–1988), President of the Massachusetts Institute of Technology (MIT), had been established by Gardner in July 1954 on the instruction of Eisenhower. Its brief was to consider US technological and intelligence capabilities. Killian was to serve as Presidential Science Adviser to Eisenhower from 1957 to 1959.

43 It was even considered whether or not the second stage of Titan, which had been confirmed as a two-stage missile, could become the basis of the IRBM; however, it was determined that this would result in a range of only $c.800$nm.

44 Armacost, *Ibid*, p.76.

45 *New York Times*, 22 May 1956, p.14.

46 IOC (Department of Defense definition): 'The first attainment of the capability to employ effectively a weapon, item of equipment, or system of approved specific characteristics, and which is manned or operated by an adequately trained, equipped, and supported military unit or force'.

47 Consideration had also to be given to the other conventional aircraft contracts that were being undertaken. Much of this effort surrounded the Air Force requirement for a Mach 3 bomber to replace the B-52. Convair was responsible for the Mach 2 B-58 Hustler, whilst Boeing-North American was working on the WS-110A 'Chemical Bomber' and Convair-Lockheed on the WS-125A 'Nuclear Bomber'. Convair also had the contract for Atlas whilst Martin was engaged in preliminary work on Titan.

48 Armacost, *Ibid*, p.85.

49 Armacost, *Ibid*, p.91.

50 Lonnquest, John C. and Winkler, David F., *To Defend and Deter: The Legacy of the United States Cold War Missile Program*, November 1996.

51 Armacost, *Ibid*, p.134.

52 Hartt, *Ibid*, p.53.

53 Hartt, *Ibid*, p.56.

54 While Thor had four prime contractors, Atlas had five, Titan had eight and Minuteman five.

55 The US Army still did not give up its efforts to operate long-range nuclear missiles, even seeking exotic solutions such as Project Iceworm, a proposal to site missiles under the arctic ice cap. See: *Journal of Cold War Studies*, Vol.3, No.3.

56 Armacost, *Ibid*, p.50.

57 The launch site is usually referred to as Baikonur. This was essentially 'disinformation' about the exact location of the site, as the town of Baikonur, Kazakhstan, is 400km to the north east of the Cosmodrome. The launch complex was built close to the railhead of Tyuratam. Only when US U-2 Spy Planes were able to fly over the Soviet Union was the true location identified. It is still the main Russian launch complex.

58 The actual designation of Sputnik-1 was PS-1 (Elementary Satellite–1).

59 At the time the terminology 'Missile Lag' was used, but 'Missile Gap' is the generally used current terminology.

60 Sergei Pavlovich Korolev (1907 (Gregorian calendar)–1966). Korolev was born in the Ukraine, and it was his leadership that was largely responsible for early Soviet successes. He was appointed Chief Designer in the Scientific Research Institute – 88 (NII-88), set up in 1946 by Stalin to develop the captured German rocket technology. Such was the secrecy of the Soviet space programme, that Korolev was only identified publicly after his death in 1966 as a result of unsuccessful colon surgery whilst being treated for cancer.

61 Neil H. McElroy (1904–1972). Secretary of Defense in the Eisenhower Administration from 9 October 1957 to 1 December 1959.

62 Armacost, *Ibid*, p.177.

63 *The Times*, London, 18 January 2000.

CHAPTER TWO
EARLY DISAPPOINTMENTS AND SUCCESSES

On 7 November 1956 the United States, for the first time, placed some of its missile forces on full alert.[1] The history of the 701st Tactical Missile Wing confirms that this was in response to 'the world situation'. Prior to that, on 31 October, British and French forces followed up an earlier attack by Israeli forces[2] and launched an attack against the Suez Canal with the objective of occupying the Canal Zone.[3] This action had been initiated without the knowledge of the US, whose response was distinctly unfavourable. The Russians, seeking to protect their client interests, threatened missile attacks against the United Kingdom and France,[4] and US NATO Forces would have been obliged to respond. US displeasure was actively demonstrated when aircraft of the US Navy 6th Fleet, operating in the eastern Mediterranean, harassed Royal Air Force (RAF) aircraft routing close by the American Carrier Task Force and jammed radio communications. Operation Musketeer Revised, ill-conceived and not fully supported by the military chiefs, was uncoordinated, unsuccessfully carried out and became a diplomatic disaster. On 6 November, under intense pressure from the United States, the threat of intervention by the Soviet Union, adverse world opinion and a run on the pound threatening the UK's gold reserves, a ceasefire was put into place.[5] It was a humiliating political defeat and its effects were to influence British attitudes to the use of military force for the next quarter of a century. Britain's role as a significant player on the world scene had suffered a severe blow and it was apparent that US international dominance was such that it could assume a power of veto on any independent action of which it disapproved. The American intervention was to leave a bitter taste amongst the ranks of the British Tory Party. It is interesting to note, if only in passing, that Soviet Premier Josef Stalin, who had died three years previously, had predicted a falling out amongst the Western Allies after the end of the Second World War. In this view he was reiterating Lenin's belief that the uneven distribution of wealth endemic in a capitalist system would lead to a falling out of capitalist allies. He had believed that this disaffection would lead the way to an expansion of Soviet interests towards Western Europe. To further raise international tensions, on 4 November, Warsaw Pact forces had invaded Hungary resulting in a bloody suppression of the subsequent uprising. The world was an uncertain, and a potentially unsafe place.

The missiles placed on alert were Martin (TM-61A) Matador surface-to-surface missiles operated by the United States Air Force in Europe (USAFE). The Matador was the first missile to be operated by the USAF. It was a winged, subsonic air breathing cruise missile which could carry a W-5 nuclear warhead. It had a range of 690 miles, a radio-controlled guidance system which was not immune to jamming, and could only reach supersonic speeds in the final dive to its target.[6] Nearly cancelled in 1949, the Matador had been saved by the advent of the Korean War.[7] It had reached operational capability by 1955 but was never a fully satisfactory weapon, being unreliable and inaccurate.

However, progress was rapidly sidelining Matador. The first two Douglas Thor missiles were flown in Douglas C-124 Globemaster IIs from Santa Monica to Patrick AFB in late 1956. These were both instrumented test vehicles. For the Douglas engineers the constant travel between Los Angeles and Cape Canaveral became an arduous aspect of their work until the BMD managed to obtain a Douglas C-118 Liftmaster transport from the Military Air Transport Service and set up a regular coast-to-coast shuttle service, known as Hebner's Airline after the colonel who set it up.[8] Thor had been classified by the WDD as a 'maximum risk' programme. This meant that the initial series of test flights could be conducted under minimum requirements for performance and reliability without, of course, compromising basic safety needs. The Air Force was keen to establish its superiority over the other two services and needed a successful first flight. They were to be disappointed.

The launch operations were under the control of Project Director Dr Dolph Thiel from Space Technologies Laboratory.[9] Thiel had been one of the V-2 engineers brought from Germany so had some experience of the complexities of a missile development programme. The Associate Director was Arnold Anchordoguy. The first launch took place on 25 January 1957 from Launch Complex 17B (LC-17B) at the Air Force Eastern Test Range (AFETR) at Cape Canaveral. The missile was Thor T101 (Air Force Serial 56-6751), a Series One[10] Research and Development missile, although under the concurrency concept this was a quasi-production missile. It was radio guided and had a dummy warhead, the latter much more aerodynamic in shape than the blunt cone of the actual warhead. Contaminated liquid oxygen caused the failure of a check valve leading to thrust decay. The missile lifted 6in off the pad, fell back onto the pad and exploded violently. Unlike Soviet missile failures which were closely guarded secrets, US failures were in the public domain and could not be disguised.

A second attempt was made on 20 April. Missile T102 (Air Force Serial 56-6752) was set up on a refurbished launch pad. Launch was successful but thirty-five seconds into the flight the Range Safety Officer (RSO) initiated the missile destruct command. Those watching the missile saw it start on its trajectory and begin arcing over the Atlantic. However, unknown to the observers outside who were in fact witnessing a successful launch, a fault in the wiring of the Beep-Beep DOVAP Plotter was giving a signal to the RSO inside his bunker that the missile was 180 degrees from its actual course. To him, it appeared to have started to fly inland, and without any visual means of verification available to him he determined to destroy the vehicle.

The third attempted launch took place on 22 May. This time the missile, T103 (Air Force Serial 56-6753), blew up on the pad four minutes before launch, after a main fuel valve fault which caused the fuel tank to over pressurise and then rupture. The fourth launch on 30 August from Launch Complex 17A was a partial success. Missile T104 (Air Force Serial 56-6754) lifted off successfully and was ninety-two seconds into the flight when a poor signal to the yaw actuator caused the engine to go hard over. Despite this, the auto-pilot and vernier control continued to function and correct the swing. The missile was subject to severe right and left yaw and broke up.

It was not until 20 September that a fully successful launch and subsequent complete flight profile was demonstrated. Missile T105 (Air Force Serial 56-6755), still radio guided with a dummy warhead, lifted off from LC-17B and flew a 1,300nm trajectory. However, the next launch on 3 October from LC-17A ended when missile T107 (Air Force Serial 56-6757) lifted-off 10ft and exploded after an electrical malfunction delayed the opening of the gas generator valve. Worse was to follow when, on the following day, the Soviet Union took the world by surprise in launching an R-7 booster from the Tyuratam Cosmodrome, and took the first artificial satellite, Sputnik-1, into space. It was no longer necessary to speculate about Soviet missile capability. Nor did the next Thor test do much to redress the balance, although the launch of T108 (Air Force Serial 56-6758) from LC-17B, four days after the launch of Sputnik-1, was classed as a partial success. This was the first flight with the production thrust motor developing 150,000lb thrust. There was a premature engine cut-off two minutes and thirty-two seconds into the flight, after a turbo-pump quill shaft failed.

Now desperate for a totally successful launch, if only to maintain the project's credibility, the Douglas crew readied T109 (Air Force Serial 56-6759) on LC-17A for a launch on 24 October. Air Force Chief of Staff General Thomas D. White had given instructions to launch a missile to maximum range and this missile had been stripped down to reduce its weight. It still retained the dummy warhead, although this had had 4,100lb of ballast removed, and radio guidance. After a flawless lift-off, the missile completed a fully successful flight profile with a range of 2,350nm, well in excess of the design range of the missile. Thor had at last proved itself.

With things at last looking better, there were high hopes for a successful US Navy Vanguard TV3 launch on 6 December.[11] This was designed to place the first US satellite in orbit. Unlike events at Tyuratam, the Vanguard launch took place in the full glare of live TV coverage, but it was the glare of the rocket exploding on the launch pad having only lifted off inches that horrified the American public.

The following day saw the next Thor test flight. Thor T112 (Air Force Serial 56-6783) was the first Series 2 missile and was equipped for the first time with an AC Spark Plug all-inertial guidance system. However, this guidance system failed to give a cut-off signal and the RSO was obliged to destroy the missile one minute forty-seven seconds into the flight. The last launching of 1957 took place from Pad 17A on 19 December. Missile T113 (Air Force Serial 56-6784) was classed as an overall success although it impacted some 5nm from the target.

Whilst the US was suffering these problems, the Soviet Union was demonstrating a more successful capability, thereby reinforcing the fears of the increasing missile gap. On 3 November Sputnik-2 had carried a dog called Laika into orbit. It was clear in which direction the Soviets were headed.

The first launch of 1958 took place from Pad 17A, which had been updated to incorporate an operational launch mounting. T114 (Air Force Serial 56-6785) was another Phase 2 missile, and the launch proved a partial success when the RSO had to destroy the missile two minutes thirty-two seconds into the flight after a loss of guidance caused by electrical supply instability. Three days later it was the US Army who restored some of America's prestige by successfully launching Explorer 1, the first US satellite, using a modified Jupiter-C (RS-29).[12] The early history of rocketry had been characterised more often by failure rather than success, but as the Soviets' list of 'firsts in space' increased there was increasing concern at the repeated failures of Thor. The US Army, on a lesser budget, seemed to be able to achieve more and had, in the full glare of publicity, successfully entered space, an arena that the Air Force had presumed would be its domain.

Exactly one month after the flight of T114, the flight of Thor T120 (Air Force Serial 56-6791) was even shorter. The missile suffered premature engine shutdown after one minute forty-nine seconds. Another Phase 2 missile, it was the first to carry a Mk2 RV.[13] On 19 April, the next missile, T121 (Air Force Serial 56-6792) destroyed itself on the launch pad from what was believed to have been a collapsed fuel duct, leading to fuel starvation on ignition.

That Thor would earn itself the reputation of being one of the most reliable US launch vehicles would presumably never have been guessed at the time by the engineers trying to make it work, but the 23 April launch of T116 (Air Force Serial 56-6787) presaged the other role to which Thor would be put. This was the first test launch of Thor as a satellite launch vehicle. For this purpose, a second stage 'Able' booster was added. The purpose of the launch was to trial a General Electric Advanced Re-entry Test Vehicle (ARTV). To prove the ability of animals to survive such flights, the Thor-Able (Re-entry 1) carried a diminutive passenger – a mouse called Mia-1 (Mouse in Able-1). After a successful launch a quill shaft failed in the turbo-pump and the vehicle exploded after two minutes twenty-six seconds.

Over a month elapsed before the next launch on 4 June. T115 (Air Force Serial 56-6786) was designed to test the effect of windsheer. It also tested the Bell guidance system for the Titan ICBM. Despite losing two of the four vestigial fins around the base of the missile, the flight was deemed a success. It was also the first to take off from a launch pad replicating the operational configuration of the combat launch emplacements. At last things looked more promising. Nine days later, T122 (Air Force Serial 56-6793), the first Phase 3 missile, completed a successful mission which included the recovery of the RV data capsule. Another mouse, called Laska, took to the skies on 10 July on Thor-Able T118 (Air Force Serial 56-6789). Laska survived an astonishing 60G acceleration and was weightless for forty-five minutes before re-entry. This was the first RV to make its re-entry at ICBM speed. The flight was considered a success, despite the fact that the RV sank and was not recovered.

The next test of a Phase 3 Thor, T123 (Air Force Serial 56-6789), which lifted-off on Launch Complex 17B on 13 July, was partly successful. The Main Engine Cut-off (MECO) signal was not received, nor was any confirmation that the RV had separated successfully from the main vehicle. The third and last mouse to be launched aboard a Thor-Able was Wickie Mouse,[14] the miniature passenger on T119 (Air Force Serial 56-6789). Taking place on 23 July, the flight was successful but like its predecessor, the RV sank and could not be located. Launch Complex 17 was a busy place. Only three days later, T126 (Air Force Serial 56-6797), a Phase 3 missile, was a partial success. It had broken up just under a minute after launch following the early closure of the LOX valve. On 30 July the programme suffer a tragic setback when a seal in a valve that was not compatible with LOX failed on the test rig at the Douglas Test Facility at Scaramento. The resulting fire severely burning six Douglas employees; three of them were subsequently to die.[15] Another Phase 2 Thor, T117 (Air Force Serial 56-6797), followed on 6 August. This was a further windsheer test and was a complete success.

On 17 August the US made its first attempt to reach the Moon. This time the Thor-Able T127 (Air Force Serial 56-6798) payload was not a mouse but the Lunar probe Pioneer (1).[16] Success would have given the US at least one 'first' in the space race. The Soviets had not yet launched anything out of Earth's orbit. But it was not to be. The vehicle failed even to reach Earth's orbit. An explosion seventy-four seconds into the flight was the result of the first stage turbopump failure, leading to the shedding of turbine blades and almost certainly the puncturing of the LOX tank. A second attempt was made on 11 October. The launch of Thor-Able T130 (Air Force Serial 56-6801) was partially successful, although an error producing insufficient thrust and incorrect orientation of the second stage meant that the vehicle again failed to reach orbit. However, a new altitude record of 120,000km was established.

The next launch from LC-17B, on 5 November, was a significant one in the development program of the IRBM. T138 (Air Force Serial 56-2646) was the first launch of an IOC (Initial Operational Configuration) missile. This was essentially the missile that was being deployed in Britain. In fact, the first of the initial fifteen missiles for the first squadron had already been airlifted to RAF Lakenheath in August, although the Air Ministry, still nervous that Thor's operational capability was as yet unproven, had accepted these missiles for training purposes and to allow the launch facilities to be tested. These concerns were realised when the missile, fitted with a dummy warhead, had to be destroyed after forty-five seconds due to an autopilot failure. Fortunately the second IOC missile, T140 (Air Force Serial 56-2648), was launched on 26 November and declared a success, even though it overshot the target by 22nm due to guidance power failure. The third IOC launch of T145 (Air Force Serial 56-2256) on 5 December was declared a partial success. This time, the missile fell 20nm short of the target due to LOX tank pressurisation failure. Despite this, the need to demonstrate Thor's operational capability was growing. On 16 December 1958 two Thors were readied for launch. The first, at the AFETR at Patrick AFB, was the fourth IOC missile, T146 (Air Force Serial 56-2257). This launch was an unqualified success. A short while later on the west coast of the United States, the AFWTR Vandenberg AFB would witness its first launch of a ballistic missile, Thor T150 (Air Force Serial 56-2262). This was significant in that it was undertaken by a USAF launch team that had been undergoing training since early in the year and had originally been designated to operate the first squadron of missiles in the UK until the RAF launch teams were up to speed. The missile for the launch, appropriately called Operation Tune Up, was given the operational number '1001'. The launch was a success, which must have come as a relief to those present, as the event had been witnessed by around 200 media representatives. However, the point had been made. SAC had demonstrated that Thor was operational.

Notes:
1 The missiles were based at Bitburg, Hahn and Sembach Air Force Bases but, like the V-2s, they were mobile and would have been moved to undisclosed alert sites.
2 Operation Kadesh.
3 The original plan was codenamed Operation Hamilcar. This evolved into Operation Musketeer which, after a final revision in August 1956, became Operation Musketeer Revised.
4 It has never been completely clear as to whether the Soviet threat was against the countries of the UK and France, or against their formations in the Suez area of operations, although recently released documents tend towards the latter (see Peter Hennessy's book, *Having it so Good: Britain in the Sixties*).

5 Speaking on CBS Radio on 10 December 1956, the Honorable C. Douglas Dillon, the US Ambassador to France, expressed his opinion that it was principally the Soviet peril that had caused the British and the French to back down. The Soviet threat, orchestrated by Khrushchev but administered by Bulganin, was overt; the US threat was covert, with the result that it appeared that it was Khrushchev's intervention that had caused the withdrawal. This, too, was the Soviet interpretation and tempted Khrushchev to adopt this as a political policy.

6 In the 1951 USAF classification of missile types, the Matador was assigned the prefix XB, signifying an unmanned bomber and an indication of the cultural thinking of the USAF at the time.

7 'The wrong war in the wrong place at the wrong time', and the first war that the United States had lost. The Korean War had caught the United States unawares. It had also emphasised that there were still scenarios for limited conventional wars. The possession of nuclear weapons had provided little benefit to countering the North Koreans, although commanders on the ground did at least consider the use of tactical nuclear weapons.

8 Hartt, Julian, *The Mighty Thor*, p.70.

9 Space Technology Laboratories was originally called the Ramo-Wooldridge Corporation after its two founders. It assumed the role of civilian project management for the Thor programme.

10 The Thor R&D launch programme was split into four series of launches:

Phase 1: starting in January 1957 with missile 101 tested the functional operation and compatibility of the simplest flyable configuration – airframe, propulsion and control systems.

Phase 2: starting in December 1957 with missile 112 tested the functional operation of the inertial guidance system and its compatibility with the airframe, propulsion and control systems configuration.

Phase 3: starting in June 1958 with missile 122 tested the functional operation of the nose cone subsystems during the separation, re-entry, arming and fusing phases and evaluation of the airframe, propulsion, control and guidance subsystems.

IOC: starting in November 1958 with missile 138 demonstrated the functional operation of the IOC missile.

11 Vanguard 1 did succeed in placing the second US satellite in orbit on 17 March 1958.

12 Problems with Vanguard had prompted the SecDef, on 8 November 1957, to request von Braun's team at the Army Ballistic Missile Agency to restore American morale by launching a satellite by March 1958. It is perhaps no surprise that he achieved this target two months early. Explorer 1 did make a significant discovery when it identified bands of high radiation surrounding the Earth. These were to be called the Van Allen belts after Professor James A. Van Allen of the State University of Iowa, who had developed the instrument package for the satellite.

13 The Mk2 RV had been developed by General Electric for the Thor, Jupiter and Atlas missiles. It was a heat-sink blunt body design.

14 The mouse was named after a well-known Cape Canaveral space journalist, Mercer 'Wickie' Livermore.

15 Hartt, *Ibid*, p.180 and corresspondence with Dick Parker, Oct 2008.

16 After the failure the Pioneer designator 1 was cancelled and given to the next Pioneer spacecraft.

CHAPTER THREE
THE THOR AGREEMENT – FINDING THE BASES

The first time that the question of placing US IRBMs on UK soil was discussed officially was during the visit to London by the US Secretary to the Air Force (SecAF) Donald Quarles in mid-July 1956.[1] There had already been correspondence on an unofficial level between the USAF and the Ministry of Supply (MOS) and although the Air Force clearly saw the basing of missiles on UK soil as desirable, it had at that stage received no official approval from the US Government.[2] Quarles was therefore to raise the issue on an official basis. The identity of the missile the US had in mind was not confirmed, because at that stage both Thor and Jupiter, the US Army's IRBM design, could have been contenders. But the possible basis for the deployment was identified. The draft proposal was to locate the missiles:

> ...on present USAF bases in the United Kingdom with the intention of ultimate transfer to the RAF as soon as our own longer range ballistic missiles are available. They would prefer to use existing USAF bases ... for obvious security and logistic reasons but appreciate that we may prefer the bases to be as near as possible to the coast to reduce risk to the civil population becoming involved in accidents. The USAF will want to fire missiles with dummy warheads occasionally from their operational bases.[3]

The nature of the deployment had been developing in the minds of the USAF planners since early in 1955 with a suggested ORBAT of eight squadrons with fifteen missiles each. Initially, it appears that the US plan was to site all the missiles at one US base in the UK. This evolved into a two-base concept, as the vulnerability of a single base was realised.[4] A three-base scenario is also mentioned. Obviously, the USAF would favour the RAF as its partner, although it was the British Army that at that time had the greatest degree of experience in operating missiles as a result of a joint US/UK agreement, signed in 1954, to supply 113 Corporal Type IIA[5] SSMs to be operated by the Royal Artillery. Therefore, there was to be none of the inter-service rivalry that was to frustrate matters on the other side of the Atlantic. It was offered that, in exchange, Britain could be supplied with advanced fighter aircraft, the aircraft in question being the Convair

F-106 Delta Dart.[6] This seems to have been a somewhat informal offer although the United Kingdom representatives did appear to have registered a serious interest.

However, President Eisenhower's fiscal restraint dictated that there appears to have been little urgency in moving matters forward. The deployment would have meant a considerable cost increment to the US Defense Budget and some believed that the progress of the Atlas ICBM was advanced enough that there may well not be a need to field an IRBM as an interim measure.

However, things changed following the unpleasantness between the two nations some months later over the Suez Campaign. Prime Minister Anthony Eden, his tenure at Number 10 mortally wounded, resigned in January 1957 and was replaced by the discreetly ambitious Harold Macmillan, fortuitously an old wartime friend of Eisenhower.[7] The President was keen to repair the severely damaged 'Special Relationship' in the knowledge that anti-American feelings in the UK were at a post-war high. Yet the alliance between the two countries was vital to America's needs. In the same month, a visit to Washington by the UK Minister of Defence, Duncan Sandys[8], revealed that the US still had the deployment of missiles in mind, although by then the number had halved to sixty missiles distributed between four squadrons. In fact, Sandys and US Secretary for Defense (SecDef) Charles Wilson agreed a draft outline of how the missiles might be based. The plan called for the first ten missiles to reach IOC by October 1958 with the full arsenal available by July 1959. Although there were to be a number of subsequent variations on this theme, the total number of sixty missiles did not thereafter change. On 30 January Sandys telegraphed Macmillan from Washington commenting that the US was 'most anxious in view of progress of Russian ballistic rockets that [a] rocket deterrent should be established in Britain as soon as possible'. They had, by then, in mind an operational date of 1960, a date that General Schriever, Head of the AFBMD, felt more realistic and more in line with Douglas' expectations, based on the number of launch failures so far experienced. It was also agreed that a US/UK Summit Meeting would take place in the spring as a public assertion of the willingness to restore friendly relations between the two countries.

The Bermuda Conference, the second Summit Meeting held on the Caribbean island, took place from 21–24 March 1957 at the Mid Ocean Club at Tucker's Town, and did ultimately lead to the joint agreement to deploy Thor; however, the attitude of Eisenhower at the conference was not indicative of total commitment, if for no other reason than he was not, in general terms, a particularly enthusiastic supporter of the IRBM programme. His administration was increasingly keen on fiscal prudence. Thor had still to prove itself and the ICBM issue still hovered unhelpfully in the background. Once Atlas was operationally ready the case for Thor and also Jupiter would be very substantially weakened and there were undoubtedly elements within the US Administration who believed that neither IRBM would in fact be necessary. The UK contingent, however, was more enthusiastic. In early April, Sandys was to present to Parliament a policy document, 'Defence: outline of future policy',[9] which placed a significant reliance on missile technology for the future military protection of the UK. He was therefore pro-IRBM. Although Sandys did not enjoy a close relationship with Macmillan, he was seen as having a 'cassant' manner and was good at doing any job he was given. His document was bound to give rise to controversy, particularly in the ranks of the RAF. His predecessor, Anthony Head, a former Army officer, had been unable to effect a radical pruning of Britain's armed forces still bloated from the Second World War. In Sandys' plans, something akin to a British version of Eisenhower's New Look policy, and more fitting to the medium-size power that Britain now was, an IRBM would fit rather neatly into this policy and provide the UK with 'off the shelf' experience of handling ballistic missiles. There were some voices of concern, however, that it may undermine the case for Blue Streak, the British MRBM under development by de Havilland and Rolls-Royce but proving to be a difficult project both technically and financially.[10] Another view on this, however, was that the agreement would provide technical knowledge that would assist the Blue Streak programme. Conversely there were some in both Britain and the US who would have been very glad to have seen Blue Streak cancelled as they believed that the considerable funds consumed by the programme that would thereby have been released on termination of the project, which was falling behind in technological terms in any case, could then have been better spent on other projects; perhaps on more conventional weapons which would have been to the overall benefit of NATO.

Other issues were covered during the Bermuda talks so the negotiations on the IRBM issue were not imperative to the successful outcome of the conference *per se*, but an understanding was reached and the end of conference communiqué set out the broad terms of agreement under which IRBMs could be deployed in the UK. The agreement made in Bermuda, nonetheless, was only an agreement in principle. It gave no indication on how the project would be managed or funded. Was it analogous to the lease-lend programme of the Second World War? Would it be funded by the mutual aid program or by some other means? Indeed, on 20 April Macmillan wrote to Sandys, under the heading 'Rockets', asking, '[what] do you conceive to be the next stage? Do we try to make an agreement with the State Department? I feel in my bones that the Americans are going to be difficult about it. I may have to take it up directly with the President. Perhaps you will consider this and let me know what had best be done.'[11] In fact, a draft agreement had already been sent on 18 April by Wilson, although Sandys consumed much red ink thereafter as it went through successive re-drafts. It took until mid-June for Sandys to write to Wilson:

> We warmly welcome your proposal. We much appreciate the spirit in which you have made it and we are confident that this project will make a valuable addition to the strength of the Western Alliance. I am glad to be able to inform you that the draft is acceptable to us as a basis for detailed negotiation.[12]

The full agreement would not be signed until February 1958, following approval by Eisenhower and the National Security Council (NSC) on 30 January 1958.

In anticipation of an approach being made to the UK, the WDD had been given the task of defining the IRBM IOC ORBAT on 24 March 1956. Their initial proposal, put forward on 14 June 1956, was to place the missiles on one sizeable base incorporating squadrons of fifteen missiles, but the vulnerability of one site to a single incoming warhead had resulted in the number increasing first to two, the plan originally presented to the UK, and then to three. Responsibility for the programme rested with the ARDC and SAC. Broadly the ARDC responsibility covered all activities in the US whilst SAC would be responsible for coordinating the deployment of Thor in the UK. SAC would therefore be responsible for agreeing the location of the bases. Understandably, SAC initially favoured using existing USAFE bases with all the missiles being manned and operated by USAF units. The missiles would be operated under a single IRBM Wing consisting of eight squadrons. As eight does not divide exactly into sixty, was this number a hark back to the original fifteen missiles per squadron scenario? In the three-base scenario, each base would field twenty missiles in four clusters of five launch emplacements, giving a total of sixty missiles. A total production run of 120 operational missiles was anticipated. This would cover sufficient rounds for training purposes as well. Questions had also been asked about the feasibility of placing the missiles in underground silos, as was the plan for the RAF's Blue Streak; however, Douglas engineers confirmed that this was not an option as the missile was not engineered to withstand the somewhat different stresses, both structural and acoustic, that an underground launch would place on it. In any case, it was also accepted that 'in view of the timescale it is quite impossible to provide underground sites in time'.[13]

Douglas did suggest that the missiles might be stored in protective revetments but would still have to be raised for launch. In any case, silo technology was still in the design stage and completely unproven. The missiles, whether Thor or Jupiter, would necessarily be very visible and thereby, by their very nature, vulnerable. SoS(A) George Ward counselled caution when he wrote to Sandys, reminding him that as the Americans did:

> ...not intend to provide above ground protection [for the missiles] their operational value to the United Kingdom is little, while they increase our attractiveness as a target. We must be careful that we do not pay too much for the principal advantage of the deal, i.e. its contribution to the development of Blue Streak in terms of R & D knowledge.[14]

An Air Ministry note to Sandys in January 1957 confirmed the spin-off that was expected to help the Blue Streak programme:

> We are getting help in developing Blue Streak as a result of the Wilson/Sandys agreement. We should aim to get all possible assistance from the Americans, but we should insist on continuing to keep it in our programme not only because we want it but also because, politically, we cannot afford to be dependent upon America for this vital weapon. Operationally and technically we must be free, since the continuing interplay of counter measures and counter counter measures will be involved, to develop and modify the weapon to meet our appreciation of the operational situation.[15]

It would therefore appear that, by this stage, the question of receiving advanced fighter aircraft had already slipped from the agenda. It was agreed that as much equipment as possible would be purchased in the UK, although it was recognised that this would reduce the burden of costs to the Americans.

The perception of continued vulnerability to Soviet warheads, however, prevailed and an in-depth deployment of the missiles with four squadrons of fifteen missiles was eventually confirmed as the preferred option, although this was not finally promulgated until March 1957. During the informal discussions in July 1956 in which the basing issue was considered, it became obvious to Quarles that the British wanted and may insist on a degree of active participation in any missile deployment, possibly to the extent of full RAF manning for some of the squadrons. This potentially added a further dimension to the question of bases for the missiles, a subject that was to prove surprisingly difficult to resolve and something that furthermore could clearly be used as a bargaining lever by the UK. The RAF counselled caution in the selection of suitable locations. They believed that a dispersed deployment was preferable, but in accepting the US point of view agreed a four-base concentrated deployment as a compromise. Furthermore, the RAF was keen to select sites suitable for continued operation post-Thor but it was recognised that this might well conflict with US requirements. On 10 November a meeting of the AFBMC agreed to consider a joint US/UK ORBAT with squadrons operated by both countries, possibly two each. SAC was unhappy about this proposal and demanded the right of control over all missiles regardless of which country's air force may man them. Either way, the revised plan essentially expanded the deployment so that the use of US bases only was impractical and the use of RAF stations would have to be considered. By the beginning of 1958, the RAF plan had further evolved. The four concentrated bases and the dates for US and RAF operations were to be.[16]

Table I: Thor Bases – Initial Plan using RAF Stations and assuming initial USAF manning

Location	USAF	RAF
Feltwell/Methwold ★	July 1960	January 1962
Hemswell	November 1960	June 1962
Driffield	N/A	March 1961
Stradishall ★★	N/A	July 1961

★ A joint site was planned as Feltwell, chosen because of its proximity to Lakenheath, was too small on its own to accommodate fifteen missiles.
★★ It was noted that the road access to Stradishall was not ideal.

If the RAF view prevailed and a dispersed ORBAT was approved, then there would be twenty sites, each with three missiles. There would be four 'Central Sites' (in bold in the following table), each with four satellites. In this scenario, Stradishall would be replaced by Dishforth.

Table II: Thor Bases – Revised Plan

Feltwell	Marham	Watton	Honington	Witchford
Hemswell	Scampton	Ludford Magna	Bardsey ★	Kirmington
Driffield	Full Sutton	Holme	Carnaby	Hornsea ★★
Dishforth	Leeming	Neasham	Marston Moor	Sherburn-in-Elmet

★ It is presumed that this was meant to be Bardney.
★★ Hornsea was an Army establishment which was soon to become available.

Total costs at this stage were estimated at £7.15m for either deployment scenario.

It is interesting, therefore, to see that at this relatively early stage with little or no survey work done, and with the exception of the Dishforth Wing, this plan roughly equated to the final deployment. It was still, at this stage, accepted that the USAF would be an active participant in the deployment. This was soon to change as the political implications of the plan and the possible sensitivities of the UK population to the whole issue of Thor became more apparent.

The question of bases for the missiles would progress slowly even after the Bermuda Conference had given a much clearer profile of UK involvement. However, the continuing delays would lead to one significant consideration.

At its 10 November 1956 meeting, the AFBMC had examined a plan for 'IRBM Emergency Capability'. This would 'allow an experimental unit equipped with about five missiles to be deployed on an American airfield in [the UK]',[17] and would have the missiles on operational alert by mid-1958. This was a full year in advance of the IOC predicted at the time. However, this early capability was of questionable military advantage and must be viewed primarily as a political gesture, as the missiles would be interim models still in the development stage and the launch procedures would rely on joint operations with the contractors' staff forming part of the launch team. Although the plan was endorsed by Quarles and Wilson, there were varying and divided views within the Air Force. Whilst some thought it of little military significance, others saw it as a way of projecting US capability to the Soviet Union, and it would also act as a prototype to the later-expanded deployment and might even help to resolve the many differences between the US' and the UK's views on the missiles. On reflection, although demonstrating SAC's enthusiasm for moving the Thor deployment ahead, the idea would have been complex to realise within the necessary limited time-frame. The plan was incorporated in the early post-Bermuda discussions as a way of accelerating the deployment, but the continuing delays over the basing issue effectively rendered the plan obsolete and it quietly withered on the vine.

Two key factors affecting the WDD's management of the ICBM and the IRBM Programmes were the anticipated IOC date and the budget allocated to the missiles. The latter was a constant reminder of the fiscal restraint practiced by the Eisenhower administration, and the balance accorded to the IRBM against the ultimately more important ICBM programme was a recurring problem in allocating priority.

Meanwhile, in the US, the infrastructure to operate the missiles was already being constructed. The ARDC had made the request that an Air Division (AD) be formed to coordinate training and operations of the missiles and this led to the formation of the 1st Missile Division on 15 April 1957.[18] It was initially co-located with the WDD at Inglewood, California. A suitable site from which to test launch the missiles had already been identified following a survey that had started in January 1956. The chosen location was Camp Cooke, a largely derelict Army disciplinary establishment on the central Californian coast, originally chosen in 1941 as a suitable armoured unit training facility. There were some who favoured extending what was to become the Eastern Test Range at Patrick Air Force Base, but Camp Cooke had the favourable attributes of remoteness, size and a relatively ambient climate without seasonal changes that might affect operations. In November 1956 Wilson directed that 64,000 acres of North Camp Cooke be transferred, without public disclosure, from the Army to the Air Force and, although the formalities were not completed until 21 June

1957, Air Force access had been permitted since the start of the year and work on converting the place was already underway by 6591st Support Squadron. The area was given the name Cooke AFB. It was to be renamed again on 4 October 1958 as Vandenberg AFB.[19] Operations at Cooke were to be carried out by 392d Air Base Group, a unit also activated on 15 April 1957 to replace the 6591st Support Squadron. On 15 September the 392d Missile Training Squadron was formed. Its initial role was for an assignment to the Matador missile deployed in Germany. However, it was still only a skeletal unit with little for its personnel to do until they were sent, somewhat unexpectedly, to the Douglas Aircraft Company in Tucson to start training on Thor. After a year at Douglas the unit returned to Cooke AFB, by which time Douglas contractors were constructing five Thor launch pads developed from a layout mock-up, which had been built at the Douglas facility in Culver City. Numbers 1 and 2 were 'Wet Pads' (75-1-1 and 75-1-2, later to be called SLC-2E (pronounced 'Slick 2E') and SLC-2W as part of Space Launcher Complex 2) which could be used for both live and captive launches. For the latter a water-protected flame trench was added to the pad. Pads 3, 4 and 5 (75-2-6, 75-2-7 and 75-2-8, later SLC-10W, SLC-10E and LE-8) were development pads configured to reflect the evolving design of the combat launch pads or Launch Emplacements (LEs) to be built in England.

The matter of which missile would be stationed in the UK was still not officially determined. Intriguingly, in a letter of 24 September, Sir Richard Powell advised Sandys that 'it is not yet settled which weapon the Americans will supply, but it seems likely to be [a] new weapon embodying the best features of both Thor and Jupiter which are said to be [too] similar technically to be worth developing separately'.[20] Quarles had, in fact, made reference to this in correspondence with the British Ambassador in Washington, Sir Harold Caccia, but it seems an extraordinary idea which would surely only have resulted in further delay to the IRBM programme.[21]

Although the Eisenhower Administration played down the significance of the launch of Sputnik-1, the US public were alarmed and embarrassed by this unexpected Soviet success and demanded both a response and an explanation as to why a peasant-based population ruled by an authoritarian and repressive regime could outwit the technically sophisticated might of the US. Although the Soviets had come a worryingly close second in the race to develop both the atom and the hydrogen bombs,[22] they had now conspicuously won the race to develop the first intercontinental rocket. It was quite clear to see that if they could launch a satellite into orbit, then they could reach out to any part of the world's surface. The continental United States was no longer protected by distance from attack. This changed the view on its strategic position and also altered how that the Western Allies saw the possible way in which the US may now respond to any attack on Western Europe, an attack which would almost inevitably be matched by a concurrent attack on the US. However, coordinating such an attack was a challenging task to get right and might in fact have been too difficult for Soviet planners to attempt.[23]

The warnings of the impending Soviet capability had been there but had apparently gone unheeded.[24] However, Sputnik-1 did resolve one issue that had taxed US legal agencies, namely the right to overfly in orbit the above-atmosphere space of other nations.

Under public pressure the administration's response was commendably rapid. Within twenty-four hours, the production plan for the IRBM had been agreed. Various proposals were rapidly put forward by the WDD to accelerate missile IOC, but the vexed question of 'Thor or Jupiter' was still beyond resolution. In fact, on 31 October SecDef Neil McElroy, although a supporter of the role of the IRBM, further muddied the waters by granting Jupiter full IRBM status, which reduced the lead that the Air Force believed Thor already had ahead of Jupiter. Thor's IOC now largely depended on the rate of production allowed to Douglas.

Meanwhile, the joint agreement between the US and the UK was being drafted in Washington. Originally called somewhat starkly 'Intermediate Range Ballistic Missiles', the document underwent numerous re-draftings and by the fourth proof had been re-titled 'Supply of Ballistic Missiles by the United States to the United Kingdom'. It was broad in its outline but conveyed little specific information. Effectively this was a summary of the information that could be made public. A parallel document covered the elements of the agreement that were classified. The missiles – no reference was made as to which missile it was to be – would be used only for defence of NATO areas. The Cabinet approved the draft agreement on 18 February and a 'dummy' White Paper was laid before Parliament on 21 February 1958. The previous day the NATO Council had been informed in strict confidence of the impending announcement. Only the Permanent Representative for Norway, Jens Boyesen, voiced concerns, not, as he explained afterwards, to be difficult but only because the question of IRBMs was at that time a very sensitive issue in Norway. Australia and New Zealand had also been given advance warning because paragraph five of the document gave provision for the missiles to be fired, by agreement, from the British-Australian rocket-launching facility at the Long Range Weapons Establishment at Woomera, South Australia.

The official announcement was made in the House of Commons on the following Monday, 24 February,[25] during a session in which the major debate was on unemployment and in which the design of the new £5 note was also discussed. Thereafter, the media was invited to Conference Room D, where Sandys was available for questions, but it had been made clear that this would only be to clarify the statement and nothing further would be added. Over 100 members of the media were expected to attend, covering British national and provincial, American, Foreign and Commonwealth interests and including an anticipated attendance by TASS and *The Daily Worker*. Only the French media, because of diplomatic differences, and *Peace News* were highlighted as likely to be 'troublesome'. A letter from Freddie Bishop, Macmillan's highly trusted Personal Private Secretary, to Derick Ward at the Ministry of Defence commenting on the 'Questions and Answers' briefing notes for the press conference, emphasised the line that the Prime Minister wished to take. Hansard reported the statement: 'The Missiles will be manned and operated by personnel of the Royal Air Force. The Agreement provides that the missiles shall not be launched except by joint positive decision of both Governments'.[26] The missiles were not identified in the agreement but could, if required, be revealed as Thor and, anticipating questions on the location of the missile sites, Sir Richard Powell had felt:

> ...satisfied that it would be right to announce the general areas where the missiles are to be sited. There has been tremendous speculation in the Press, and if we give no indication where the missiles are to be, this will all be renewed. Moreover I feel sure that the Press would not accept a D-notice asking them to refrain from mentioning even the general

areas in which the missiles will be disposed; it will be difficult enough to persuade them not to mention the precise locations of the separate launching sites.[27]

It was therefore agreed that the bases could broadly be referred to as being in Yorkshire, Lincolnshire and East Anglia. No mention was made of the five-year duration of the agreement.

Emrys Hughes, the left-wing MP for South Ayrshire, enquired after Sandys had made the announcement, 'What about Scotland?'. Sandys replied that it 'would obviously not be in the public interest to disclose the number of missiles, or the number of sites or their precise location',[28] although he was prepared to reveal the locations in the press conference if pressed. Yet it was George Brown, MP for Belper, who touched a raw nerve when he asked, with reference to the RAF personnel to be trained in the US, 'does it mean that there will be no sites operated by Americans while our men are being trained'?[29] Lieutenant Commander Stephen Maydon, MP for Wells, after congratulating Sandys on achieving agreement so swiftly in this most difficult problem, asked if 'the Agreement mean[t] that the Americans c[ould] deploy and launch missiles under their own control from British territory?'. Sandys replied 'No, sir'.[30] The questions continued until the Speaker brought matters to a close, commenting that 'the time for East Anglia to protest, if it wants to, is on Wednesday and Thursday', the dates for the full defence debate.[31]

The Americans, who had been training their personnel since January, were still expecting to operate the first squadron, and SAC was anticipating an operational date as early as July[32] for the first three missiles, a time-frame which would scarcely permit the RAF to identify and train its first Thor personnel, let alone prepare the sites. However, endorsement of the idea had come from the highest authority, as Eisenhower had telegrammed Macmillan on 22 February: 'it will be necessary for United States personnel to man initially the IRBM Squadron scheduled for deployment in the United Kingdom this year'.[33] There was tacit understanding at this stage that the USAF would indeed operate the first squadron, handing over at a later date to the RAF. This was not what the Air Ministry wanted and would, it was predicted, realise a host of political problems. Matters were made worse when the Washington correspondent of *The Daily Telegraph* reported on 27 February, under the headline 'Mobile Thors Problem For British Roads', that 'Colonel Zink, who commands the first Thor intermediate range ballistic missile squadron that will be stationed in Britain by the end of this year told me to-day that his units are fully mobile. This was subject to roads being suitable for heavy equipment.' Zink commanded the 672d Ballistic Missile Squadron and had been addressing a meeting of the Air Force Association. A rebuttal to Zink's indiscretion was swift: 'Reports to the fact that Colonel Harry Zink, USAF, Commander of 672 Strategic Missile Squadron, will command operational units in the U.K. are in error. [...] Zink will be responsible for training activities in preparing the units for deployment'.[34]

There was a keen desire to temper SAC's enthusiasm with what the UK saw as the realities of the situation. On 24 February SoS(A) Ward had written to Mr E. Broadbent (PUS to SoS) at the Air Ministry:

In view of the fact that Thor has a long record of unsuccessful launches in public, it seems premature to imply satisfaction with its existing state of development, and it might be better to say, 'The missiles are still under development, but we are satisfied that they will make an effective contribution to the deterrent by the time they are deployed in the United Kingdom'.[35]

From a US standpoint, what effectively was procrastination was most unhelpful. Ambassador Sir Harold Caccia, when advised that 'for political reasons we may use this provision as a method of delaying deployment', warned, 'This is dangerous ground'.[36] The Foreign Office appeared to take a different view, being seen as 'mealy mouthed in the interests of pleasing the Americans at almost any price'.

However at this point, British crews still had to be selected and trained. Once the first intake had completed their training they would still be relatively few in number. Could a group of sixteen RAF personnel command a unit of 250 to 350 US servicemen? Would this in fact be a *bona fide* British unit? In any case SecAF Quarles had already vetoed any thought of British command of any US personnel early in February.[37]

In March Major Jamie Wallace, who was in charge of the GSE element of the programme, visited the UK to discuss the various aspects of the civil engineering works that would be required. East Anglia was a very long way from Santa Monica and no proper communications between the sites and Douglas had been worked out. The Air Ministry was rightly sceptical, believing that Thor would not be fit for deployment by July given the problems that were besetting it, but the Americans were clearly going ahead as if it would be ready.[38] Their considered view, communicated to Sandys, was that if the bases were ready by July, then there would be a gap of at least three months before the first RAF personnel would be ready. To speed things up, the Air Ministry suggested taking some of the Americans off the training course, allocating the places to the RAF. Alternatively the whole programme could be allowed to slip, but this would involve telling the Americans already in training that they would not be needed in the UK. Yet underlying the whole issue was the feared dilemma, outlined by the CAS in a letter to Sandys on 20 June 1958:

> ...that we shall be subject to pressure from the Americans to deploy Thor in this country before we can be satisfied that it has achieved a satisfactory operational performance, as evidenced by a series of successful test launches.[39]

SecDef McElroy sent Sandys a cutting from *The New York Times* outlining the Thor announcement, which including a photo of Sandys. Sandys' letter of thanks concluded with evident relief, 'As you know, there has been a good deal of excitement here over our IRBM agreement, but it is beginning to quieten down, thank goodness'.[40]

Consideration now had to be given to the location, construction and commissioning of the Thor sites. After the civil engineering works were completed – this would be done by UK firms – the sites would be handed over to Douglas technicians who would install all the specialist equipment and bring them up to a ready state. Special security conditions would apply during the construction, testing and handover phases for the protection of individuals and equipment. These were outlined in the 'Agreement Concerning the Physical Security of the Thor Missile Units in the United Kingdom'.[41] 'Condition Normal' would start with the installation of the weapon system. 'Condition Prepare' started on completion of the installation and at the start of the first 'wet' countdown. 'Condition Final' started with the presentation of the Certificate of Technical Completion by the Project Command (AFBMD) to the Contracting Officers, Air Matériel Command, and it ended with the handover of the completed Launch Emplacement to the RAF. Strictly speaking, up to this point there was to be no RAF involvement but No.77 (SM) Sqn ORB noted that 'DAC personnel were experiencing difficulty in meeting their schedules and RAF personnel were attached to their working teams to assist. Their contribution ... was of paramount importance during the Installation and Checkout phase'.[42] The warheads, however, as was required by the US MacMahon Act, would remain at all times under direct US control. Launch would be a joint decision by both countries, thus by implication giving each country the right over the other to veto a launch. Initially, the USAF favoured an in-depth dispersal of the sites but this gave rise to concern within the ranks of the RAF, particularly about the US wish to use their SAC base at RAF Brize Norton, which also had the necessary attributes for an airhead for bringing in the necessary equipment. This conjured up the nightmare scenario of an errant missile blowing up over London, to say nothing of the 'dreaming spires' of nearby Oxford.[43] However, none of these situations seemed to take into account that if the Thors were ever launched, then a massive Soviet pre-emptive strike was almost certainly already underway. The option of Thor being used as a first-strike weapon was not easy to envisage. Fortunately there was no shortage of alternative possible locations, although in the end, for a variety of reasons, it proved quite a complex task to finalise selection of the sites.

The RAF expansion periods of the 1930s and the 'aircraft carrier' that England had become during the Second World War had seen the construction of dozens of airfields to accommodate the thousands of Allied aircraft based in the UK. Of the many stations used by RAF Bomber Command and the 8th and 9th US Army Air Forces, many were still in Ministry ownership, some still operational, others mothballed but capable of restoration to a ready state. Most of these were on the east coast stretching from Yorkshire to East Anglia. With only the initial trajectory over land before the North Sea was reached, these presented a more acceptable solution to the problem of population vulnerability, although the bases would undoubtedly be targets for incoming Soviet missiles, a factor not missed by many local residents to the bases which gave rise to some limited local opposition. There were some doubts about the reasons for choosing these sites. On 5 March in Oral Answers in the Commons, James Harrison, MP for Nottingham North, referred to previous declarations that the bases were to be dispersed along the whole eastern seaboard of England and Scotland. Ward replied that he knew of no such declaration. George Chetwynd, MP for Stockton-on-Tees, asked if the concentration was 'entirely due to operational reasons, or is it because there are objections from a neutral country, Sweden, which objected to rockets going over its territory if the bases were stationed further north'. Ward assured him that the 'criteria which determined the siting of the bases [was] entirely operational'. Concerns about the whole programme were voiced by Geoffrey de Freitas, MP for Lincoln, when he suggested that there was a 'grave doubt as to the effectiveness of these missiles', but Ward did not accept these concerns, commenting that he thought 'they will greatly strengthen the effectiveness of the Western deterrent as a whole'.[44]

The USAF had identified a need to nominate certain airfields as airheads into where the missiles and all the related equipment could be flown. The eventual plan was for four airheads serving four main Wing HQs, each of which was to have four satellites, and each location having three Launch Emplacements giving a total of sixty missiles. SAC eventually conceded to the political sensitivities of the deployment, and although not totally without protest, accepted that the scenario of US squadrons operating the missiles was not going to be acceptable. As the host nation, the UK wanted the sole right to operate the missiles, thereby giving at least some demonstration of control over the use of the weapons. So the agreed ORBAT was that Thor would be operated by four RAF squadrons, each with four attached flights – the original RAF preferred solution. The squadrons would come under the aegis of Bomber Command.[45] The northern squadrons would be under No.1 Group based at Bawtry Hall, near Doncaster, and southern ones under No.3 Group based at RAF Mildenhall.[46] Although there was consideration given to using a completely new series of squadron number plates to reflect the novel role of the squadrons, CAS, at a meeting on 3 March 1958, declared that he would rather see the resurrection of disbanded squadrons, of which there were plenty, and this plan was adopted.

A maximum of thirty miles and a straight line minimum of twelve miles or an optimum of fifteen road miles was specified as the distance between the four outlying satellite sites and the Wing HQ – the minimum distance specified so that no one incoming warhead could take out more that one base. There was compromise on this as it was later calculated that a single accurately placed 1MT airburst could have simultaneously eliminated Driffield, Carnaby and Catfoss.[47] At least twenty Soviet warheads, and in practice more, should therefore have to be tied up in targeting the Thor sites. Site accessibility for the 60ft-long missiles was a consideration, as was the overall ability to protect the sites not only from the more obvious threats, not excluding the threat from the IRA, but also recognising that the Campaign for Nuclear Disarmament (CND) movement was gathering momentum.[48] Definition of the sites was requested by Sandys[49] and this was confirmed after meetings between the RAF and the USAF at the Air Ministry between 20–24 January 1958. The resulting draft Technical Agreement identified the following provisional ORBAT (the chart shows the users at that time):

Table III: Original Thor ORBAT. Initial choice of bases and usage at the time.

(Main bases are identified in bold. Stations which were eventually to become Thor bases are underlined.)

East Anglia Complex	First Squadron	
Feltwell ★	Flying Training Command	Operational
Honington	Bomber Command	Operational
Witchford	Inactive	
Watton	No.90 Group (Signals)	Operational
Marham	Bomber Command	Operational
Lincolnshire Complex	Second Squadron	
Hemswell ★	Bomber Command	Operational

Ludford Magna	Maintenance Command	Operational
Waddington	Bomber Command	Operational
Caistor	Inactive	
Bardney	Inactive	
South Yorkshire Complex	3rd Squadron	
Driffield	Fighter Command	Operational
Leconfield	Fighter Command	Operational
Holme-on-Spalding Moor	Inactive	
Riccall	Inactive	
Full Sutton	Inactive	
North Yorkshire Complex	4th Squadron	
Dishforth	Transport Command	Operational
Leeming	Fighter Command	Operational
Scorton	Inactive	
Marston Moor	Inactive	
Sherburn-in-Elmet	Occupied by MTCA	

★ The US had originally wanted East Kirkby and Sturgate, already used by the USAFE and the latter due to be vacated in mid-August 1958, but these were replaced by Hemswell and Feltwell. The RAF had vetoed use of both locations. There would be insufficient alternative dispersal stations in the area when the RAF took them over, the standard of domestic accommodation was well below standard and the access roads were inadequate to allow proper servicing and maintenance operations for a dispersed complex.

All these sites were owned by the Ministry of Defence so that no problems were anticipated in recovering those that were inactive and invariably being leased for agricultural use. A note was made that no search for Thor sites was being made in Scotland. This was added because it was expected that Scotland would be the site of a new 'special kind of defensive radar'[50] and Scottish MPs were taking a critical interest in any survey work that was identified. Initial survey work on the Thor sites had started in February 1958 but the political sensitivities of the program were recognised in the low-profile approach taken. Surveys of operational stations did not present so much of a problem, but great care was exercised on the non-operational sites so as not to arouse public attention. This care was evident when site assessment visits were undertaken. Feltwell had by then been identified as the lead site, and surveyed on 4 and 6 February 1958, mainly because of the convenience of its location close to Mildenhall. With the final ORBAT agreed, the earlier need to have a joint site at Feltwell with nearby Methwold was no longer required as only three missiles would now be based there. It was confirmed that all flying from Feltwell would cease on

1 May 1958. Two possible site layouts to the southern edge of the airfield, adjacent to each other, were drawn up.[51]

It was now necessary to identify suitable sites for the 2nd, 3rd and 4th Squadrons. These visits were made by a fifteen-man survey team consisting of representatives of the RAF, USAF, Air Ministry and the GPO; the latter was included because of the communications links that would need to be installed on the inactive sites. Journeys were to be made separately in six cars – air transport had been contemplated but was considered to be impractical – so as not to attract undue attention, and everyone wore civilian clothes. The list of six provisional locations on existing stations identified as potential Wing HQ sites had been submitted to the Air Ministry on 13 February 1958, and were all assessed in gruelling weather conditions between 24 and 28 February. The sites were: Waddington, Hemswell (where the group was temporarily snowbound), Leconfield, Driffield, Leeming and Dishforth. The criteria against which the sites were assessed were:

- Suitable area for launch pads.
- Suitable building to be used as a RIM (Receipt, Inspection and Maintenance) Building.
- Suitable building to be used as a Technical Storage Building.
- Dog Compound for thirty dogs.
- LOX Plant – local production of LOX was still being considered.[52]
- Segregated conventional storage building.
- Provision of Special Storage Area (SSA).

Assessments were also made as to the suitability of the proposed access routes.

So bad was the weather that at one stage the officials broke their own rules and travelled in convoy 'as a measure of self-protection against appalling road conditions'. The purpose of the visits was known only to the Station Commanders. Certainly, in the case of Hemswell, visited on the very day of the announcement of the Agreement in Parliament, this did not seem to have stopped the local civilian population, based on its own native intelligence, having already worked out the likelihood of the station becoming a dedicated missile base. Hemswell's Station Commander had to emphasise that there was 'no question of a security leak'.[53] Notwithstanding the need for secrecy, the Station Commander at Leeming had received permission from RAF Fighter Command to bring the three station Wing Commanders into his confidence as they would be able to offer much useful advice.[54]

The Sitings Board, which included members of the survey team, were thereafter to consider their criteria:

- No missiles were to be within 1,500ft of an inhabited dwelling or within 750ft of any public road.
- No missile was to be within 700ft of the Launch Control Trailer (LCT), Crew Rooms/Guardroom or SSA.
- Cable ducts between the missiles and the LCT were not to exceed 1,500ft.
- The distance between missiles must be greater than 700ft. (This could be reduced to 300ft if the LEs were protected by revetments.)
- Access to the site was to be by only one gate in the security fence.

- The inner fence was to be at least 150ft from the LEs and ideally 200ft.
- There was to be a gap of 225ft between the inner and outer security fences, inside which the dogs would patrol. This gap could be reduced if it proved difficult to achieve.
- The Crew Room was to be within 200ft of the LCT.
- All turning circles must have a minimum radius of 50ft.
- The LCT should ideally be sited uprange of the missiles (although as many were not, this requirement must have been relaxed).
- The LOX Plant was to be a minimum distance of 300ft from any carbohydrate source and ideally upwind.

It can be seen that only three locations survived this 'first cut' to become operational. In planning the locations it was necessary to make sure that the plan allowed for the maximum de-conflicting of the V-Bomber main bases, which weakened the case for Waddington which already housed a Vulcan squadron and was earmarked for SAGW Stage 1½.[55] V-Bomber dispersal sites had to be considered and also the protective coverage that would be given to the Thors by the Bloodhound Mk1 SAGW, operated by Fighter Command. In addition, increasing public opposition and political considerations had to be taken into account over certain proposed locations. The advantage of the east coast sites was that it avoided launchings over large areas of population, took full benefit of the missiles' range by placing them closer to their target and reduced the possibility of any radioactive fallout resulting from an enemy attack on the bases drifting over areas of population. Sandys was advised that it was:

> ...proposed to deploy the squadrons on four RAF airfields in Yorkshire, Lincolnshire and East Anglia. There will be none in Scotland. Some of the airfields are disused and land will have to be recaptured from agriculture.[56]

Anticipating the speed with which the sites would have to be constructed, preliminary discussions had taken place with the Ministry of Works. Hugh Molson, the Minister of Works, apparently misinterpreted what was to be built. On 23 January he wrote to Sandys suggesting the practical answer was to extend the work already being done at Spadeadam[57] in Cumbria in support of Blue Streak. The workforce there was already well skilled in the type of work he foresaw as necessary for Thor. There was a 'sterilised area of land at Spadeadam' that could be used and would minimise the effect on the public of the 'appalling noise of testing the device'.[58] He also advised Sandys that he was 'trying very hard to counter inflationary tendencies in the building and civil engineering industries'. In reply he was told that all testing of the missiles was to be undertaken in the US and that the UK constructions would be limited to the twenty planned sites.

The Technical Agreement still confirmed that the USAF would operate the first squadron, only handing over to the RAF when the latter 'was prepared to operate the weapon'. This was an unfortunate ambiguity of expression given the less than wholehearted support for the missile in certain UK corridors of power. It also reinforced the appearance of the whole deployment being to the benefit of the Americans, again something that was believed by many to be the case. The USAF desire to move the project forward was understandable. The discussions to deploy Jupiter elsewhere in

NATO were not going well and in any case Jupiter had become largely a political rather than a military issue.[59] But Thor had not yet proved itself as anything close to becoming an operational weapon. It would cost the UK Treasury £10 million and would take a total of c.4,000 personnel away from other duties, and in this context anything that would divert attention away from Bomber Command's V-Bombers[60] was likely to produce opposition within the higher ranks of the RAF. The prioritising of the needs of the V-Bombers was a recurrent theme which would run in the background of the Thor operations throughout the deployment of the missiles. There was also the question of Blue Streak, although by this time it had been publicly acknowledged that the UK MRBM Programme was experiencing considerable technical problems. Some saw the attitude of the Americans and SACEUR towards the project as indicating that the missiles would be allocated to SACEUR's control; this was not what had been agreed.[61] Indeed, it was partly that the Jupiters would be under the operational command of SACEUR that was causing problems within the NATO countries invited to accept them. The Air Council had a clear view on SACEUR's involvement with Thor:

> CAS was concerned at the way matters were developing. We should be required to man the sites and pay for installations but operational control, it was now being suggested, shall be vested in SACEUR. In the event the principle of an independent British contribution to the deterrent would be materially weakened, and from a purely practical point of view SACEUR's responsibilities to the individual NATO countries might involve unacceptable delay in giving operational decisions.[62]

Slight leeway was given to this latter matter by accepting that 'General Norstad as US CinC [could] control the use of the weapons'.[63]

The final choice of stations was outlined in the Air Ministry Quarterly Liaison Report for January to March 1958, although final agreement was not signed until 26 June. Even by May when the first contracts were drawn up, only the Feltwell and Hemswell Wings, which had been given final confirmation by ACAS at the Thor Meetings on 15 April and 20 May respectively, had been definitively agreed. In the case of Feltwell, all the original satellite locations, of which Marham and Honington were already used by the V-Bombers, had been replaced by alternative locations. The Feltwell survey team had completed a first survey on the provisional Feltwell satellite sites between 4–7 February. They had recommended Marham, Tuddenham, Shepherds Grove and Witchford, although they had not actually visited the latter during that survey, assuming from their knowledge that it would present no problems. Both Honington, because of the extensive demolitions that would be required, and Watton, because it came inside the minimum distance required between sites, were not recommended although it was noted that Watton could be used should Witchford prove unsatisfactory. A survey of North Pickenham and Witchford on 6 and 7 March 1958 with an overnight stop at Feltwell was completed. This found at Witchford that two of the three existing runways would be sterilised, but as there was no operational requirement for the runways this would not present a problem. A possible attraction of Witchford was that its runway was aligned at 150 degrees which allowed the three LEs, which had to be aligned at 60 degrees to true north, to be incorporated into the existing runway in line abreast. However, all the unpaved land was let to agriculture and the leases relating to this land, on which eight months' notice had to be given, would have to be terminated. This proved to be the site's Achilles heel, and the proposal was turned down by the Director of Operations Bomber and Reconnaissance (DofOps (B&R)) Air Cdre J.H. Searby,[64] who commented that, 'In view of the fact that the lease of this airfield cannot be terminated in sufficient time to enable the "Thor" timetable to be kept I recommend this airfield shall not be used'.[65] But there were other problems with Witchford. It was only two miles from Ely Cathedral and the former owner of the site had been the Church Commissioners, a body sensitive to its legal and political rights. Furthermore, the site had been bought expressly for agricultural use under the Labour Government's post-war policy, not for defence. Nearby Mepal suffered from none of these problems. A survey of possible satellite sites for Hemswell was carried out on 10/11 April. The eleven-man team – eight RAF/Air Ministry and three USAF, again travelling incognito – visited Digby, Coleby Grange, Caistor, Kelstern, Ludford Magna and Bardney with an overnight stop at Hemswell. Digby proved unsuitable. Kelstern would require various demolitions including the watch office and the possible reinstatement of roads. Ludford Magna was an explosives storage containing 10,000 tons of bombs and was considered doubtful. Like Bardney it lacked good drainage. Only Coleby Grange and Caistor were considered to be 'excellent' sites for the missiles.[66]

Driffield was provisionally agreed as the third base, with visits taking place in early May and encompassing all the potential sites for the Driffield complex. Still travelling discretely, the visit schedule was Sherburn-in-Elmet, Church Fenton and Marston Moor on 5 May; Riccall, Breighton, Holme-on-Spalding Moor, Catfoss and Carnaby on the 6th with an overnight stop at Driffield; Pocklington, Full Sutton and Elvington on the 7th with an overnight stop at Leeming; Catterick, Scorton, Wombleton and East Moor completed the list on the 8th. The initial list of preferred satellites was Carnaby, Holme-on-Spalding Moor, Pocklington, Catfoss, Full Sutton and Breighton. Holme-on-Spalding Moor, however, was leased to the nearby Blackburn Aircraft Company.[67] The discussions surrounding the choice of Breighton emphasises the continuing severe problems over adequate accommodation. Part of the difficulty in providing accommodation was the knowledge that Thor would only be operational for a relatively short time – at that time considered to be possibly until 1965/7 – and there was 'no guarantee that succeeding generations of ballistic missiles will be sited at, or even in the vicinity of Thor sites',[68] so building specific accommodation was not justified on a cost basis. AOCinC Bomber Command, Air Mshl Sir Harry Broadhurst, was actively promoting Elvington as a more suitable location. It had been one of the SAC expansion airfields, had the longest runway in the northern part of England and was well equipped with buildings vacated by the USAF when they left in 1958. In comparison, Breighton had no existing or local amenities. However, Elvington was a V-Bomber dispersal airfield and it had been agreed that these sites would not be used for Thor. It was close enough to Full Sutton that one warhead could have eliminated both stations. It would also delay the building programme and compensation would have to be paid to the Breighton contactor.[69] The case for Leconfield had by this time been dropped as an option as two runways would have had to be closed and a taxiway cut, although the station was subsequently to be used for Thor operations as the airhead for Driffield. The fourth squadron was even more provisional as North Luffenham was being considered as an alternative to Dishforth because of radar scatter and signal-masking problems caused by the Yorkshire Dales. The North Luffenham sites were the last group to be visited: Kimbolton, Harrington, Desborough and Polebrook on 24 May and Melton Mowbray, Folkingham and Market Harborough on the following day. Chelveston had been deleted from the list at the last minute as the USAF had indicated they would not give it up for Thor use. North Witham and Harlaston were also deleted. All the sites were considered as possibles except Market Harborough, which was used by the War Department as an Unfit Vehicle Depot and was full of vehicles in various states of disrepair. North Luffenham became increasingly seen as a better option than Dishforth. It would be much cheaper to implement as it was becoming clear that the costs of relocating No.242 OCU Transport Command, the resident unit at Dishforth, would be significant. However, the potential satellite sites for North Luffenham did not provide an ideal solution.

A problem existed over Polebrook for which Kimbolton was an alternative, but a poor one as it was thirty-six road miles from North Luffenham and shift transfers from the Wing HQ would occupy up to four hours travelling time per shift. Ninety acres would be needed for Polebrook which would leave 100 acres for the two farmers who were farming the land. A more difficult issue was potentially HRH The Duke of Gloucester who owned Barnwell Manor, situated only three miles from the proposed missile site, and spent much of his time there with his family. An initial approach was made by George Ward to Major Michael Hawkins of the Royal Household at St James' Palace and thereafter a full presentation was arranged for the Duke, who fortunately raised no objections. In fact he 'showed great interest in the project'.[70] Fortunate indeed because it was considered that 'if Polebrook is not selected the entire North Luffenham complex will be jeopardised'.[71] AMSO, ACM Sir Walter 'Tubby' Dawson, advised Sandys:

> as there is no alternative the selection of Polebrook was automatic and unavoidable. If Polebrook is not selected, the Fourth Squadron deployment will have to be considered afresh, in which case we may find that we shall be forced into the use of Dishforth, which will be very costly and much less desirable operationally.[72]

A further problem was that engine manufacturers Messrs Perkins occupied one of the J-Type hangars and habitually used the runway for 'motor demonstrations'. This was, however, not the final problem for the North Luffenham Wing, as a motoring problem of a different sort affected Folkingham, which was leased by Rubery, Owen & Co. Ltd as a test track for their BRM racing cars: engine development took place at nearby Bourne. The company used the control tower and the runways. Site alterations for Thor would sever part of the track and Rubery Owen confirmed they would need the whole circuit and would therefore need to find an alternative facility. However, six months' notice was required. Fortunately, however, this did not seem to have held up the building schedule. Similar notice had to be given to a flying club that used Bardney.[73] There was sympathy that a flying club could not simply just 'shut up shop and go somewhere else and they will probably make representation through their MP if we give them notice without offering them alternative access'.[74] In fact, there were only three aircraft based there and the owners were quite happy to find an alternative home.

The Thor Agreement – Finding the Bases

Two proposals were put forward for the North Luffenham Wing, which represented the greatest degree of compromise in the five chosen Wing proposals, with airfields from Proposal 1 eventually being chosen:

Table IV: North Luffenham Wing Proposals.

Unit	Proposal 1	Proposal 2
Wing HQ	North Luffenham	North Luffenham
1 Flight	Folkingham	Folkingham
2 Flight	Melton Mowbray	Melton Mowbray, Desborough, Harrington
3 Flight	Mkt Harborough, Desborough, Harrington	Polebrook
4 Flight	Polebrook, Kimbolton	Kimbolton

The case for North Luffenham was further strengthened when air defence coverage shortcomings for the Yorkshire sites were identified. The Dishforth complex proposals were far from ideal and the eastern sites proposed as satellites for Driffield would not be covered. The solution, after the deletion of Dishforth, proved to be the decision to co-locate a SAGW squadron at Carnaby. Had this remedy not been implemented it seems likely that Riccall would have been chosen instead.

The final ORBAT, in which the Dishforth Wing was indeed deleted and replaced by one based on North Luffenham, was as follows:

Table V: Final Thor ORBAT.

Feltwell	Shepherds Grove	Tuddenham	Mepal	North Pickenham
Hemswell	Caistor	Coleby Grange	Bardney	Ludford Magna
Driffield	Catfoss	Carnaby	Breighton	Full Sutton
North Luffenham	Polebrook	Harrington	Melton Mowbray	Folkingham

Starting on 30 May 1958, detailed surveys of the chosen sites were conducted by the Army under Captain R.C. Gardiner-Hill of the Royal Engineers with three NCOs.[75] Feltwell in Norfolk would be the first operational Station.[76, 77, 78] The USAF were using both Tuddenham and North Pickenham but these were to be vacated by 1 July and 1 December 1958 respectively. Ten thousand tons of bombs stored at North Pickenham would have to be removed. Of these satellites, only Mepal would have to be reclaimed. After due consultation with the Ministries of Agriculture and Housing, who presented no objections, the chairman of Ely District Council was duly informed but not told the reason. There was no local opposition. Target dates for start and completion were:

Feltwell	No.77 (SM) Sqn/A Flight	1 May 1958	30 August 1958
Shepherds Grove	B Flight	1 May 1958	30 September 1958
Tuddenham	C Flight	31 May 1958	31 October 1958
Mepal	D Flight	31 May 1958	30 November 1958
North Pickenham	E Flight	31 May 1958	31 December 1958

It will be noted that the original ORBAT envisaged only four squadrons. As already mentioned, consideration was given to creating a completely new series of number plates for these squadrons, but it was decided to re-form previously disbanded Bomber Command squadrons. There was a proposal to call these squadron locations Strategic Missile Bases (Feltwell would have therefore been called No.1 Strategic Missile Base) but this complicated the existing Bomber Command structure and was vetoed. Taking Feltwell as a model it was suggested that 'No.77 Squadron RAF Feltwell' was an acceptable title, but this would mean that the squadron would be the Station Commanding Unit, which would be the command of a Group Captain who would also perforce be the Squadron Commander, a scenario which was in conflict with all other RAF squadrons. The satellite stations would be termed Flights, commanded by flight lieutenants reporting to this Station Commander. New titles would also have to be introduced for the station administration and technical wings as it would not be appropriate for a squadron to be controlling station wings. As a solution to this problem it was decided that the lead site could be called 'RAF Station Feltwell'. The operations wing would be replaced by a missile squadron with a Wing Commander responsible to the Station Commander, but in this scenario the squadron would be commanded by a Wing Commander. He would receive administrative and technical support from the appropriate Wings. However, by July 1959 it had been decided that '[in] the light of practical experience, Bomber Command have recommended that "Thor" stations should be organized on the same lines as "V" Bomber Stations, and that each launch position should be given squadron status'.[79] This was duly instituted from 1 September 1959.

The announcement for those squadrons under No.1 Group was made by the AOC No.1 Group at a dinner held at Hemswell on 10 September.[80] The squadron OCs would be squadron leaders and would report to Wing Commander (Ops) at the Wing HQ. The twenty Thor squadrons thus formed represented the biggest single expansion of RAF squadrons to take place in peacetime. Each squadron was designated 'Strategic Missile' (SM) on a proposal of CAS. The press had been freely using the suffix 'Bomber Squadron' in its reference to the reformed squadrons but this was not considered an appropriate designation.[81] The move to full squadron status seemed popular amongst the squadrons themselves. No.104 (SM) Sqadron's ORB noted that '[forming] the Squadron has increased morale and has greatly improved team spirit'.

The personnel establishment for the squadrons was estimated to be 809 officers and airmen and 107 civilians. In addition, about 400 US personnel were involved although this number would go down as the RAF training requirement reduced.

The Thor Agreement – Finding the Bases

The missiles would be airlifted into the substantial USAFE Base at RAF Lakenheath in Suffolk.[82] Lakenheath was conveniently adjacent to Mildenhall, to where the Military Air Transport Service (MATS) had recently moved from Burtonwood near Warrington. It was the latter organisation that would undertake the 'Thor Hauls' to fly in the tons of equipment needed for the operation.[83, 84] The Airheads for Hemswell, Driffield and North Luffenham would be Scampton, Leconfield and Cottesmore respectively, all of which had suitable runways and facilities for off-loading the missiles and *matériel*. Hemswell and Driffield would come under No. 1 Group, and Feltwell and North Luffenham under No. 3 Group.

As far as the splitting of costs was concerned, the US would pay for all the missile hardware costs, along with the associated equipment, facility requirements and all necessary training of the maintenance and launch crews. The UK would pay for the construction of the bases and the manning costs of the RAF personnel and any associated civilian support. Whilst UK contractors would be responsible for the civil engineering works involved, Douglas engineers would thereafter install all the specialist equipment on site and prepare and verify all the systems prior to handover to the RAF. Most of this – it ended up at about 69 per cent – would have to be flown in on the Thor Hauls, although some of the larger items were brought across by sea. In all, a total of over 11,000 tons was to be airlifted by 1607th Military Air Transport Wing of Eastern Transport Air Force, MATS. Things were made a little easier when the Douglas C-133 Cargomaster came into service in January 1959. This bigger aircraft, the largest turboprop aircraft to be used by the USAF, allowed the missile to be airlifted and mounted on its transporter. The missiles for North Luffenham, Driffield[85] and Hemswell were flown in directly to the sites. After the final missiles were delivered the runways were closed and all subsequent flights operated via the respective airheads. The risk of an aircraft crashing once the squadrons were operational was too great.

Following the MOD practice of providing somewhat incongruous names for projects, the Thor deployment was, perhaps surprisingly, not given a 'rainbow code' designation but was allotted the codeword 'Emily' on 27 March 1958. This codeword was unclassified but its meaning was to be kept secret.[86, 87] The USAF was to centralise its management of the project at Lakenheath via the 705th Strategic Missile Wing, formed on 20 February 1957 and essentially a paper-only organisation. Bomber Command's No. 3 Group was next door at Mildenhall. 705SMW came under the 7AD based at South Ruislip and was in due course to move there to be co-located. It was determined that Feltwell and its four satellites at Shepherds Grove, Tuddenham, Mepal and North Pickenham would be the first operational units.

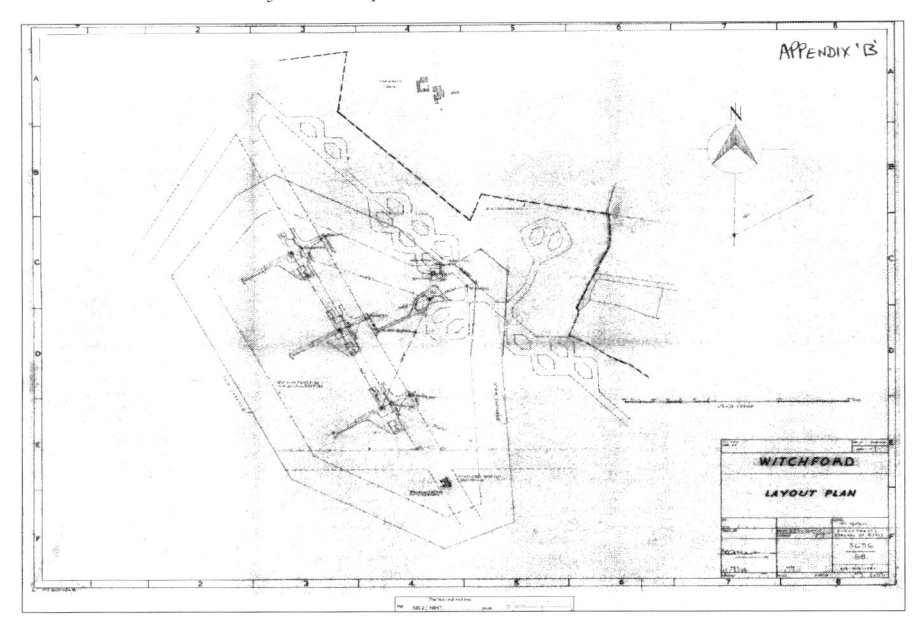

A draft layout for a proposed Thor site at RAF Witchford (replaced by RAF Mepal). (TNA AIR2/14947)

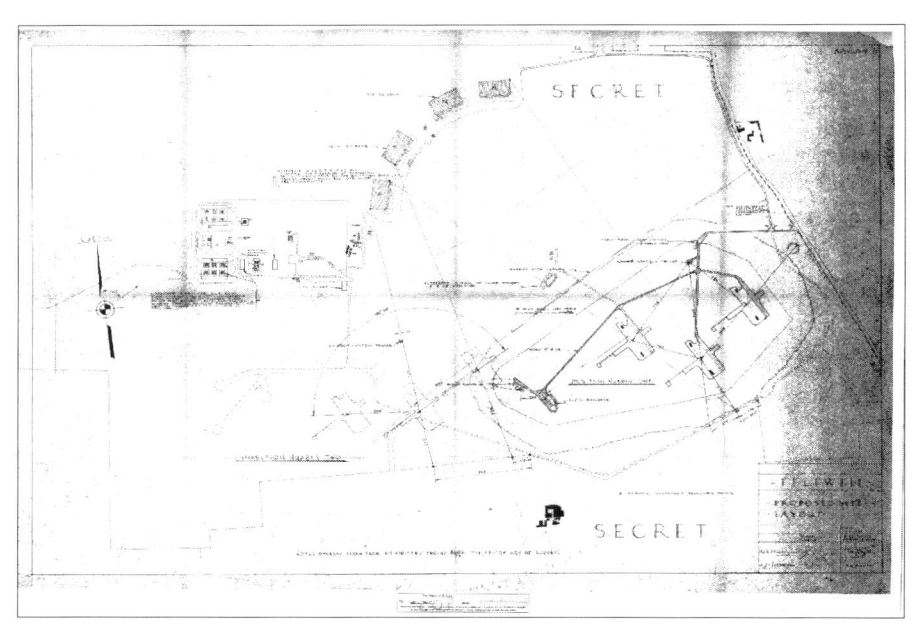

Draft plans for two proposed layout options for the Thor Wing at RAF Feltwell. (TNA AIR2/14947)

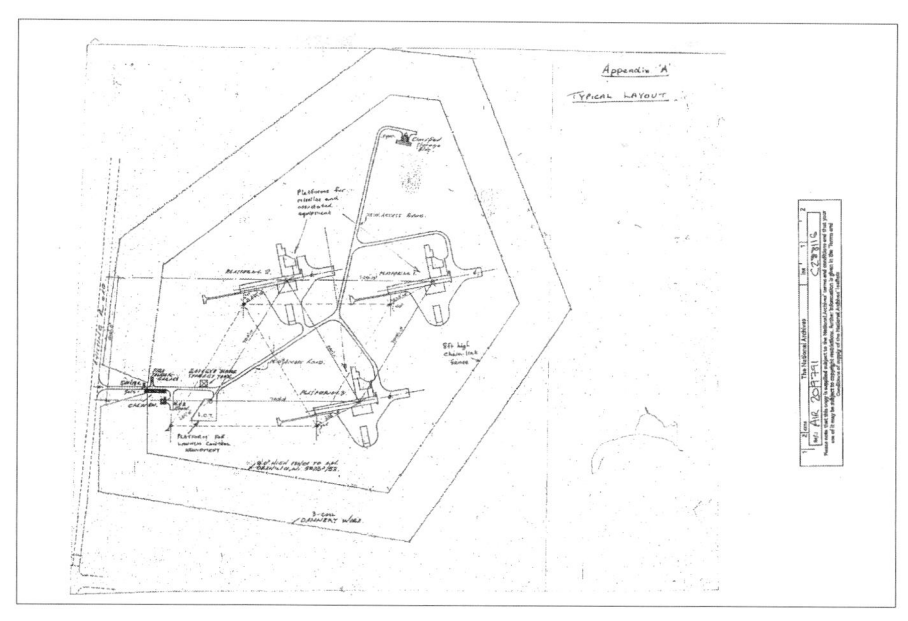

A diagram of a typical Thor site. (TNA AIR 20/9791)

Notes:
1. TNA, Air Council Conclusions of Meeting. AIR 6/111: G.18651/MGH/2/58/75, 30 January 1958.
2. TNA, AIR 2/13373. f.1A. Telegram BAFS Washington to Air Ministry, 10 July 1956.
3. *Ibid.*
4. It was estimated that a 1MT burst within 15,000ft of a site would destroy it. See AIR 2/13337. f.2B.
5. The Firestone Tire & Rubber Co. MGM-5 Corporal SSM was the first US missile to be approved, in December 1950, to carry an atomic warhead. It was developed as an offshoot of the US Army White Sands V-2 Programme. First issued to the US Army in July 1954 it was operationally deployed in Germany from February 1955. It had a ninety-mile range but was notoriously inaccurate and was phased out in mid-1964. A Memorandum of Conversation between Eisenhower and Macmillan, dated 22 March 1957, confirms that the Corporals would be assigned to SACEUR and that an amount of $30.5m, the equivalent cost of the missiles, would be used to finance projects to modernise the RAF's Plan K.
6. The RAF was keen to acquire the F-106 to replace, on a one-for-one basis, its 160 Gloster Javelin all-weather interceptors, which were proving technically disappointing. The records are ambiguous as to which variant was wanted. AIR 2/13374 emphasises that it was the single-seat F106A that was being considered, whereas other references point to the two-seat F-106B, a seemingly more obvious choice to replace the Javelins. The F-106 was superior to the Javelin but superior to both was the Canadian Avro CF-

105 Arrow which would have been the RAF's preferred choice had it not been more expensive and two years behind the US fighter. The CF-105 was abruptly cancelled in 1959. In the end the RAF soldiered on with the Javelins. The order for the F-106 would have included 5,000 Falcon AAMs – the British Blue Jay equivalent was incompatible – but it was considered unlikely that the RAF would have been allowed to acquire the N.B.1. Special Weapon also fitted to the F-106.

7 Macmillan had been Eisenhower's British Political Adviser during the North African Campaign.

8 The Rt Hon. Duncan Edwin Sandys (1908–1987). A Conservative politician who was married to Churchill's daughter. During the war he had been chairman of the committee charged with countering the German rocket and flying bomb programme.

9 Cmnd.124, HMSO, April 1957.

10 The Blue Streak MRBM was being developed under Air Staff Requirement No.OR1139, dated 8 August 1955. In many ways similar to Thor it was designed to be launched from silos and in this respect pioneered this form of missile protection. Much of the test programme and associated work on the prototype silo, U1, was undertaken at RAF Spadeadam in Cumbria. To many it had the advantage of being an independent deterrent which Thor would never be, but 'it was clear that the development of this weapon had suffered from lack of money in 1957' (Air Council Meeting, 23/24 January 1958, G.18600/EF/1/58/75 paragraph 6). For further information on the U1 silo see *Prospero No.3, The Spadeadam Blue Streak Underground Launcher Facility U1*, published by the British Rocketry Oral History Programme 2006.

11 TNA, DEFE 13/593. f.E4. M 147/57.

12 TNA, DEFE 13/594. f.E27. Letter, Sandys to Wilson, 1 June 1957.

13 TNA, AIR 2/13337. f.2B.

14 TNA, DEFE 13/594. f.E33.

15 TNA, AIR 2/13373. f.36A.

16 TNA, AIR 2/13337. f.53B.

17 TNA, DEFE 13/593. f.E8A.

18 The 1st Missile Division was re-formed from what had originally been the 1st Bombardment Division, formed in August 1943 and based in the UK. Since the end of the Second World War it had been re-designated the 1st Air Division. It was to be further re-designated the 1st Strategic Aerospace Division on 21 July 1961.

19 Named after General Hoyt S. Vandenberg (1899–1954). Second Chief of Staff of the US Air Force.

20 TNA, AIR 14/4293. f.15.

21 Wynn, Humphrey, *RAF Nuclear Deterrent Forces*, p.286.

22 Much of the success of the speed of the Soviet development of nuclear capability had been as a result of the information passed to them by the spy Klaus Fuchs, who had worked at Los Alamos as part of the British nuclear team helping to develop the first atom bomb. To many Americans this was adequate enough proof to limit the transfer of nuclear knowledge to Britain.

23 Armacost, Michael H., *The Politics of Weapons Innovation*, p.185.

24 The Soviet Union had made known in late August 1957 that it had successfully tested an ICBM, but little interest seemed to have been taken by the US.

25 Hansard, 24 February 1958. Vol.583, No.59, Col.29.

26 *Ibid.* Cols 29–30.

27 TNA, DEFE 13/123. Letter from Sir Richard Powell to Minister of Defence, 19 February 1958. RRP/196/58..
28 Hansard *ibid*. Col.30.
29 *Ibid*.
30 *Ibid*. Col.32.
31 *Ibid*. Col.36.
32 SAC was working on the basis that the first squadron with five locations of three missiles each would become operational on 1 July, 1 September, 17 September, 19 October and 17 November.
33 TNA, DEFE 13/123. Serial T.29/58.
34 *Ibid*, Letter from Sir Richard Powell. RRP/216/58, 27 February 1958.
35 *Ibid*, Letter E Broadbent to George Ward. 24 February 1958.
36 TNA. DEFE 13/394. f.E3.
37 TNA. DEFE 13/123. Telegram 242 from Washington, 4 February 1958.
38 'The Americans are still making great exertions to achieve the July deployment originally discussed.' TNA. DEFE 13/120. f. E27. Letter Air Ministry to Ministry of Defence, 23 April 1958.
39 TNA. AIR 2/14981. CAS to SoS Defence. Minute 74, 20 June 1958 .
40 TNA. DEFE 13/123. Letter from Sandys to McElroy. February 1958.
41 TNA. AIR 20/10081. Document C-4010. May 1959.
42 TNA . No.77 (SM) Squadron ORB. AIR 27/2952.
43 *Journal of the Royal Air Force Historical Society*, No.26, p.25.
44 Hansard, *Ibid*, Wednesday 5 March. Col.1155.
45 RAF Bomber Command was formed on 14 July 1936, and from March 1940 until it was merged into the new RAF Strike Command on 30 April 1968 it was to have its Headquarters at High Wycombe. By the time of the Thor deployments, it had reduced from its wartime ORBAT of five operational Groups and one training Group to just two, which were to each control half of the Thor force. No.1 Group also controlled the Command Bombing School at RAF Lindholme, the Command Development unit at RAF Finningley and the Canberra and Vulcan OCUs. No.3 Group controlled the Central Reconnaissance Establishment as well as the Victor/Valiant OCU and the PR Squadrons. Its Air Officers Commanding in Chief during the Thor period were Air Marshal Sir Harry Broadhurst and, from 20 May 1959, Air Marshal Sir Kenneth Cross.
46 All USAFE Bases in the United Kingdom were classified as RAF Stations, nominally under the command of an RAF Station Commander.
47 TNA. AIR 20/10325. Letter from VCAS to AOCinC Bomber Command, 16 February 1959. VCAS.DO.37.
48 The Campaign for Nuclear Disarmament was launched in London on 17 February 1958. It was supported by a wide section of the community though most were educated, non-violent, sympathetic to the left and sought unilateral disarmament by the UK. Much annual publicity was generated by the Easter Aldermaston Marches – the annual turnout peaked in 1962 at 150,000 marchers. Its well-known badge, originally made in ceramics as a material capable of surviving a nuclear explosion, was based on the semaphore flag positions for the letters 'N' and 'D'. Its eventual significance was largely undermined after the Test Ban Treaty was agreed.
49 TNA. DEFE 13/120, Letter from Sandys to CAS, 24 January 1958.
50 *Ibid*.

51 TNA. AIR 2/14947. Drawing No2906/58.
52 The proposals for local production of LOX were cancelled but a T2-Type hangar being dismantled at RAF Turweston, north of Bicester, was initially destined for re-construction at Feltwell to house the LOX Plant.
53 TNA. AIR 2/14947, f.15B, TS2049/DDO1.
54 *Ibid.*
55 This was an improved Red Duster (Bloodhound) SAGW Mk 1, called Green Flax and later Yellow Temple, embodying a Ferranti Type 86 (Indigo Corkscrew) or AEI Type 87 (Blue Anchor) continuous wave seeker.
56 TNA. DEFE 13/120. RRP/89/58. Letter from Sir Richard Powell to Sandys, 27 January 1958.
57 *Ibid.* f. E3. Letter from Molson to Sandys, 23 January 1958.
58 With the demise of the UK's missile programmes, the Spadeadam complex was eventually handed over to the RAF in April 1976. It thus became the largest RAF Station in the UK. Its current use is as an electronic warfare range; one of only two in Europe.
59 The proposal to site Jupiter IRBMs in Europe proved a vexed and thorny issue. The offer of Jupiter was announced during the high profile NATO Summit meeting in Paris in December 1957. After months of entrenched negotiations, Italy agreed to take thirty missiles (two squadrons designated NATO 1 operated by 36 Aerobrigata IS based at Gioia del Colle) and Turkey fifteen missiles (one squadron designated NATO 2 based at Cigli). Misjudging certain areas of European public opinion, the US was surprised that the take up of the offer of missiles was not more popular and experienced vocal antagonism from Denmark and Norway, who wanted to open channels of rapprochement with the Soviet Union. France, although initially very receptive to the basing of three Jupiter squadrons on its soil, particularly if Britain was to have IRBMs, dramatically changed course with the election of President Charles de Gaulle and the creation of the Fifth Republic. France immediately became a thorn in NATO's side and vehemently said 'non' to the missiles. Unlike Thor, however, the Jupiters would be placed under the NATO command of SACEUR.
60 The RAF had ordered three different designs of the V-Bomber. The first, the Vickers Valiant, entered service in 1956 and had been used for the British nuclear tests at Maralinga. It saw active service with No.148 Squadron during the Suez Campaign. The Valiant had been ordered because the other two designs, the Avro Vulcan and the Handley Page Victor, were more advanced designs which would take longer to develop. Whilst Thor was controlled by joint UK/US agreement, the Bomber Command V-Bombers were under UK national control until May 1963, when they were assigned to SACEUR.
61 SACEUR had held a watching brief over the Thors. In a memo to the Secretary General of NATO on 18 August 1959, he was to comment: 'SHAPE believes that the achievement of a quick and timely introduction of the weapons system in our common defence is of great importance. Therefore SACEUR will recommend that when IRBMs are accepted by a country, they will be assigned such priority as to assure their earliest operational capability.' (TNA. DEFE 13/120. f.E33).
62 TNA. Air Council Conclusions of Meeting. 23–24 January 1958. AIR 6/111. G.18957/VK/1/58/120.
63 TNA. DEFE 13/594. f.E7. See also: Control of Intermediate Range Ballistic Missiles. (COS(58)12), 30 January 1958.

The Thor Agreement – Finding the Bases

64 Air Cdre John H. Searby had been a prominent bomber pilot during the Second World War. He had been a flight commander at No.106 Squadron under Sqn Ldr Guy Gibson and took over command when Gibson moved to form No.617 Squadron. He then took command of No.83 Pathfinder Squadron. He had already had a connection with missiles as he had been the 'Master Bomber' on the Peenemünde raid, for which he received the DSO.

65 Report of the Board of Survey by Sqn Ldr E.R.G. Haines, 7 March 1958. AIR 2/14947.

66 TNA. AIR 2/14905. f.89B.

67 *Ibid*. f.84B/3A.

68 TNA. AIR 2/14908. Memo from DCAS from AOCinC Bomber Command, 12 December 1958.

69 TNA. AIR 20/10325.VCAS.DO.37. Letter from VCAS to AOCinC BC.

70 The presentation reassuringly assured that '[t]here will be no annoying or noxious activity within the launch position. There will be no static test firings of rocket motors there is no possibility of inadvertent firings of missiles. The possibility of missiles exploding is negligible and there can be no discharge of radio active material beyond the confines of the launch position, even if a missile were destroyed by fire'. TNA. AIR 2/14907.

71 TNA. Memo in File AIR 2/14907.

72 TNA. AIR 20/9791. AMSO to SoS Memo, 10 July 1958.

73 TNA. AIR 2/14907. The flying club at Bardney had to vacate by 14 July 1958. Loose minute MS.1949/57/D.D.O.P.

74 TNA. AIR 2/14906. f.12A. Loose Minute S.3 to DDCP, 23 April 1958.

75 TNA. AIR 2/14947. f.58A.

76 Confirmation of the Feltwell Wing was made in the Air Ministry Quarterly Liaison Report (AMQLR) for January–March 1958.

77 No one seemed to have told the Feltwell Station Commander, Gp Capt. Leigh Rankin, what was going to happen to his station. He wrote to Air Cdre J.D. Melvin (D of Org) at the Air Ministry on 3 April 1958:

> ...wonder[ing] if anything could be done to coordinate the activities of the many individuals and departments of the Air Ministry who seem to be involved in arranging the future of Feltwell, and especially to ensure that the station and the two commands concerned are kept informed about things which effect them? I think 7 Works area would make a plea for similar treatment, too. I do get occasional bits of information from one or two more thoughtful officers, like Wg Cdr Knight (B. & R. Ops) and your Wg Cdr Wherry, but apparently there is a lot going on that we should be told about. Two examples will show what I mean. A few days ago, a Post Office engineer arrived and told us that, on 19th May, he is coming here to begin installing a 400 line automatic exchange, and will require the whole of our existing orderly room for the purpose. ... [N]obody on the A.M.W.D. side, from 7 Works area downwards, knows anything about the matter, nor does anyone on the service side. Somebody ought to tell us soon, through official channels – in fact ought to have told us before now. Yesterday, a Col. Davis, of 7th Air Div., U.S.A.F. arrived with a civilian, Mr Bauer, of the Douglas Aircraft Corporation, to see if we could possibly provide them with some covered working and storage space from about 15th April onwards. ... What is needed is some co-ordinating authority ...

He received a sympathetic reply but it is unclear if anything was done to set up a system to provide him with the necessary information.

78 Co-located with the Missile Wing at Feltwell were 721 Mobile Signals Unit, based at nearby Methwold, and the Upper Meteorological Research Unit, a shadowy organisation with, apparently, little interest in meteorology!

79 TNA. DEFE 13/121. Thor Project 14th Progress Report, 6 July 1959.

80 TNA. No 269(SM) Sqn ORB, September 1959.

81 An alternative suggestion which was not adopted had been to describe the Bomber Command squadrons 'Defensive Missile Squadrons' and the Fighter Command SAGW Squadrons 'Air Defence (Rocket) Squadrons'.

82 Lakenheath was acquired by the Air Ministry as an alternate station to Mildenhall. It supported Bomber Command operations until in 1944 it was upgraded to a Very Heavy Bomber Base to support USAAF B-29 bombers. It became a SAC base in 1950.

83 The largest single items flown in on the Thor Hauls were, by weight, the LOX tank (50' long x 8' wide x 9' high and weighing 35,000lb) and, by overall dimensions the missile erector (68' x 10' 6" x 13' 6" and weighing 17,500lb).

84 Some of the missiles were flown directly into the Wing HQs. This usually happened after dark for security reasons. However, little could be kept from the local population. When an incoming aircraft suffered brake failure at Hemswell, ending up just short of the Gainsborough road, the emergency services were beaten to it by the local population who had a grandstand view of events from the roadside. Conversation with David O'Flanagan, September 2007.

85 For example, the first inbound flight to Driffield arrived on 3 April 1959 and the last on 3 November 1959, whereafter the runways were closed.

86 For full details of the Rainbow Codes see www.skomer.u-net/projects/colour.htm.

87 TNA. AIR 2/14905. f.63A. Memo from A.I (S)1b K.D. Bannister. For policy on use of codewords see: A.P.3086, Chapter 2, Paragraph 16 et seq.

CHAPTER FOUR
BUILDING THE INFRASTRUCTURE

Once the twenty RAF Stations had been identified, the contractors could move in and prepare the groundworks. Whilst the bases conformed to a standard requirement, no two were the same as their layout was determined by the existing runways, incorporated into the format to minimise the need for extra road construction. The four Wing Headquarters locations were all on well-established stations with hangars and permanent accommodation, whereas the satellite sites usually lacked even basic facilities. Because of the mobile concept of the missile, the requirement for fixed buildings was limited, the major constructions being the three concrete launch emplacements. These were to a common, irregular, but roughly cruciform design constructed in 6in reinforced concrete, differing individually only in the extension of the pad area to the access roads, this being dictated by the existing layout of the adjacent runways or taxiways that were utilised. The pad, built to a level tolerance of $^1/_{100}$ of 1ft, was in size approximately 500ft by 425ft. It was oriented within ± ½ degree of a pre-set angle to true north. The original orientation of the pads to true north was as follows:

1st Wing	60°
2nd Wing	78°
3rd Wing	42°
4th Wing	68°

After the first ten sites were under construction it was seen that these angles gave an unequal coverage of targets, with gaps in the middle, too liberal a coverage of targets in the north and poor coverage of the more important targets in the south. The first ten LEs of the 1st and 2nd Wings were aligned at 60 and 78 degrees respectively, but the second ten LEs had a varying degree of orientation which allowed for more selective target coverage:

Driffield	42°
Full Sutton	42°
Carnaby	55°
Catfoss	60°

Breighton   70°
Harrington   75°
Folkingham   75°
Melton Mowbray 80°
North Luffenham 85°
Polebrook   85°

Appendix 1 shows the degree of target coverage obtained at varying ranges. One hundred and thirty-one targets had been identified, but these could only all be covered by missiles with a range greater than 2,000nm. Missiles of 1,500nm range allowed for sixty-four targets to be covered, so with only sixty missiles there was not full target coverage, even at this range. However, when it came to priority targets, only twelve of the most important twenty targets were within range. The 1,500nm range was therefore considered 'insufficient for a number of important targets' and the desire was to 'pursue development of a 2,000nm [range capability]'.[1] The ability to cover Moscow, 1,400nm distant, was considered politically essential from the outset.[2]

In the centre of each LE was the launch structure. The hardstanding was of 6in-thick concrete set on 'dry lean' concrete. This incorporated US-supplied grillage and mounting plates which weighed 7 tons. The coordinates of the launch point had been surveyed with great accuracy and the location was confirmed with a brass stud set in the concrete. The sites were periodically re-surveyed during the operational period of the sites. Normally the missile lay horizontally on its Erecting Transporting Boom, its nose pointing downrange. It was protected by a retractable environmental shelter (100ft x 24ft), of relatively lightweight construction, made from pre-fabricated panels on a steel frame. Messrs Guest Keen Iron and Steel Ltd of Cardiff supplied the steel rails on which it moved. Inside this shelter and mounted on a platform were the two short-range electrotheodolites, one for each of the two stored targets, used for aiming the missile via an access panel to the guidance section, situated just below the nose of the missile. Three retractable servicing platforms allowed access to the various missile subsystems. The Re-entry Vehicle (RV) with or without the warhead was also fitted under the protection of the shelter, an operation nominally carried out only by USAF personnel from 99th Munitions Maintenance Squadron, but it was not unknown for this operation to be witnessed and even assistance provided by the RAF staff. A purpose-built, four-wheel trailer was backed through the opened end of the shelter and then raised on a scissors mechanism to bring it to the height of the waiting missile. The Munitions Officer attached to the 99MMS signed off the installed warhead and certified the height of the burst settings. The shelter could be retracted 200ft on cables powered by two-speed electric motors. A tractor was on standby to pull the shelter open in the event of failure of these motors. After it had been retracted 93ft it was clear of the missile and erection could begin. A warning light operated if the shelter was not clear of the missile. The downrange vertical end of the shelter moved sideways on rails to allow the separated main part to uncover the missile. At right angles to the axis of the missile and on each side of the launch pad were the 6,500 US gallon fuel tank (to the north) and the larger 13,500 US gallon LOX tank diametrically opposite. The problems of storing LOX (at -183°C) effectively required the tank to be a very large double-walled thermos container. Cylindrical in shape, it was fabricated by the Cambridge Corporation in Lowell, Massachusetts. Made of stainless steel it was, at the time, the largest air transportable storage vessel.[3] Plans that the tanks for the third and fourth squadrons would be spherical were not ultimately realised. Both tanks were set into concrete pits for protection and also to allow a catchment area should either of the liquids leak or spill.

Difficulties were experienced in keeping rainwater out of these pits, the standard pumps proving, at times, insufficient.[4] From the remains still visible today, it is evident that on some of the sites there was no retaining wall on the outer end of the LOX tank pit. There was an additional square catchment area for LOX dumping via an overflow pipeline adjacent to the pad itself. Beside this was a shower cubicle operated automatically when the door was opened. This was to be used if anyone was inadvertently splashed with the super-chilled liquid. The 6in pipes carrying the fuel and LOX to the missile were suspended on gallows-type brackets which allowed for expansion and contraction of the liquids, particularly the super-cooled LOX. The missile was pressure fed with fuel and LOX at a very high transfer rate. Nitrogen was used for this although at the US launch sites helium was used; however, the supply of helium in the UK was evidently a problem. The cylinders of gaseous nitrogen used to pressurise the LOX tank were kept in two trailers, each carrying thirty-eight cylinders of 50,000scf holding liquid nitrogen at 2,500psi. These were parked close to the tank, usually on the up-range side but occasionally on the other side. In total it was estimated that 184 specialist vehicles would be required, and the regular movements required amongst the complexes was, in itself, a potential problem. Where possible, and when an equivalent vehicle was available in the UK, these would be used, but around half of the vehicles still had to be sourced from American manufacturers and brought across on the Thor Hauls.

Extending 400ft to the west of the LE was a concrete path that led to the Long Range Electrotheodolite (LRT) Building. This was a 9in brick construction with a corrugated asbestos-sheeted roof. The position of the doors and windows, other than the window in the side facing the launch pad, which allowed aiming to take place once the missile was erect, were determined by the positioning of the theodolite targets which were mounted on pillars, the position of which differed from site to site. Early on in the layout of the sites, it was agreed that these pillars would all be sited within the security fence. These plinths were re-surveyed by the Army from time to time, as on the accuracy of their positioning did the accuracy of the targeting depend, as both the short- and long-range theodolites were aimed at targets on these survey points. Problems were experienced in seeing these targets at night and in October 1960 a trial system was approved using a white-painted parabolic shield illuminated by a tilly lamp and placed behind the target.[5] The long range theodolites were used for maintaining the target gyros once the missile was vertical, but would only be needed if the missile was held in the vertical position for any length of time, during which the gyros would tend to wander. This targeting was done via a window in the guidance section.

The most prominent features of the pads that still survive are the two L-shaped blast walls, which gave protection to the Hydraulic/Pneumatic, Electrical, Air Conditioning and Fuel Tank Nitrogen Semi-trailers, as well as the High Pressure

Gas Storage Tank. In tests at the US LEs at Vandenberg AFB, mice placed behind these blast walls during launch survived the experience, apparently with no ill effects. The purpose of these blast walls was to provide protection to the equipment behind them if a missile exploded on the launch pad and also for the brief period between engine start and the launch of the missile. They were constructed from 20cm-thick concrete with a sandy ballast infill.[6] Should the missile have been launched in anger and with no re-loads available, the pads were effectively redundant until they were almost certainly vaporised by incoming Soviet warheads a short time later, providing of course they had already survived long enough to launch their missiles. At some distance, between 1,000 and 1,500ft from the LE, was the Launch Control Area (LCA), a reinforced concrete hardstanding from which the launch operations for the three missiles were controlled. Two trailers accommodated the power management and the launch control operations. All launch control operations were conducted from the Launch Control Trailer (LCT). Initially, the USAF Authentication Officer (AO) who armed the warhead was accommodated in the somewhat cramped environment of the LCT, but at some bases later on, a separate hut was provided. At No.98 (SM) Squadron at Driffield, a system of mirrors was rigged so that the AO could see what was going on in the LCT. Also, on the LCA were the four Cummins diesel generators, similarly mounted on trailers, and their associated 5,000-gallon fuel tank. High intensity illumination was provided by lighting units mounted on masts around the pads. RAF pilots flying into nearby stations remember well the eerie blue lighting that flooded the Thor bases during the hours of darkness. Physical protection was by an 8ft-high 'unclimbable' chain-link fence with double overhead angle bars mounted with barbed wire.[7] At a distance of 225ft from this was a second 'Dannert' wire stock proof fence consisting of five strands of plain wire and three coils of Dannert wire set out in a triangular cross section from 4–6ft in height, secured on concrete posts 9ft apart. Further rolls of Dannert wire were considered but deemed to be a risk to passing members of the public, as many of the areas were used for hunting. Barbed wire placement was still controlled by the Barbed Wire Act of 1893![8] Between these two fences was the sterile zone patrolled at night by RAF Police dogs.

A further chain-link fence protected the US part of the site where the warheads were stored in a Classified Storage Building. This building had two bays at the main sites and one bay at the satellite sites. Alongside this building was a Pyrotechnics Store where igniter squibs for the missiles were kept. These two buildings were protected by an 'E', 'F' or 'T'-shaped revetment. There was also provision for a 10,000-gallon water tank. Entry to this restricted area was permitted only to personnel from the USAF 99MMS and USAF Police and was protected by a small US double-manned Picket Post. At the Wing HQ in addition to a two-bayed Classified Storage Building there was an additional S&I (Surveillance and Inspection) Building not found at the satellite stations. The Classified Storage Building was a 350sqft steel-framed structure in-filled with 'Hi-Rib' panels, cement plaster walls with concrete and asbestos troughing and a triple-felted roof. The floor was dust-proofed and there was both ventilation and heating. The Pyrotechnics Building was of similar but smaller construction. The S&I Building was part brick, part steel framed again with 'Hi-Rib' panels and cement plaster walls.

Building the Infrastructure

Each site had only one entrance closed with two 16ft double-hung manually operated gates. A similar single gate provided entry to the US warhead compound. Access was from public roads and the entrance was protected by an RAF guardroom, constructed from standard B-Type prefabricated hutting. In the case of Feltwell this hutting came from surplus hutting dismantled at RAF Cranwell. This guardroom accommodated the Provost Office, WO's & SNCO's Office, a 12ft x 12ft Ops Room and an Orderly Room as well as the telephone exchange, crew off-duty quarters and messing facilities.[9] Subsequently the GPO advised their requirement for two 8ft x 10ft rooms to house their Auto-PBX 400 or 500-line telephone exchanges. Outside and external to the site entrance was a parking area which could accommodate one missile on its Transporter Erector Launcher (TEL) trailer and the support vehicles which accompanied it on its convoy. Next to the guardroom was a brick-built garage for a Police car, and opposite was a further larger garage for the fire tender, while nearby was an electrical Power Conversion Building. This accommodated transformers which altered the 60cps on which the whole Thor electrical system was designed to operate from the UK National Grid standard 50cps. Wing HQs had a dog compound to kennel thirty dogs. Water for firefighting came from one or more 20,000-gallon storage tanks dug into the ground, usually adjacent to one of the runways. Later on, after a re-appraisal of firefighting requirements led to a need to provide improved facilities, water was ducted directly into each LE, transferred by electric pumps and accessible from various hydrants situated around the LEs. Some sites acquired a 'terrapin hut', often, it seems, left over by the Douglas contractors which provided a better quality than the standard huts. Coleby Grange was one of these. In February, No.142 (SM) Squadron recorded:

> The new terrapin hut is now erected and the work to turn it into a Squadron Operations centre is in hand. It is disappointing that so much time is expended in the approval of the electrical services of the buildings. The existing electrical supply to all the huts at all the squadrons leaves much to be desired. One is exposed to so much safety propaganda that one hesitates to ponder the possibilities.[10]

On-site chefs provided food for each shift, although initially the night shift was usually supplied with food brought in from the Wing HQ. There was no accommodation on site and crews who had not found local hirings were bussed to and from the Wing HQ. This placed a strain on the MT requirement, to say nothing of the miles that would be covered. For the Feltwell Wing, efforts were made to find accommodation at nearer locations; Marham and Watton (North Pickenham), Mildenhall (Tuddenham), Honington (Shepherds Grove) and Wyton and Waterbeach (Mepal).[11] Nonetheless, displaying the ingenuity for which servicemen are renowned, many found their own accommodation. Because of his requirement to be available at short notice, at satellite sites only, a house was provided nearby for the Squadron Commander. The influx of personnel resulted in the inevitable paperwork and documentation and, of course, the question of paying everyone had to be addressed. The Pay Section at Hemswell alone accounted for around 100 Disturbance Claims.[12]

Table VI: Thor Base Facilities (based on AIR 2/14947. f.77).

Item	Wing HQ	Satellite
Missile Launch Emplacements (LE)	3	3
Launch Control Area (LCA)	1	1
US Warhead Compound	1	1
Classified Storage Building	2 bay	1 bay
Pyrotechnics Storage	1	1
RIM Building	1	–
Technical Storage Building	1	–
Surveillance and Inspection Building (S&I)	1	–
Power Conversion Building	1★	1
Guard Room and Crew Room	1	1
Fire Tender Garage	1	1
Police Vehicle Garage	1	1
Dog Kennels (x 30)	1	–
Static Water Reservoir	1+	1+
Fire ring main system (from 1960)	1	1
Chain Link/Dannert Wire fencing	★	★

★ As needed

By May 1958 contracts had been signed with Sir A. McAlpine & Son Ltd for the building and civil engineering works for the sum of £968,950 5s 10d, and with G.N. Haden Ltd for heating & ventilation work in the RIM and S&I buildings for the sum of £73,221 15s 0d.[13] Work was to start as soon as possible. The construction of Feltwell started on 19 May. Not surprisingly, some additional work had to be done over and above the basic requirements. At Feltwell the access road between the RIM (agreed as one of the C-Type hangars, Building 73, which had been used by an Army Air Corps squadron whose approach to everything in general, and the Feltwell Landing Strip in particular, was a source of puzzlement to all RAF types[14]) and the main public road to the site was too narrow and an urgent requirement to widen this road by 5ft was identified. Also recognised was the need for extra messing facilities to cope with the imminent arrival of the US personnel. The size of the equipment that would be arriving at the bases was a further factor:

> The Dual purpose trucks are large 4 x 4 vehicles 7' 6" wide with no rear vision. Reliance when reversing must be placed on mirrors. I cannot imagine anything more difficult

than reversing this truck, possibly in the dark, along the narrow access road through 180° ... in emergency in the excitement of the moment, even a good driver would find difficulty in keeping to the road.[15]

HQ Bomber Command had estimated that around 230 vehicles would be in regular use, accounting for fifty vehicle movements per day of vehicles averaging 8ft wide.[16] Consideration was given to multi-shift working but it would have been 'almost certainly obvious that we are using special works procedures of greater urgency even than those used for the "V" bomber airfields. How can we justify these publicly?' was the response.[17]

The influx of hundreds of DAC personnel gave rise to a problem for which an adequate solution was never really found. This was the question of accommodation. There simply was not enough in the right places. A variety of solutions were found. Unaccompanied personnel were easier to accommodate and whilst priority was given to employing single people for the jobs, the variety of required skills meant that many married people came and they had to be found accommodation with their families. Some of the Feltwell personnel found themselves living in the faded splendour of Lynford Hall, a Jacobean-style mansion near Thetford once offered to Queen Victoria as a country home.[18] Accommodation ships were even considered but where these were likely to have been berthed is not easy to work out. For the majority however, US-style trailer (caravan in British parlance) parks provided the solution as *ad hoc* married quarters. This solution was not without its problems as such complexes were unpopular with local authorities and Norfolk County Council was expected to raise objections.[19] It was hoped that these caravans would be sourced from British companies forming a useful export order for a contract of c.£250,000 although it was noted that this could not be insisted upon. There is no record of the final outcome on this matter, although the contemporary photographs of the camps suggest that the caravans were brought in from America. RAF personnel arriving at RAF Driffield were surprised to see a sign to 'Santa Monica on the Wolds', the Douglas employees' trailer park, with all the trailers arranged neatly in herringbone formation. The park for Hemswell, which suffered severe overcrowding, was located at Sturgate, originally considered as an alternative site and already used by the USAF. Methwold (at one point shortlisted as a potential Thor site) was considered as the trailer park for Lakenheath but a suitable area was found at the latter base. Kirton-in-Lindsey maintained on a care and maintenance basis was also used. Inevitably, the American influence was evident and the RAF personnel benefited from this presence, experiencing, amongst other things, the first bowling alleys to be established at RAF stations. The reverse was also true. Feltwell's station newspaper, *Rocket Review*, reported 'The advent of three USAF officers to the Rugby XV has been interesting, to say the least – the days of the Wing Forward are numbered and the new laws appear to be tailor-made for the Left Tackle'. The arrival of the US construction teams is still remembered by older members of the local populations, and some still resolutely believe the 'misinformation' of the time that the missiles were stored in huge underground silos.

With the dispersed area represented by the Thor sites, communications was an important aspect and so a twice-daily C-47 service operated out of RAF Northolt on an airline basis with a set timetable. Originally the service went only to Lakenheath which covered Feltwell, but as work started on the other sites the flight schedule included these as well. The route was to become Northolt – Lakenheath – Hemswell – Driffield – North Luffenham. The return to Northolt was to be no later than 7.00p.m. After the initial flurry of activity these flights settled down to a thrice-weekly profile of Monday, Wednesday and Friday.

Then, on 10 January 1959, the *Daily Mail* reported:

> Delays in building Thor rocket sites in East Anglia have been caused by labour problems among highly skilled and FBI-cleared American workers. Dissension amongst these VIP technicians has resulted in hold-ups at some of the secret sites and a top-level reorganisation in the U.S. management of the job. Mr Errol (sic; actually Earl) M. Neff the Douglas Aircraft Corporation's Chief rocket expert in Europe was secretly replaced on December 19.

Neff had indeed been replaced by William (Bill) A. Duval following a low-profile visit to England by Leo A. Carter, DAC's vice president and general manager. He had found dissatisfaction amongst the workforce exemplified by homesickness, long hours – typically sixty-hour weeks – poor discipline and no duty-free allowances on cigarettes and spirits such as was available to the USAF servicemen. The workforce accommodation was split between RAF camps, hostels and hotels. Sandys' Office was reassured by the Ministry of Works that DAC was 'concerned solely with the installation of equipment. Consequently the work programme has in no way been affected'.[20] However, it was admitted that there was some slippage at Feltwell, the lead site. This was attributable principally to DAC underestimating the task to install and check the equipment far from their headquarters. BMD had been concerned over this and had despatched Major Wallace to the UK with a small team to report on what was happening. Wallace reported that the set-up operations in the UK had been seen as a production problem, whereas in fact it had become an engineering problem.[21] Until the handover of the installations, DAC staff nominally had sole control over the site and no RAF personnel could assist with the commissioning of any of the technical equipment although, in practice, RAF assistance was gratefully accepted.

Generally speaking, there was inevitably some limited integration between the local population and the RAF personnel. Overall the relationship seems to have been good even though the mere presence of the missiles almost guaranteed the annihilation of the local population in a nuclear exchange, although the finality of this was sometimes misunderstood. A farmer local to North Pickenham requested of the OC that he be given suitable warning of an attack so that he could move his cattle to a safer location. Local pubs were frequently used for social events and squadron parties.

The headquarters of each wing was co-located with the squadron closest to the four chosen airheads. These HQs would be responsible for the administration, handling and final testing of all missiles before they were transferred to the associated squadrons. This was done in a RIM (Receipt, Inspection and Maintenance) Building which was located in one of the existing hangars, suitably refurbished with separate bays containing dozens of grey steel cabinets which housed the Douglas-supplied

Figure A equipment used for servicing the missiles.[22] The RIM Building consisted of four elements:[23]

- Offices.
- The Operations Room or Missile Control Centre (MCC). This was permanently manned by an RAF Squadron Leader (the Missile Controller) and an USAF AO of Major or Captain's rank. It was equipped with telephone and radio communications links with Bomber Command, Nos 1 and 3 Groups, USAF SAC Headquarters at Omaha, Nebraska and to all the squadron stations.
- A large floor area for servicing missiles and GSE, most of which was in self-contained mobile trailers.
- Servicing bays for special equipment (Guidance sets, CEAs, LOX and gaseous nitrogen pipelines).

The RIM Buildings were all converted from existing C-Type hangars, except at North Luffenham where the hangars were J-Type. This latter type required extra work to strengthen the roof trusses to take the overhead crane that would be installed in all the RIM Buildings. The interior was converted with brick-built bays for the various Thor servicing operations. To maintain cleanliness, the floor was, after various solutions had been tried unsuccessfully, covered in 1ft sq. white 'Duromit' tiles laid on a concrete screed. A proposal to convert only two hangars as RIM Buildings with two Wings (i.e. 10 squadrons) using each one was briefly considered as a cost-saving measure[24], but the idea 'horrified' A/DD Ops (BM)[25] as the distances involved to the further sites were considered too far and would subject the missile to excessive risk of deterioration. A further hangar adjacent to each RIM Building was converted into the Technical Storage Building. This involved the sealing of the doors so that only the two centre doors opened.

One further consideration was the nature of the UK road system, which had not been designed with the need to transport a 65ft-long missile on its TEL. The original TEL had a fixed rear axle and the manufacturers, the Food Machinery and Chemical Corporation in California, were asked to modify the design to incorporate rear wheel steering with separate drivers along the lines of the US City Fire Department's rescue ladder vehicles. The modified vehicle was tested in secrecy on the perimeter roads of Moffett Naval Air Station.[26] Meanwhile, oil drums and aircraft wheel chocks were arranged on the remoter taxiways at Lakenheath, the nominated lead airhead, to replicate the more tortuous bends that would be encountered. The majority of road works consisted of widening the access to the sites themselves. The size of the vehicles required some cutting back of overhanging branches and this task was arranged with the various local authorities. Colonel Harry Zink, Commander of SAC's 672nd Ballistic Missile Squadron,[27] was concerned that:

> many minor roads and bridges and much of the terrain of Britain and Western Europe would not stand up to the weight of a Thor unit. Each individual Thor [unit] needs some two dozen pieces of heavy or comparatively heavy equipment to render it operational.[28]

In fact, the TELs proved more manageable than had been originally expected and just minimum road widening or strengthening was required. In some areas Perforated Steel Planking (PSP) was all that was used. The first flight of the Thor Hauls on 24 March had brought in a TEL vehicle and the use of this vehicle to prove the routes to be travelled was reported to the Air Council Meeting on 27 March 1958. As a contingency the USAF had already considered the use of helicopters to transport the missiles in the UK, the possibility of flying the Thor Hauls direct to some of the proposed satellite sites (this may have been possible at Honington, Marham and Watton, none of which was eventually selected), or to expedite the land transfer the practicality of mating the propulsion and aft-end package to the front end on site. US vehicles were re-painted RAF blue-grey when they ventured onto public roads to minimise public curiosity. The US-made prime mover was eventually replaced with a right-hand-drive Leyland tractor unit as this was considered more suitable. During the route-proving, American personnel were disguised in civilian clothes and all communication was to be done by accompanying RAF personnel. If this disguise was compromised the cover story was that the Americans were from SAC concerned with the USAF bomber Reflex programme.[29]

In addition to the Thor Hauls was the ongoing need for logistic support and servicing spares for the missile. This was coordinated through the San Bernardino Air Matériel Area (SBAMA) at Norton AFB in California. Santa Monica recorded issue and usage of spares and automatically ordered re-supply. In cases of urgent need SBAMA provided a maximum delivery time of fifty hours on any required part.[30, 31]

Security, too, of both the missiles and the warheads was of paramount importance and was fully itemised in the Security Agreement. The Air Ministry was responsible for providing the necessary infrastructure and personnel to protect the classified elements of the weapon system, supported by the US Provost Marshal, 3910th Combat Support Group based at Lakenheath. Their armed personnel would always accompany ground movements of classified components. Seven types of threats to Thor were identified (and they are remarkably similar to the current-day perceived terrorist threats):

- Penetration of the launch position.
- Damage from small arms.
- Light civilian aircraft.
- Portable nuclear devices.
- Enemy submarines launching SSMs.
- Lethal chemicals dispersed upwind.
- Suicide actions by fanatics crashing vehicles into the site.

Additionally, there was a constant threat from the Provisional IRA which was known to be planning attacks on military targets to steal weapons.

Two levels of sabotage were identified, covered by a Sabotage Notification Scheme which would be escalated upwards through the chain of command.

SEVEN HIGH: This was an 'extraordinary event which appeared to be capable of adversely affecting the capability or readiness to launch the retaliatory strike force, or the possibility of enemy sabotage or covert action that could not immediately be ruled out'.

RED SKIN: This was an event capable of adversely affecting the capability or readiness to launch the retaliatory strike force and rapid investigation revealed enemy sabotage action, or an event had occurred 'which is of such a serious and suspicious nature that even without investigation, enemy sabotage or covert action appears very highly probable', or that the base was 'implementing its Sabotage Alert procedures'.[32]

The building of the bases also attracted the attention of CND – North Pickenham, perhaps by nature of its ease of access was a particular focus. Over a series of weekends in December 1958 the Direct Action Committee Against Nuclear War had besieged the site. The protesters, however, had failed to understand the enthusiasm with which the workers on the site were prepared to evict anyone trying to force an entry. At one stage the local Police had to be summoned to rescue a number of demonstrators who had scaled the perimeter fence: 'Yelling abuse, the workers grabbed men and women alike and hurled them into a six-inch deep mixture of mud and wet concrete. Women were dragged along by their hair and many were trampled on while trying to release themselves from the mud'.[33] Although arrests were made, the protesters praised Supt. Arthur Canham, the Head of the Downham Police Division, for the sensitive way in which he had handled the episode. Some of the jailed prisoners staged a hunger strike in Norwich Prison, and there was a public outcry when it was revealed that two of them had been forcibly fed.

Inevitably, however, the programme suffered slippage and the mid-1958 date proved hopelessly optimistic. A number of launch failures had been caused by turbine shaft fractures and this delayed the programme by a further month. Because of the commonality of components with Jupiter the problem also affected that programme, thereby vindicating those who had wanted the two missiles to be developed along separate tracks. Sandys and his UK delegation were advised of this during a series of meetings at the Pentagon from 22–24 September 1958. The UK missiles, some of which had already been delivered to Lakenheath (see Chapter Five) would have to be modified with new turbines.[34] This raised the issue of the operational state of the missiles. The Thor Agreement was to last for five years, but when did the clock start ticking? The Atlas programme was by this time clearly going to deliver and with its operational deployment there were clearly fears that the US would lose interest in the IRBM programme, leaving the UK maybe stuck with missiles that fell short of requirements. Concerns about the safety of the warhead had also reached the ears of the Air Ministry. The possibility of a nuclear accident, however small, could not be contemplated.

Briefing notes for the press conference which followed the announcement of the Thor Agreement confirm that there 'was no intention of developing a British warhead for the Thor Weapon. British efforts [were] being directed towards the development of an all-British weapon – a more advanced type capable of launching from underground'. But the question of a UK-built Thor warhead was, in fact, to be considered later, in the context of a 'without strings' follow-on Thor proposal to provide an independent UK strategic deterrent.

Table VII: Launch emplacement equipment inventory.

Item	Code	Group
Trailer-Mounted Hydropneumatic Systems Controller	AF/M46A-1	Ground Support
Trailer-Mounted Launching Control Group	AN/MSQ-22 or AN/MSA-22	Ground Support
Trailer-Mounted Ballistic Missile System Checkout Station ★	TTU-36/M, -36A/M or -36B/M	Ground Support
Trailer-Mounted Launching Countdown Group	AN/NSQ-23 or AN/MSA-21	Ground Support
Trailer-Mounted Power Switchboard	JEU-2/M	Launch Control
Trailer-Mounted Diesel Engine Generator Set x 4	AF/M32A-12	Launch Control
Hydraulic Pumping Unit	AF/M42A-1 or AF/M42A-1A	Launcher Erector
Erecting-Transporting Boom	GSU-33/E	Launcher Erector
Ballistic Missile Erecting-Launching Mount	MTU-1/E	Launcher Erector
Compressed Gas Cylinder (Nitrogen) Semitrailer x 2	AF/M32A-17	LOX System
Liquid Oxygen Storage Tank	TMU-3E	LOX System
Liquid Oxygen Pipeline Outfit	GSU-5/E	LOX System
Overflow Pipeline	GSU-20E	LOX System
Compressed Gas Cylinder (Nitrogen) Semitrailer x 2	AF/M32A-17	Fuel System
Fuel Storage Tank	TMU-4/E	Fuel System
Trailer-Mounted Fuel Filter Unit	GSU-7/M	Fuel System
Fuel Pipeline Outfit	GSU-6/E	Fuel System
Immersion Electric Heater	HDK-5/F24A	Fuel System
Trailer-Mounted Air Conditioner	AF/M32C-1	Launcher
Trailer-Mounted Missile Launching Equipment Simulator ★	SMU-18M	Power Distribution

Building the Infrastructure

Skid Mounted Power Switch	JEU-1/E	Power Distribution
Power Driven Reciprocating Compressor	A/M32A-26	Electrical Supply
Liquid Oxygen Side Junction Box	GSU-8/E	Electrical Supply
Fuel Side Junction Box	GSU-9/E	Electrical Supply

★ These units (x 2) were also used in the RIM Building.

Notes:
1 TNA. DEFE 13/593. f. E14B.
2 TNA. DCAS to SoS, DCAS 1383/58, 1 April 1958.
3 *Flight*, 5 December 1958, p 872.
4 TNA. No 142(SM) Sqn ORB, January 1960. 'Some difficulty is being experienced in keeping the RP1 tank area clear of rain water. The present hand pumps are not adequate nor are they proof against frost damage.'
5 TNA. No 142(SM) Sqn ORB, October 1961.
6 NMR. Swindon. Survey Report on RAF Mepal. NMR ID 1156384.
7 To Air Ministry Drawing G.No 5033A/53.
8 TNA. AIR 2/14905. f. 87A.
9 TNA. A full listing of the works carried out at Hemswell can be found in Appendix C to Air Ministry letter A.302973/58/W.H.1, dated 17 July 1958 contained in AIR 2/14907.
10 TNA. No 142(SM) Sqn ORB, February 1961.
11 TNA. AIR 2/14905. f.86B.
12 Correspondence with Peter Rich, former Sgt Pay Accountant, June 2007.
13 TNA AIR 2/14947. f.42A.
14 *Rocket Review*. Vol.1, No.1, RAF Feltwell, April 1959.
15 TNA. AIR 2/1497. Air Ministry File A 304450/58.
16 TNA. AIR 2/14947. f.115A. Letter HQBC to USoS Air Ministry, 7 October 1958.
17 TNA. DEFE 13/120 f. E16.
18 Lynford Hall still exists today as a country house hotel and conference centre. See www.lynfordhallhotel.co.uk.
19 TNA. AIR 2/14906 f.12A.
20 TNA. DEFE 13/120 f.E35. Letter from D. Hanson to H. Godfrey.
21 Hartt, Julian, *The Mighty Thor*, p.182.
22 Although in many cases a standard high-grade Avometer Type 8 was all that was needed and was the preferred option. Correspondence with Sgt Dave Jones, August 2007.
23 TNA. No 77(SM) Sqn ORB. AIR 27/2952.
24 Loose Minute 472K/DDWP2, 22 May 1958.
25 TNA. AIR 2/14906. F.118A. A/DD Ops (BM), Wg Cdr T. Knight, 30 May 1958.
26 Hartt, *Ibid*, p.159.
27 The 672nd Ballistic Missile Squadron had been activated on 1 January 1958 to operate Thor.
28 *The Daily Telegraph*, 27 February 1958.

29 The USAF Reflex Programme allowed for forward basing of US-based bomber units in Europe and North Africa normally on a ninety-day duty basis.
30 RAF Museum. X002-5491/006.
31 But sometimes things would go wrong. On one occasion a Chf Tech. ordered a replacement bolt for one that was badly worn. Realising that it was a low-cost item he ordered six. Part of the ordering procedure was to identify the next higher assembly for which the ordered part was required. In this case it was the boat tail assembly at the rear of the missile. In due course a storekeeper arrived and asked him to sign for delivery. He commented that it seemed unnecessary for such a small part and he was therefore invited to go outside where six boat tail assemblies were waiting on BRS lorries. The UK taxpayers were not asked to pick up the bill!
32 TNA. AIR 20/10081. Document C-4010, May 1959. Annex VII, p.2.
33 *The Eastern Daily Press*, 26 March 1999.
34 TNA. DEFE 13/194. f. E18.

1. Missile No.214 being unloaded from a C-124 Globemaster II at RAF Mildenhall prior to being flown to Vandenberg AFB for CTL-10. (RAF Museum)

2. Missile No.214 is removed from the RIM Building at RAF Hemswell. (RAF Museum)

3. Erection Phase 1. (Author's collection via J. Atkison)

4. Erection Phase 2. Note the emergency shower unit on the right of picture. (TNA)

5. Bill Duval and Douglas staff brief Lt Gen Schriever and RAF officers. (RAF Museum)

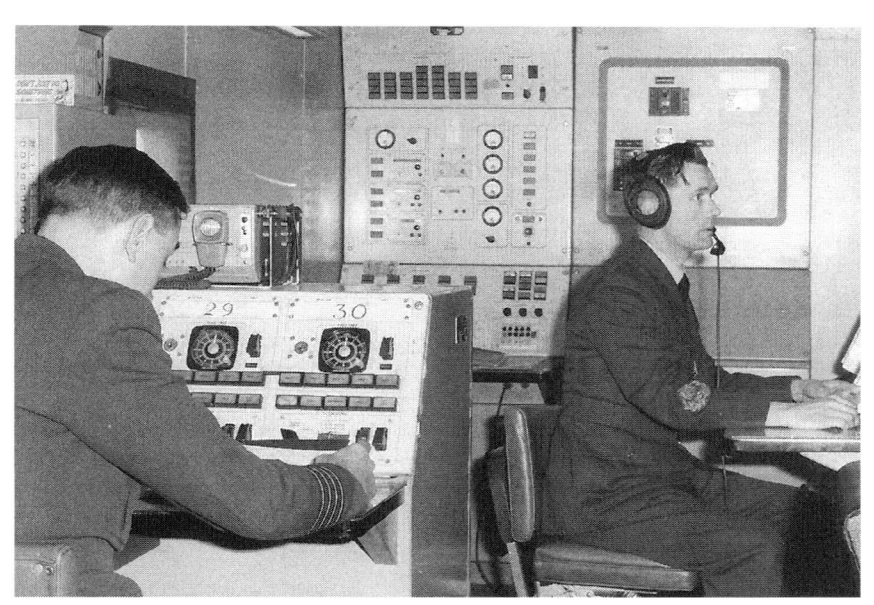

6. Inside the Launch Control Trailer during a countdown. (RAF via R.Pratt)

7. Erection Phase 2. (RAF Museum)

8. LOX Loading Phase 3. Note the high pressure venting as tank is filled. (RAF via R. Pratt)

9. Technicians in the 'boat tail' of the missile give a good idea of the size and complexity of the engine. (RAF via R. Pratt)

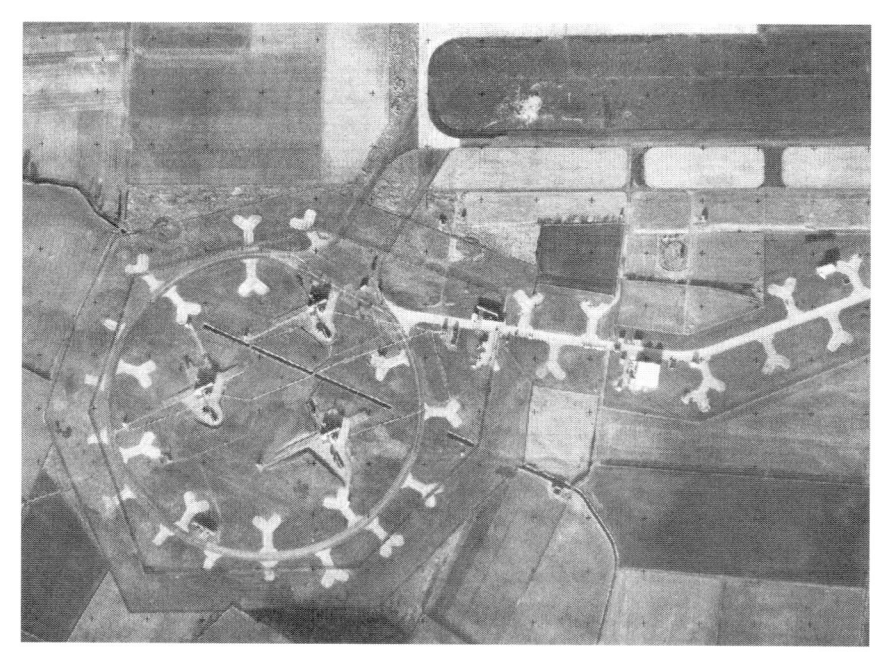

10. Aerial photo of RAF Carnaby. (English Heritage)

11. Awaiting its CTL-10 launch at Vandenberg, AFB missile No. 214 receives a fly-past from a Handley Page Victor B1 (XA928). (RAF Museum)

12. 'Acton Town', 13 December 1960. Missile No.267 launched by a crew from the North Luffenham Wing.

Top: 13. B-Type hutting, guardroom, administrative offices and crew room – Caistor, 2006. (Author)

Middle: 14. Fire tender and Police vehicle garages – Caistor, 2006. (Author)

Bottom: 15. Shelter – Caistor, 2006. (Author)

Top: 16. Power conversion building, North Pickenham, 2007. (Author)

Middle: 17. Derelict Surveillance and Inspection Building – Hemswell, 2007. (Author)

Bottom: 18. Surveillance and Inspection Building (modified for current use) – RAF Feltwell, 2007. (Author)

19. Erection Phase 2. (AIR 27/2594)

20. Two-Bay Classified Storage Building – RAF Feltwell, 2007. (Author)

21. Pyrotechnics store – Breighton, 2007. (Author)

22. Long Range Theodolite building – Melton Mowbray, 2007. (Author)

23. Blast walls and launch pad base – Harrington, 2007. (Roger Tutt)

24. Launch Emplacement showing electrical conduits – Caistor, 2006. (Author)

25. RIM Building – RAF Feltwell, 2007. (Author)

26. Long Range Theodolite target pillar – Bardney, 2007. (Author)

Above: 27. Squadron Leader's house – Bardney, 2007. (Author)

Opposite above: 28. Lynford Hall, where many of the Douglas personnel were billeted, as it is today. (Author)

Opposite below: 29. Rocketdyne MB-3 Thor Engine – RAF Museum, Cosford. (Author)

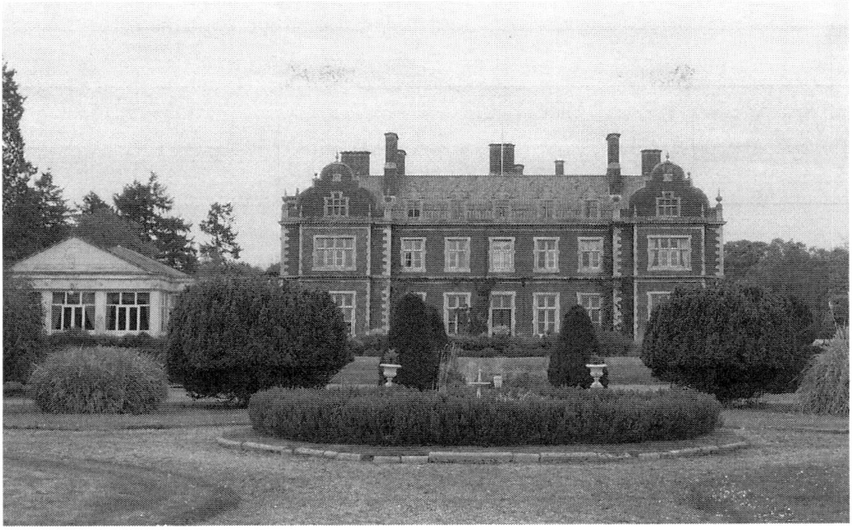

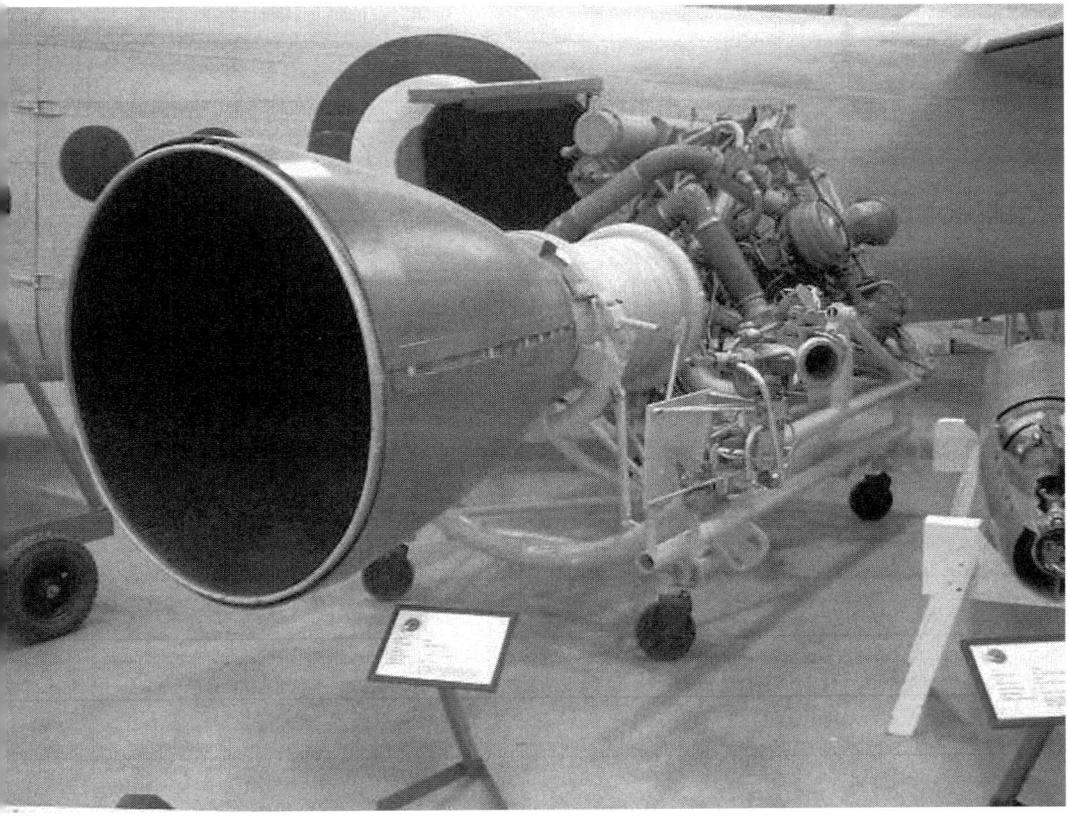

30. RAF Feltwell as it is today. It is of interest to note that the boundaries of the golf course very closely follow the perimeter fence of the Thor site. (Get Mapping)

CHAPTER FIVE
THE FIRST THOR ARRIVES

The first Thor – No.139, the second production missile – was flown into RAF Lakenheath aboard a Douglas C-124, arriving in typically early autumnal British weather and without ceremony on the afternoon of 29 August 1958. This arrival had been predicted in an article by Chapman Pincher, a regular reporter on Thor matters, in the *Daily Express* on 25 August, ostensibly written in Amsterdam, saying that the first missile was due to arrive during the course of that week. This was, for a variety of reasons, somewhat later than the Americans had originally planned. The missile had been ready for shipment on 18 July[1] and the USAF wanted to fly it in on 1 August – there were by then four missiles ready for delivery – but they had to await the 'green light' from the Air Ministry. However, the Government was by no means unanimous on how to handle the receipt of this first batch of missiles; indeed, Macmillan 'had decided that no statement should be made [about the arrival and he had also] vetoed a departmental proposal that the press should have facilities to photograph Thor in the United Kingdom'[2] when the first missile was delivered to the newly re-formed No.77 (SM) Squadron. Two main factors seem to have influenced Macmillan's thinking:

- There was a special Security Council Meeting on the crisis in the Middle East scheduled for 18 August. (In the event it was postponed.)
- The missiles were still not proved operationally.

Nonetheless, it was acknowledged that there was:

> great public interest. [There would be] great pressure to give the fullest information about each stage of the arrangements for deploying the weapons. [The Government would be] told that it was nonsensical to classify as 'secret' a weapon which would be taken on long trailers through the nearby towns and villages and will be visible on their sites.[3]

Although there was awareness that the press knew that the arrival of the missiles was in the offing, Macmillan believed that it was a sensitive time to announce overtly an increase in strategic weaponry. This had been echoed earlier in the year: 'we shall be asked why, at a time when the air is full of a talk of a summit meeting, we are in such haste to deploy these weapons'.[4]

In terms of press reporting, there was certain protection provided by the D-Notice[5] that had been placed on much of the information surrounding Thor. A revised version of the original notice issued in 1956 had been communicated via the Secretary of the Service, Press and Broadcasting Committee, Rear Admiral (Retd) George P. Thomson, on 24 February 1958.[6] No details were to be disclosed covering the number of missiles, the precise location or number of sites, any details of the layouts of the sites or the operational relationship between them. The press were also asked not to report any obvious signs of survey work which might indicate a potential site. The practicalities of the issue of site location were recognised, however:

> The Russian Intelligence will inevitably find out where the sites are because they are not hidden from public view and the broad area in which they are located is generally known. If the Press abide by the 'D' notice however we have made the Russian task a little more difficult'[7].

This approach was echoed in a reply in Parliament to Frank Beswick, who had asked about Kirton-in-Lindsey, located in his constituency, becoming a Thor base, asking if it was really thought 'possible that these great, clumsy things [could be] sited in the flats of East Anglia without any other country being aware of them'. Mr C.I. Orr-Ewing, Under Secretary of State at the Air Ministry, commented, 'there is no point in giving away information to the enemy before one [needs] to, and ... we must make the intelligence services of your potential enemies work for a living'.[8] But it seems that the Russians were already using civilian flights to monitor progress on the sites. A commercial Moscow to London return air service had been inaugurated by Aeroflot in 1958, operated by twin-jet Tupolev Tu-104 airliners.[9] It was not unknown for these flights to suffer 'navigational problems' over the North Sea which would invariably result in the aircraft making landfall over the countryside where the Thor bases were being built. The Tu-104 fortuitously had a glazed nose cone ideally suited for observing the ground below. (When asked why a civilian airliner needed what essentially resembled a bomb aimer's position a Russian engineer is reported to have replied, 'It's a design feature: the plane couldn't fly without it'.) There were concerns that if the arrival came before the Security Council meeting it might give a 'handle to hostile propagandists and criticism from the opposition'.

The most serious concern though, was the question of the operational status of Thor. Although the missiles due to arrive were IOC missiles, there were doubts about the operational capability of a missile which was still experiencing regular launch failures in America. In February a meeting at the Ministry of Defence on Deployment of Intermediate Range Ballistic Missiles in Britain had concluded that it was 'important not to accept missiles which were not operational and which could not be manned by the RAF because of lack of trained personnel'.[10] The British Joint Services Mission (BJSM) in Washington was instructed to obtain information on the operational effectiveness of the missile. On 11 August Foreign Secretary Selwyn Lloyd advised Macmillan that it was acceptable for the delivery to go ahead. However, on 13 August Sandys advised the SoS(A) that:

Thor should not be regarded as operational at the present time. The Americans themselves had said that its reliability would not be firmly determined for another twelve months by which time a further 28 test firings would have taken place in the United States.[11]

Of the twenty-five test launches that had taken place up to July 1959, only ten had been classed as successful. Four had been partially successful and eleven had been failures. Reliability was still a sensitive subject. In late March Sandys had set the operational requirement that 50 per cent of the missiles must land within two and a half miles of the target (relaxing somewhat the USAF design parameter of two miles) and this had still to be demonstrated. The British concern was that acceptance of the missile without question in its present state of development may make the Americans less enthusiastic in their efforts to perfect it. Also, Britain wanted operational missiles not training rounds.[12] However, it was also acknowledged that there was an advantage in having at least some of the weapons. It would enable the first squadron to be trained, gain experience with the equipment and assess the operational aspects of handling the missile. Sandys therefore authorised the RAF to accept the first fifteen missiles, the allocation to the Feltwell Wing, but he also made quite clear once again the limit of American involvement:

> I should perhaps explain that there is no intention that the first squadron of Thor missiles should be manned and operated by the Americans. The Royal Air Force will be in charge from the start, and the Americans, who have now arrived in the country in considerable numbers but without any publicity, will give the Royal Air Force training on the spot, particularly in the problems of technical maintenance of the site installations and the missiles themselves.[13]

With the first missile now safely in Lakenheath, shortly to be followed by the subsequent fourteen, deployment to the actual sites could begin. The first three would be taken to Feltwell as the lead site followed by one to Shepherds Grove as the first satellite installation. But the missiles would have to be transferred on public roads to these bases. Whilst the missiles would be covered up, the convoys would be not inconspicuous and it was going to be impossible to conceal the event from the media. Despite the D-Notice covering the bases, the identity of at least the first five bases was quite widely known – their construction was in practice difficult to hide – and a protest march had already taken place at Mepal on 24 August. It was noted that 'in practice ... the Press have been allowed to mention Feltwell'.[14] As *RAF Flying Review* magazine later pointed out:[15]

> ...there is understandably some secrecy about the precise location of these launch sites. Apart from the one at Feltwell and another at Driffield, Yorks, no *official* indication of location has been released. It *has* been stated, however, that each main base is situated on a permanent RAF station and that the subsidiary bases have been sited on disused wartime airfields; so it is not difficult to arrive at a reasonably accurate picture of the network of twenty sites.

However, it was acknowledged that the East Anglian press were aware of the locations of the sites.[16] Macmillan was still sensitive to formal media coverage but was advised by the Ministry of Defence that the '*Daily Express* ha[d] gone so far as to pre-empt the most suitable location in Feltwell village from which to photograph [the missile's] arrival. As things stand they are likely to get a "scoop" and we cannot prevent its publication'.[17] On 12 September Macmillan agreed to a press facility being provided for the arrival of the first Thor at Feltwell. On that day the Ministry of Defence issued a press release announcing the event:

> The first Thor ballistic missile will be moved to its site near Feltwell on or about 18 September, 1958 where it will be handed over to the RAF for training purposes. This is a routine operation in accordance with the schedule resulting from the February agreement and foreshadowed in the statement by the Minister of Defence on 25 August, 1958.

Accordingly the press was invited to Feltwell on 19 September to witness the arrival of the first missile.[18] The members were to be advised that:

1) The Thor program in Britain was basically British.
2) USAF participation extended only to technical assistance and the provision of equipment.
3) The US-manufactured warhead would remain under US control. (The nature of the two key systems had been fully detailed in the original press announcement following the Thor agreement.)
4) The D-Notice provisions were to be observed.
5) The Thors were not yet operational and had been supplied for training purposes.

Photography was permitted using the following guidelines:

1) Photographs of the covered missile being transported on public roads could be taken provided there was a neutral background which would not identify the location.
2) Photographs of the uncovered missile could be taken at Feltwell where it would be put in No.2 storage hangar (occupied by the Technical Supply Flight, as the RIM Building was not yet ready). These pictures must be taken at sufficient distance so that no details of the missile were disclosed.

The missile would bear RAF roundels[19] and a yellow band indicating that it was a training round. It would carry a prominent distinguishing number, namely '01'.[20] The TEL on which the missile would be carried would be painted USAF blue-grey but with all USAF markings removed. The tractor unit would be a USAF vehicle painted 'airfield yellow' but, again, with all USAF markings removed, and it would carry RAF number plates (on the day, however, an RAF Morris tractor was used, painted blue-grey and with RAF number plates and No.3 Group markings. Later convoys would see some yellow US tractors used). It would be driven by RAF personnel and the convoy would be escorted by RAF and civilian Police motor-cyclists.[21] The yellow training band was also never applied as it was pointed out that this would be a misuse of the standard yellow band applied to RAF training aircraft. It was also noted that operational squadrons did not use the yellow band during the period when they were working up to operational readiness and this may lead the press to question the operational state of the squadron.[22] Once inside Feltwell, the presence of the missiles was far from obvious. On 17 October, only a few days after his appointment as director general of Organisation, AVM Walter Pretty visited Feltwell – this was two days after a further three missiles had arrived. He did not see them nor did he hear mention of them. Only one missile was in the RIM Building. 'Please check' was his request.[23]

The missile that the press saw quite clearly had no warhead. Major-General William H. 'Butch' Blanchard, commander of 7th Air Division, advised DCAS, Air Marshal Sir Geoffrey Tuttle, that the 'warheads are scheduled to arrive this fall'.[24] More specifically, DofOps(B&R) Air Cdre J.H. Searby had advised DCAS(Ops) that 'we have been informed by 7th Air Division that they plan to bring in the first warhead on the 14 October. On arrival the warheads will be stored in their storage at Lakenheath whilst awaiting transport to Feltwell'.[25]

There was, of course, much press interest in the warheads and how they would be treated. This was a difficult path to tread. On the one hand there was the concern over US-controlled warheads mounted on missiles in the UK, but the conditions of launch were clear. The warheads remained at all times in US custody, but the authority to launch the missile was subject to a 'joint decision in the light of the circumstances at the time and having regard to the two Governments' obligations under Article 5 of the North Atlantic Treaty'.[26] To many the only proper deterrent that the UK should have was a truly independent deterrent under UK control. On the other hand, if the warheads were not mounted on the missiles, the deterrent effect of Thor was severely diluted. The press was generally aware by then that the missiles would be capable of launch within about fifteen minutes. Bomber Command had been less certain. In February 1958, AOCinCBC Air Chf Mshl Sir Harry Broadhurst (not by the tenor of his correspondence a particular fan of Thor) had written to DCAS:

> You said on the 'phone that it would be possible to hold these things at fifteen minute readiness. Everything is possible, of course, but I would remind you that we are not yet beginning to solve the problem of holding the 'V' bombers at any state of readiness. The 'V' bombers present a relatively simple problem because having brought them to readiness, I can order them off at the first warning, but I am still left with well over an hour in which to obtain a decision as to whether they should carry on and complete their attack or be recalled to base. On the other hand, as I see it, we will need two Governments to agree before the IRBMs can be fired but even then they could not be launched at first warning. This could only be done when the radar plots were definitely identified as hostile or, what is much more likely, after the Soviet bombs or missiles had started to fall on this country. In sum, it seems to me that given the same state of readiness i.e. fifteen minutes, whereas the 'V' bombers can be controlled through our present chain of command the IRBMs present an entirely different problem because the military readiness and the political decision to fire must coincide if we are to avoid having our 'deterrent' destroyed before it can be launched. I do not know how much thought has been given to this problem but I do urge most strongly that we know exactly what we are aiming at

before we commit ourselves to any agreement with the Americans on a specific operational set-up.[27]

Under Project E, unhelpfully similar in title to Project Emily, but in fact completely separate from it, the US had allocated some of their nuclear weapons to the RAF in the event of hostilities. This was to provide a stop-gap whilst the RAF built up its own stocks of Yellow Sun nuclear weapons. The Project E weapons were held strictly under US custody until they were released to the RAF. SACEUR controlled the release of the weapons for the Canberra Light Bomber Force whilst the V-Bombers' weapons were under the control of the Pentagon with orders coming from SAC HQ via 7AD:

> A somewhat similar procedure for holding and releasing the [Thor] warheads [was] being written into the agreement. ... There is one difference between this procedure and that for atomic bombs for aircraft, necessitated by the fact that, to achieve a high state of readiness, the warhead may need to be actually joined up with the missile.[28]

To be effective, therefore, the warheads would have to be in position. This fact was assumed in an article which appeared in *Aviation Week* following a US press visit to Feltwell in July. Despite certain differences in the approach to the media between the two countries, the joint Anglo/US agreement on the release of information clearly stated, *inter alia*, that 'no inference or speculation will be made concerning the presence or absence of nuclear warheads'.[29] What was actually inside the RV was therefore a closely-guarded secret. Even the squadron COs were not aware of whether their missiles were armed. Assurances were given both as to the security of the warheads on their way to the Thor bases and the safety aspects once they were mated with the missiles. The warhead was an integrated unit which could not be split into different components. Their transport on public roads was therefore a particularly sensitive matter with closely-guarded warhead convoys. The arming system was very elaborate and was not fully completed until the final stages of re-entry. There was, therefore, no risk of a nuclear explosion on the ground, a matter fully explained to the press from the beginning. Yet it was all too easy to get drawn into revealing too much and hackles could all too easily be raised. On 7 August the *News Chronicle* claimed that the warheads were not in place. The reporter Angus MacPherson had telephoned Brigadier Hobbs at the Ministry of Defence suggesting that if the Thors were at fifteen minute readiness then the warheads must be in place – a not unreasonable assumption. Hobbs was between a rock and a hard place and sought advice from Sir Frederick Brundrett who instructed him to say that the warheads were not in place. The reason given 'was that to answer otherwise would be to leave the impression that [the missiles] were operational, which was politically unacceptable'. This was, however, a direct contravention of the Anglo-US agreement on the warheads which stated that:

> no inference or speculation will be made concerning the presence or absence of nuclear warheads. We have ourselves taken a stand at high level on this document, and have complained about American disclosures which violated it. Now we are convicted on the same count ourselves.

The loose minute concluded on a caustic note: 'I suggest that the opportunity should be taken to put out to the Ministry of Defence, at a suitable level, that difficulties like this can be expected to arise so long as they persist in attempts to deal with RAF matters without a proper background of knowledge and without consulting us'.[30] A conciliatory reply was received from the Ministry of Defence on 11 August.[31]

In fact, it was not until May 1960 that permission to fit the warheads was finally given.[32]

The press were a constant source of concern. On 1 December 1958 Macmillan wrote to Sandys about an article by the defence correspondent of the *Sunday Times*. This claimed that Thors were being airlifted into the UK at the rate of thirty a month, which implied that the full quota would be in the UK by the end of the year: 'These journalists are usually very well informed and often seem to know more than I do. ... I must say that I am not very happy at the thought of a large number of these missiles being given to us before we are sure of their performance, especially if they are complete with warhead.'[33] Sandys' reply was reassuring:

> The report in the *Sunday Times* has no foundation in fact. ... Up to the present 10 missiles have been delivered. Three of these have been installed on their launching pads at Feltwell, and one has been installed at Shepherds Grove. The rest are still in hangars at Feltwell. ... A further 5 missiles are due for delivery to this country by the end of he month.[34]

Even General Schreiver had fallen foul of an American TV interview when he stated 'of course we expect to have a few missiles blow up on the stand; if we didn't we wouldn't need a Research and Development programme'. Furthermore, Schreiver had also said that the 'initial operational missiles will be about 50 per cent reliable [and] we are putting our first missiles overseas fully a year before we thought we could'. Not everyone bought into the interpretation that only 50 per cent of the missiles would reach their target with extreme accuracy and that it was the technical success of the programme that meant the missiles were *in situ* a year early.[35] Even later in the programme there was concern that a uniform message may not be given to a group of UK defence correspondents who were to visit US Thor facilities in April 1962. As well as seeing the Douglas manufacturing facilities, the correspondents were also expected to meet RAF personnel under training and witness a live firing of the missile. This visit, however, proved a great success and generated much positive publicity.[36]

The ongoing press interest was not restricted to the arrival of the missiles. The US media had seen Thor production at Santa Monica on 28 January 1959. They were welcomed by Donald Douglas Jr and Lieutenant Colonel Sidney Greene from the AFBMC.[37] Yet more parochially in the UK, the press naturally wanted to see a countdown in progress. Whilst there was still a reluctance to show too much, it was recognised that a proper press facility at one of the bases would eliminate, to a great extent, the 'ferreting about for information and so on by other means' that was the natural instinct of the media. The facilities granted would be 'of no wider scope that those given to a party of visiting US correspondents' that was scheduled for the summer of 1960.[38] The press had, in any case, assumed that there would be a progression of facilities following the arrival and a subsequent pooled facility[39] which covered the erection of a missile. As always there was sensitivity to photography, but this would be controlled and was considered a better option than thwarting the efforts of photographers with long lenses seeking vantage points around the bases. It was considered possible that such photos could reveal too much. Therefore, a pooled visit to witness the erection of a missile was decided upon.[40]

By the autumn of 1959 the first squadrons were completing their training and pressure continued to declare the missiles operational. DCAS had given permission to fly in the missiles for the Driffield and North Luffenham sites on 21 July[41]. There was a backlog of essential modifications to the pads at Feltwell that had been reported in June but would occupy 120 contract workers until the end of the year, and each LE would be out of action for ten days. These problems had their origins in the early part of the year. The 10th 'Thor' Project – Progress Report[42] had noted, referring to Feltwell, that DAC technicians had not allowed enough time to complete their preliminary work properly and the 7AD were asked to ensure that they took a more careful approach. However, there was much concern over an article in the *Daily Express* of 3 November 1959 by Chapman Pincher. *Britain Keeps Thor Rockets 'Inactive'*, was the headline. It continued: 'A political disagreement between Britain and the US over the Thor rockets has become so serious it could imperil future military aid from America'. Pincher had ruffled feathers before, when he had arguably breached the D-Notice on Thor. He had stated the number of missiles, the location of Feltwell and the layout of the sites. In practice, even the casual observer would have been able to identify the sites – there was no attempt to disguise their locations – indeed, it would have been an almost impossible task. CND were well aware of the locations and published advance notification of their planned demonstrations in local newspapers. As the missiles were raised for training it could be seen that there were three per site and there was sufficient public knowledge of Thor's purpose to work out that even if there were spare rounds, these were very unlikely to be capable of use as 'reloads'. Furthermore, both *Flight* and *The Aeroplane*[43] magazines had published comprehensive drawings of the pad layouts, apparently without raising official eyebrows, and the latter had published a photograph of the trial pad layout at Douglas' Culver City facility.[44]

Aware of the previous sensitivity in the US to the question of Thor's operational status, it was decided that a statement should be made 'in the broadest terms ... that the Thor weapon system can be made operational whenever we wish to make it'.[45] However, it was clear that a specific declaration of the system's operational capability was now necessary and Minister of Defence Harold Watkinson (who had succeeded Sandys in October) wrote to Macmillan on 29 November, 'I am satisfied that Thor has reached acceptable standards of performance and that the House of Commons should be advised that it is operational'.[46] SoS(A) George Ward confirmed on 2 December, 'As a result of test firings which have taken place in the USA and in light of the progress made in the training programme, we are satisfied that Thor is able to take its place as part of the operational front-line of the Royal Air Force'.[47] At last, and no doubt much to the relief of the Americans, the green light had been given to the Thor squadrons. The announcement came on 9 December in the form of a reply to a question tabled by the pro-Soviet MP Konni Zilliacus, MP for Gorton. Ward repeated the text of his 2 December letter but omitted a paragraph included in the original draft statement: 'I consider that the joint project with the United States has been crowned with a success which reflects great credit upon the combined effort and the spirit of collaboration and understanding of the United States and ourselves'. However, to be a credible deterrent, the missiles had to have their warheads fitted. Known to CAS and DCAS and, seemingly, very few others, if anyone at all, were concerns admitted by the Americans about the safety of the warhead.

Chapman Pincher had sensed something of a problem when he reported in the *Daily Express* of 19 November, 'I can report that in spite of insistent US pressures to get them delivered, all the warheads are still in storage under US control at Lakenheath, Suffolk'. Yet he had failed to identify why they were not being delivered.

The design of the warhead was such that it was one integrated unit which could not be broken down into sub-assemblies. The whole warhead, including the fissile material, was assembled at the factory. The design was inherently safe from the point of view of a nuclear explosion, but the Americans acknowledged that there was a very small risk of an explosion from the conventional explosives in the warhead which could give rise to some localised radioactivity. Macmillan, however, appeared very sensitive to the possibility of any form of nuclear contamination and wanted reassurance. Sandys had clarified the content of the warhead in a memo to the Cabinet: 'The nuclear warheads will always be in a fully assembled state and will normally be permanently positioned on the missiles. The missiles will incorporate a number of safety features designed to prevent an inadvertent nuclear explosion'[48].

Insofar as the safety of the warhead in transit was concerned, stringent safety precautions would be observed. The warhead convoy would have a Provost escort and would be accompanied by a specialist team suitably equipped to deal with any accident. The route would be carefully chosen to minimise the risk of accidents, and transfers would only take place in favourable weather conditions. Had there been an accident it would have been classed as a Broken Arrow incident if there was any chance of nuclear contamination. Confusingly, the Broken Arrow codename was American terminology – the equivalent UK codename was Fortnum. Should the incident have resulted in identifiable nuclear contamination it would have been classed as a Marco event. In fact, the Americans had originally wanted to keep the warheads in secure storage in Lakenheath and only take them to the squadrons in times of increased tension. However, it was calculated that it would take fifty-two hours to transport the warheads, considerably more than the twenty-four-hours' warning of attack that was anticipated. For similar reasons a modified proposal to store the warheads at the Wing HQs was overruled and the RVs were allocated to each squadron site, the only practical solution to maintaining an effective readiness capability. All the crews knew was that an RV was in place on the missile. Whether or not this contained a live warhead was not revealed.

The missiles may well have been in the UK but a further problem now arose, born out of the delay in bringing the Thors to operational status. This was the question of when the five-year support agreement actually started. The agreement covered:

- Missiles.
- Specialised equipment.
- Supply of training facilities and training missiles.
- Spare parts as required to maintain the missiles and specialised equipment in an operational condition.
- As may be agreed to be necessary, modification kits, modified components or assemblies, or factory modifications of the missiles and specialised equipment.

There was a high level of concern in the Air Ministry that if the Support Agreement was initiated before the missiles were fully operational, the Americans, close to completing the initial phase of the Atlas programme which would give them strategic independence from the IRBM programmes, may lose interest in further improving Thor. The continuing proof of the operational capability of the whole system would be a series of Integrated Weapons System Training (IWST) launches, undertaken by RAF crews as part of their US-based training, and a subsequent series of Combat Training Launches (CTL), although there had already been a disappointing response to a reduction in the CTL schedule to only four a year. This had been determined by SecDef Thomas Gates, and essentially halved the initial launch rate. VCAS had been advised on 16 December 1958, but despite some fairly uncompromising exchanges of letters on the subject, the Americans would not give way on this, and so after the IWST programme (nine launches) had been completed the CTL launch rate ran at four per year. This meant that far fewer RAF personnel would take part in an actual launch than had originally been planned by Bomber Command, who had anticipated that every member of the technical and operational crews would take part in one training launch. By then, it was clear that the Americans were not going to compromise further and an effective date of 1 November 1959 was taken as the start of the support period. This meant that if the Thor Agreement ran its natural course it would terminate on 31 October 1964. The twenty-one RAF launches were as follows:

Table VIII: RAF Thor IWST and CTL launches by year.

YEAR	1959	1960	1961	1962
IWST	8	1	0	0
CTL	2	4	4	2
TOTAL	**10**	**5**	**4**	**2**

More CTLs were planned but were cancelled once the Thor draw-down was announced.

Notes:
1 TNA. AIR 2/14907. Ref. 58/8. Minute of Meeting of RAF/USAF Co-ordinating Committee, 31 July 1958.
2 TNA. AIR 20/9791. AUS(A), R.C. Kent, to PS to USofS. 29 August 1958. See also Prime Minister's Personal Minute: M286/58.
3 TNA. AIR 20/10555. Attachment from E. Broadbent to PS to SoS. M.1391, 11 February 1958.
4 *Ibid.*
5 The D-Notice (short for Defence Notice) system started in 1912 and was a way of issuing censorship notices, via the Ministry of Defence, to the media to prohibit the publication of specific information on matters considered to be against the interests of national security.
6 TNA. DEFE 13/120 E14.
7 TNA. A.I.(S) 2/501/4 in file AIR 2/14982. Letter from ACAS(I) to AVM S.O. Bufton.
8 Hansard, 26 February 1958. Col.374.
9 The advent of the Tupolev Tu-104 (NATO codename: Camel), derived from the Tu-16

(Badger) Bomber, had already caused not a little surprise and concern in intelligence circles when the prototype landed at London, Heathrow, on 22 March 1956. After the grounding of the BOAC de Havilland Comet fleet, the Tu-104 was for a time the world's only commercially operating jet airliner.

10 TNA. DEFE 13/120 E16.
11 TNA. Ministry of Defence. RRP/698/58.
12 TNA. AIR 2/14982. Minute, 12 August 1958. AM File NoCMS/2960/56(Part IV).
13 TNA. PREM 11/2633.
14 TNA. AIR 2/14982. Memo, 17 September 1958.
15 *RAF Flying Review*. Vol XV, No.8
16 TNA. AIR 20/10557. C10/17069, 12 August 1958.
17 TNA. Letter from MoD to Philip de Zulueta (No.10), 11 September 1958.
18 TNA. Letter from AUS(A) to Chief Information Officer. DD Ops (BM/S426).
19 TNA. AIR 2/14982. Letter from Gen. Blanchard to DCAS, 11 September 1958.
20 Originally it was reported that the missiles would have 'United States Air Force' painted on them. Understandably, a request was made to have them re-marked. (See also Wynn, Humphrey, *RAF Nuclear Deterrent Forces*, p.293 N.1).
21 The Missile Convoy consisted of the following vehicles/personnel:
    Lead Motor Cycle   Police Driver
    Land Rover   Convoy Commander, Escort Commander, Police, Driver,
                  Spare Driver
    Missile Transporter   Three Drivers, Guidance Technician
    Land Rover   Technical Specialist, Police Driver Police Escort
    Motor Cycle   Police Driver
    Motor Cycle   Police Driver
22 TNA. AIR 20/9791. Loose minute, P.J. Hudson, Head of S.6. BF.1746/IS/S.6/5099. 17 July 1958.
23 *Ibid*. Letter from AVM Pretty, 22 October 1958.
24 TNA. AIR 2/14982. Blanchard to Tuttle, 11 September 1958.
25 TNA. AIR 2/17401. Loose minute DofOps(B&R) to DCAS(Ops). DCAS/4235/58.
26 Whereby an attack on one or more member states is deemed to be an attack on all.
27 TNA AIR 20/10555. Letter CinCBC to DCAS, 27 February 1958. BC/TS.90325/CinC.
28 TNA DEFE 13/594. f.E2.§ 4. DCOS to Minister of Defence, 27 January 1958.
29 TNA. AIR 20/10325. P J Hudson, Head of S.6 to AUS(A). BF.1746/TS/S.6/1096, 7 August 1959.
30 *Ibid*. Head of S.6 to AUS(A). BF.1746/TS/S.6/1096, 7 August 1959.
31 TNA AIR 20/10325. DUSI/9497.
32 TNA. DEFE 13/394. f.E53. Harold Watkinson to SoS(A), 10 May 1960.
33 *Ibid*. f. E13. Ref: M 421/58.
34 *Ibid*. f. E15, 2 December 1959.
35 *Ibid*. f.E33. Quarles to Sandys.
36 *Ibid*. f.E34. R R Powell to Quarles, 6 May 1959.
37 RAF Museum. Collected papers of Wg Cdr E.R.G. Haines.
38 TNA. No.97 (SM) Sqn ORB, June 1960. A party of twenty-five US press members visited Hemswell.
39 In which journalists select from their own number a group to witness the event. The

copy and photographs produced are thereafter made available to all.
40 TNA, DCAS to Gen. Blanchard. 21 July 1959. DCAS/L835/1959.
41 TNA. AIR 20/10557. CIO to AUS(A), 12 August 1958.
42 TNA, dated 6 March 1959. In file DEFE 13/121.
43 *Flight*, 5 August 1958 pp.864-872. *The Aeroplane*, May 1959 issue, pp.597-600.
44 As a twelve-year-old schoolboy, albeit with a fascination for anything that flew, the author, on reflection now, is amazed how much he knew about Thor at the time. It was not at all difficult to identify the bases from the main road. Much knowledge was also to be gleaned from *RAF Flying Review* magazine which, though not identified as such, in the files to be found in the National Archives, also reported the progress being made with Thor in some detail, see Vol. XV, No.8, pp.23–24.
45 TNA. AIR 2/14982. D.C.A.S. 4551/59, 5 November 1959.
46 *Ibid*. Letter SoS(A) to PM.
47 TNA. In file AIR 2/14982.
48 TNA. DEFE 13/594. f.E33A §7, 10 February 1958.

CHAPTER SIX
TRAINING AND SQUADRON OPERATIONS

On the evening of Tuesday 8th April 1958 a group of GD[1] Officers consisting of 1 Wing Commander, 9 Squadron Leaders, 17 Flight Lieutenants and 5 Senior Flying Officers, especially picked from all Commands, most of them because of their educational qualifications [gathered at the RAF Flying College at Manby]. All had undergone positive vetting security clearance. Few knew what the future was to hold for them and there was considerable speculation. The address the following morning by the Commandant followed by a fortnight's intensive training provided the answer. They were the Operations Officers and the Launch Control Officers of the first Royal Air Force Intermediate Range Ballistic Missile Squadron due to form at Feltwell.[2]

These were the first officers to undergo the GD Ballistic Missile Course (also referred to in some reports as the Ballistic Missile Indoctrination Course). These courses covered all aspects of the operations of guided missiles, from their structure to the theory of ballistics and guidance, control systems and the development of nuclear warheads. (See Appendix 8 for a synopsis of the No.4 GD Ballistic Missile Course.) Whilst this course was specifically oriented towards Thor crews, a separate, more general Guided Weapons Familiarisation Course was also run at Manby to give a wide range of other officers an overall appreciation of missile developments, which included a visit to a Thor site, once they were operational,[3] to study its organisation. After completing the Manby course the officers travelled to the United States to continue their training.

Once 'Stateside' after a leisurely sea crossing of the Atlantic,[4] classroom training on the missile and its systems was undertaken at the Douglas Aircraft Company (DAC) facility at Tucson.[5] After roughly a month with Douglas and usually after a short period of leave on America's west coast, Operational Training was thereafter conducted with a two-month course at Vandenberg Air Force Base (AFB) alongside USAF personnel. Training was provided by 392d Missile Training Squadron (MTS). The 392d MTS had been formed in 1957 at the former US Army disciplinary barracks at Camp Cooke – later to become Cooke AFB and then Vandenberg AFB. The initial role of 392d MTS was for an assignment to the Martin TM-61 Matador SSM to be deployed in Germany. However, as previously noted, the squadron was only a very basic unit, with little for its personnel to occupy themselves with until they were sent to Douglas for training on Thor. By the time they returned to Cooke AFB, the five Thor launch pads were under construction, so they were able to formulate the Thor training programme with the help of Douglas staff. At this time, it was still planned that USAF personnel would form the initial Thor squadron in the UK. Yet RAF Thor personnel would also soon be arriving, so consideration had to be given to anticipating the influx of a significant number of British servicemen who would have a very limited knowledge of missiles of any sort, and certainly not missiles the size of Thor.

RAF NCOs and airmen also began crossing the Atlantic to join the training programme but their journeys often proved to be less luxurious than those experienced by some of the earlier batches of officers, although they, too, could be subject to the unreliability of the Curtis Commando.[6,7,8] Furthermore, once they arrived in Tucson they were faced with living arrangements, courtesy of Davis-Monthan AFB, that were far from ideal. Fortunately, the 'Daughters of the British Empire' provided plenty of trips off-base to various social events so off-duty life was varied and there was no need to stay on base all the time. Local girls also were not long in discovering the presence of the RAF personnel and proved generous in their hospitality, although this generosity was sometimes to result in an embarrassing visit to the base medical facility![9] Having completed the general familiarisation phase with Douglas, those concerned with the guidance system moved on to the AC Spark Plug plant in Milwaukee, where they were accommodated within the city itself, before proceeding to their ultimate destination, the launch pads at Vandenberg AFB.

Meanwhile, AVM Wally Sheen, Commander of the RAF Staff at the British Joint Services Mission in Washington (BJSM), had been reviewing the woefully inadequate domestic facilities and had advised the Air Ministry of the vary basic conditions that existed at both Tucson and Vandenberg AFB, which he described as being 'more like Iraq than Hollywood'. He was concerned that the personnel, many of whom were unenthusiastic about working with Thor and had not been adequately briefed on their career prospects, were having a 'pretty rough time and will, I fear, arrive back in England to take up their duties with a pretty poor impression of both RAF and USAF organisation and training'.

AVM Sheen's comments were reinforced in October when Gp Capt. K.R.C. Slater and Wg Cdr T. Knight visited the US. They reported inadequate training facilities, poor standards of instruction and observed that, because of differences between RAF and USAF trade structures, many of the RAF's skilled personnel were over-qualified for the tasks that they were being required to perform. Some of the men who were there at the time subsequently confirmed the impression of poor training and commented specifically on the lax and colloquial use of terminology by the Douglas instructors, a practice which led to inevitable confusion. There were too many petty restrictions. Even the poor quality of the standard RAF tropical working dress was all too evident in comparison with the much smarter equivalent worn by their US opposite numbers.[10] Many bought and wore American uniforms with the appropriate RAF insignia attached.[11] Although there was no period of leave, weekends could provide many opportunities to explore the countryside quite widely.[12]

For those going on to Vandenberg there was the added discomfort of dust and mud as the base was built on eroding soil. Yet the most serious problem that Slater and Knight identified, and one which demanded immediate attention, was 'the low morale of the trainees, the majority of whom at present regard it as a major misfortune to have been selected for the Thor programme'.[13] Simple domestic arrangements were aggravated by the fact that both officers and airmen were unaware until they embarked for the US as to where they were heading for the duration of their various courses.[14] Hardly an encouraging start. Although, on balance, officers seem to have fared better, the main problem for some seems to have been their rate of pay to cope with US costs.

Prior to all this, on 15 March, an aircraft left Northolt bound for Los Angeles with a party of RAF officers from the Air Ministry and Bomber Command on board. They had accepted an invitation from General Blanchard to visit various Thor facilities in the US and receive a full briefing on the weapon's progress. With stops at Goose Bay, Westover and Offutt the party eventually arrived in Los Angeles on the morning of the 17th. That afternoon they visited the Headquarters of Strategic Air Command's Missile Division, otherwise known as SAC MIKE. The following day they visited DAC in the morning with visits to Rocketdyne's facilities at Canoga Park and Santa Monica in the afternoon. The 19th saw a full day of discussions with representatives of AFBMD and SAC MIKE. On the following day they went again to Santa Monica but followed this with a visit to the Shrine Exhibition where, as well as seeing examples of various USAF guided missiles, there was a model of the Thor launch pad layout. The rest of their visit was taken up with more meetings except for a visit on the 24th to the Douglas Test Centre in Sacramento, where they saw Thor missile No.110.[15] They arrived back in the UK much impressed by what they had seen.

A permanent RAF presence was created once the Thor Agreement was completed when the US team was joined by four RAF liaison officers, who became the essential interface between the two air forces. Three of these, a Group Captain, a Wing Commander (GD) and a Wing Commander (Technical), were based at the AFBMD in Los Angeles, covering the Vandenberg AFB operations where Wg Cdr Peter J. Finlayson AFC, later to become OC Ops Wing at North Luffenham, came to be much respected by the Americans for his pragmatic approach to merging the needs of the two air forces. The fourth, another Wing Commander (Technical), was based at Patrick AFB. When the first group of ten RAF officers from the initial Manby course arrived at Vandenberg in July 1958 they were greeted by Colonel George P. Cole USAF, Commander of Vandenberg and later Director of Training for the 1st Missile Division, who commented to the local press, 'It is my desire that we do everything possible to make their stay comfortable and productive, just as they would if we were assigned to one of their most important bases to study a new weapon'. It was a spirit of co-operation that would be fostered throughout the Thor era. By the very nature of 'concurrency' the first two courses were 'adequate but not complete' and further support training was carried out on return to the UK by the US Field Training Detachment.

When the first RAF NCOs reached Vandenberg, it became possible to form full launch teams, and the programme became a series of generic 'Welcome' courses, the first of which – Welcome One – began in early 1959. This course provided what was known as Integrated Weapons Systems Training (IWST) and was supposed to culminate in a live launch by one of the student crews. The original plan had called for 'every member of the technical and operational crews to take part in one training launch during a tour of duty in a squadron'.[16] However, the newly appointed US Secretary of Defense, Thomas S. Gates, was prepared to support only four training launches a year, using missiles drawn from US stocks. Despite much strongly argued correspondence from the British, the Americans refused to give way on the number of missiles that could be fired but agreed that for the follow-on training courses, to be known as Combat Training Launches (CTLs), missiles taken from UK stocks would be used so as to monitor their serviceability after exposure to actual operational conditions. Only a relatively few lucky ones would therefore actually launch a missile.[17, 18]

By the time that the Welcome courses started, three of the seven Thor pads at Vandenberg had been allocated to the RAF. Two others were used for the embryonic US Discoverer[19] scientific research programme whilst the remaining two were kept on standby. In total there were nine IWST launches between April 1959 and January 1960. Although the RAF persisted with the Welcome series to identify the IWST courses, the Americans gave a less prosaic range of codenames to the actual launches (see Appendix 2). The 'Welcome One' launch was appropriately codenamed 'Lion's Roar', and took place on 16 April 1959 (delayed two days by minor problems) by Driffield's No.98 (SM) Squadron.[20] The Detachment Commander for the launch was Gp Capt. R.T. Frogley CBE DFC, the Station Commander at RAF Driffield. The launch team was Sqn Ldr P.G. Coulson MBE DFC, in this case acting not as OC but as LCO, MPlts A.E. Glover and M.H. Sloan AFM and Chf Tech. R.M. Carpenter.[21] Sqn Ldr Coulson was to return twelve months later as Detachment Commander for CTL-4. A film of the launch was made entitled 'The Lion's Roar' and this film was subsequently seen by many visitors to both Driffield and the other Wing HQs.

The IWST launches highlighted the difference between launches conducted by Douglas personnel and service crews, the latter after only a relatively short training period. In September 1959 DCAS, Air Mshl Sir Geoffrey Tuttle, wrote to General Blanchard, Commander of the 7th Air Division (SAC) at High Wycombe, commenting that:

> [t]he five launches (plus an unsuccessful attempt) so far carried out by RAF crews have been far from encouraging. ... There still seems to be a long way to go before the weapons system can be considered capable of the required accuracy and reliability when operated by military as opposed to R&D personnel. The Combat Training Launches are essential to provide us with the experience of the missile under operational conditions. Moreover they are the only means of assessing the effect on a missile of a long period of exposure to the British climate.[22]

The CTLs were to be a feature of a new sequence of six-week continuation training courses which began once the bulk of the initial crew training programme was nearing completion. The aim of these firings was to verify the operational capability of the launch teams, while, as noted above, and starting with CTL-4 in June 1960, validating the system's overall reliability by using operational rounds drawn at random from those on sites in the UK. These missiles had crossed the Atlantic twice and had been exposed both to the British weather and to regular handling by the crews. Despite DCAS's misgivings (which may well have been less to do with Thor's reliability than its accuracy, which at the time was still not good) only two of the twenty-one IWST launches were actually classed as failures. This performance provided a demonstration of the underlying soundness of the system's design and, following withdrawal as a weapon, Thor went on to become one of the most reliable vehicles in the US inventory, serving for many years in support of a variety of space and other research programmes. Nevertheless, as an IRBM guided by 1950s technology, Thor was never going to be accurate enough to attack a small target and, although the requirement that 50 per cent of the warheads had to land within two miles of the target was demonstrated, it had left little margin for error.

CTL-6 was witnessed by the AOCinC Bomber Command Air Mshl Sir Kenneth Cross,[23] accompanied by his AOA Air Cdre (later ACM Sir) Brian Burnett, who remembers that the event 'was, of course, of great interest and gave one enormous confidence in the likely effectiveness of the weapon. So I was particularly interested in them when I became AOC No.3 Group and had some of them under command'.[24] As progress was made, morale progressively improved. At the start of the CTL phase, Wg Cdr Finlayson, the Liaison Officer, commented:

> Let's make certain we no longer call this training. The training portion is complete. What we are doing here now is conducting launch preparations in line with United Kingdom procedures. Our many successful firings from Vandenberg have proved to be a great encouragement to our missilemen in England. We are building up a great competitive spirit among squadrons and each detachment can hardly wait until its turn comes up to come over here and fire.[25, 26]

The CTL sequence required a Thor to be received, checked-out, installed and launched. It therefore involved both the Operations Group and the Technical Group. The spectacle of a live launch, in this case the CLT-2 launch which took place on 2 December 1959, was described in the *Santa Maria Times*:

> The missile was visible for almost five minutes as it rose into the night sky. A Royal Air Force crew launched the night Thor under simulated combat conditions. On duty since early in the day, the RAF men were unaware of the launch until a few minutes before the execution order was relayed by Strategic Air Command headquarters in Omaha.

The launch had originally been scheduled for 30 November but a faulty CEA had caused it to be postponed. The successful launch was undertaken by B Crew from North Luffenham. Although ostensibly a no-notice exercise, the activities of the USAF personnel in preparation for the launch usually gave some warning of an imminent launch command.[27] There were certain factors in the procedures that the RAF crews found unique to Vandenberg, but the CTLs were invaluable, if not essential, exercises to ensure operational efficiency. The twenty Thor squadrons would account for around 1,200 personnel, confirmed as the approximate number to complete training in the US, but a 1957 estimate of Bomber Command manning for 1962–6 identifies the total number of personnel allocated to Thor to be around 4,000 out of a total Bomber Command requirement of 27,000. This number included the training teams and the technical, administrative and support staff at the parent sites. The total equated to roughly a third of the allocation to the V-Bombers.

Compared with life on an RAF fighter or bomber station, the remote Thor launch sites provided little comparable excitement. Access to Caistor for instance, was about 200 yards from the public highway. The whole site was surrounded by the double security fence. The only break in this fence was the one entry point. Outside this entrance was a parking area for the missile convoy. On the right of the entrance was the woodenhutted Guardroom and administrative building. Opposite these buildings were the fire tender and the Police car garages. Behind the Guardroom was the brick-built Power Conversion building. This was the largest building on site. The Launch Control Area was just beyond and behind this building and there, too, were the concrete cradle and the brick catchment pit for the diesel tank. Further into the site were the three LEs in a triangular layout. Visible too, and just inside the perimeter fence, were the three theodolite triangulation pillars used for setting the theodolites. At the far end of the site, 1,000ft from the three LEs, was the US warhead compound. Separated by another security fence, entry was again at only one point. There was a parking area outside this compound, as a number of vehicles would require access on a regular basis. Inside the US compound was the single-bay Classified Storage Building and the Pyrotechnics Building. The whole site was landscaped as there were extensive areas of grass.

Much of the time was spent on routine activities and practice countdowns. Each Thor site consisted operationally of the three LEs, the Ground Support Equipment (GSE) and the Launch Control Area (LCA). Anything else was effectively a bonus. Whilst the launch sites located at each of the four main bases could enjoy the creature comforts of a normal RAF station, this was not so for the sixteen outlying sites where, initially, there were very few facilities, with most of what was available being fairly basic. Day-to-day command and administration were the responsibility of the Squadron Commander (but delegated to the shift LCOs in his absence). He reported to the Station Commander, a Group Captain, at the parent site via the usual three Wing Commanders who were individually responsible for 'operations', including security and training, 'technical', covering missile servicing and support and signals, and 'administration', embracing supply, movements and personnel matters.

Broadly speaking, the Squadron Commander's duties reflected the functions of the three Wing Commanders. He was largely responsible for the welfare of the launch crews, organising the duty roster and shift system, paying the non-commissioned ranks, arranging the disposal of domestic swill, keeping the sites neat and tidy and providing whatever could be acquired (if necessary, in true time-honoured military fashion, by whatever means presented itself) to improve the comfort of the squadron personnel. This could be as simple as his wife making curtains for the crew rest facility, the provision of some form of quasi-NAAFI facility or the acquisition of an 'extra' trailer converted as a crew room, but subsequently and perhaps inevitably, frowned upon by higher authority. Flagpoles were erected to fly the RAF Ensign and the Squadron Leader's pennant, but these still had to be scrounged. Harrington acquired its flagpole from a US base.[28]

Finding suitable accommodation was a constant problem. Initially, the majority of the personnel for the remote sites were accommodated at the parent station and bussed to and from shifts. Personnel who subsequently failed to find local accommodation were obliged to live at the main site on a permanent basis, which necessitated the provision of a regular bus service to shuttle the crews back and forth. In fact, it is said, and possibly not without justification, that there were more MT assets per head for the Thor force than for any other part of the RAF, a claim which is borne out by the 400,000 miles per year MT estimate for the Feltwell Wing alone, nearly half of this being in crew shift transfers.[29] Bedford buses were used to transport the launch teams to and from the remote sites with a fleet of Morris J2 vans available for other duties. Of all the Wing HQs, Driffield appears to have had to rely the most on transport to and from the satellite sites. The station was all the more pleased therefore when Flt Lt W.E. Sword BEM was presented with the Bomber Command Accident Prevention Award on behalf of the Station Motor Transport Flight. Some of the vans were used to transfer the Police dogs and could be clearly identified by their own particularly distinctive smell.

Increasingly, however, many sought local living-out accommodation, but often found that the Douglas personnel had already filled up available 'hirings'. Hirings achieving suitable standards and within twenty miles of the place of work could be registered and would be managed by the RAF in the usual way. AOCinC Bomber Command, Sir Harry Broadhurst, advised AMSO, ACM Sir Walter Dawson:

> I have instructed the Stations to take on as many hirings as possible; to make their task easier. I have authorised them to extend the search to areas around each satellite. As you point out it is most difficult to find hirings in the rural districts in which the Stations and satellites are located especially in face of American competition.[30]

With traditional service ingenuity, others sought alternative solutions. At Mepal, four of the staff set up a caravan park on the adjacent, disused side of the airfield which, once equipped with the necessary facilities, made quite adequate accommodation conveniently close to the missiles.[31] There were similar caravan parks at many other bases including North Pickenham and Tuddenham. At the latter the camp was set up by some of the NCOs but a request from one of the officers to join them was vetoed by authority. Officers and other ranks still had to be segregated.[32] Some squadrons seemed to fare better than others in finding accommodation. No.104 (SM) Squadron recorded that a 'high percentage have managed to find living-out accommodation in or near Ludford Magna'. Some Hemswell staff joined their USAF/DAC colleagues at the Sturgate caravan park.[33] The only specific provision of accommodation was made for the Squadron Commander as the nature of his duties required him to be available at short notice. One of the initial, and as it turned out quite time-consuming, duties of the first appointees was to find a suitable site for this house. These two-storey houses, usually brick-built, were constructed to the common left- or right-handed L-shaped pattern which was the standard for officers' married quarters on RAF Stations, and were often built on the edge of the nearest village. Their siting, where possible, was sympathetic to local considerations and intended to integrate within the community. They represented good housing stock and were sold off into private hands on the completion of the Thor programme. They still exist today, although some have been extensively modernised, their new owners invariably aware of their original purpose. At Harrington the house was offered to one of the LCOs, as No.218 (SM) Squadron's second CO was 'unaccompanied'.[34] Not all Squadron Commanders were so lucky. Sqn Ldr Frank Leatherdale at North Pickenham was housed in an existing 'prefab' bungalow adjacent to the Second World War Operations Centre, but it did have an air-raid shelter, a throwback to the war![35]

The basic necessity of catering was not, initially, adequately provided for but proper cooks were soon added to the establishment to prepare meals for the two daytime shifts and, increasingly, for the nighttime shift as well. At RAF Driffield those on the night shift often saw, in the darkness, the shadowy figure of the Duty

Chef collecting mushrooms for breakfast. Disposal of swill was often to the benefit of the local pig farmer, but private enterprise took over at Catfoss where latent agricultural skills amongst the personnel saw the squadron keep its own pigs, geese and chickens in the old Control Tower and make a modest profit when the pigs were sent to market.[36] They were not the only squadron to embark on farming pursuits. No.102 (SM) Squadron at Full Sutton maintained a flock of geese. Penned in next to the Guardroom, they provided an extra level of early warning capability, but only, it was regretted in the ORB for 1962, 'for a short period. All but two of the geese raised by personnel to supplement the Christmas fare were duly despatched prior to Christmas Day. The two survivors decided not to be phased out with the missile force and flew away'. They took up residence in an adjacent field but a fox killed one of them; the other was recaptured, had its wings clipped and was posted on sentry duty in the US warhead enclosure. Geese were to be found at Coleby Grange as well: 'The four geese and a gander acquired a few weeks ago are now finally on the squadron strength and have laid quite well. Goslings for all for Christmas!'[37] But by the following month one of the geese was 'highly dangerous to approach. However she is sitting twelve eggs – quite a spread'.[38] Personnel at Caistor were privileged to enjoy the occasional addition to their menu when the adjacent duck farm allowed the discrete acquisition of one of their stock to supplement the rations.[39] Occasionally, shots could be heard during the hours of darkness as sentries, bored by the tedium of guard duty, 'bagged' a passing rabbit for the pot. As well as developing latent agricultural skills, life at the remote sites also provided opportunities to demonstrate expertise in the field of horticulture. At Coleby Grange, for instance, flowerbeds were set out, rockeries built and bulbs and flowering shrubs planted. Fifty trees were added, mainly flowering cherry and crab apple.[40] By June 1960 the poppy crop 'which threatened to cast doubts on our political integrity had been reaped; cricket pitches have been laid and the sound of willow on leather echo[ed] across the site'.[41] These efforts nearly came to nought when the diggers arrived to put in the firefighting ring main in August 1960, but by September the garden was looking at its best with antirrhinums, asters, wallflowers, geraniums, nasturtiums, polyanthus, alyssum and lobelias.

Then there was the traditional English weather to cope with. 'Morale high even though weather poor' No.226 (SM) Squadron recorded, ruefully, followed later by: 'Extremely bad weather conditions, snow, ice and high winds persisting for several days'.[42] Things were to get worse when, after a period of constant rain, the firemen had to pump out flooded living quarters and launch areas. The winters in the early 1960s were severe. In 1961, Harrington was all but cut off, requiring a major initiative by the CO to rescue the hungry Police dogs and return them to North Luffenham, there being no adequate provision for the dogs' welfare on site. The winter of 1962/63 was little better, as No.220 (SM) Squadron at North Pickenham noted in January: 'Severe weather conditions existed on the site throughout the month. Heavy snow falls, drifting in places to a depth of seven feet and temperatures of -12° were experienced'. Temperatures of -15 degrees were recorded by No.142 (SM) Squadron at Coleby Grange, which noted that 'Weather hampered all exercises and training during the month due to almost continual snow and ice, with occasional fog. ... These low temperatures caused severe icing on all roads and pads'.[43] At Tuddenham 'the continuous freezing weather makes wet fire practices impracticable and the personnel have been obliged to concentrate on snow and ice clearance and on keeping the fire-fighting system de-frosted and operational'.[44] At Feltwell the LOX safety shower froze after an electrical heating failure and the thick ice on the static water tank caused a rupture of the brickwork, placing dependency on water for firefighting on the static water tank in the USAF storage area. A recurrent and potentially hazardous problem was the freezing of the fire ring main, although placing protective covers over the hydrants did help. February was little better: 'Snow and ice clearance has been the major occupation of all the Squadron's personnel during the month, especially during daylight hours'.[45,46] For those still travelling to the satellite sites from the Wing HQs, the journey proved none too pleasant as the coaches, often delayed by the weather, were unheated. The weather conditions also caused a higher than expected degree of corrosion on the exposed LEs, and as early as July 1960 DAC had to complete Operation Cleanup to improve the corrosion resistance of the pads. England is so famous for its poor weather, however, that this had come as no surprise, not even to those who were more accustomed to the balmy blue skies of California – like the DAC employees.

There were occasions when the unexpected could provide a welcome diversion from the daily routine. On 21 June 1960 a civilian Percival Proctor landed on the disused runway at Polebrook. The pilot claimed that he was from a construction company based in Halifax and that he had come to attend a sale of aged Air Ministry property at the old domestic site on the airfield. After checking with the Northamptonshire Police it turned out that his story was indeed true.[47] On 3 April 1961 a civilian Auster aircraft piloted by a farmer, with a GPO engineer as passenger and both members of the nearby Fakenham Flying Club, landed outside the sterile zone at North Pickenham after experiencing problems. Squadron personnel rendered assistance by picketing the aircraft overnight. The Auster took off successfully the following day.[48] The following month North Pickenham hosted a BBC team who filmed a countdown in progress. The footage taken was to be used in a news feature showing the exchange of plaques that had taken place at Feltwell to commemorate the transfer of responsibility for all Thor training from the USAF to the RAF. Folkingham also had an unexpected aerial visitor when a crop spraying helicopter made a forced landing on the runway just outside the Guardroom. It was allowed to stay overnight until repairs could be effected.[49] Language proved a problem when two Frenchmen in a light aircraft landed at Melton Mowbray on 23 November 1960. They had got lost and believed that they had landed at RAF Cottesmore where they had intended to re-orient themselves.[50] These unscheduled visits were not always without their problems. 'On 12th August 1960, a glider pilot from the Doncaster Gliding Club landed on the airfield outside the security fence. Subsequent press reports of his treatment by No. 106 (SM) Squadron were unfavourable and unjustified. These allegations have been referred to, and are now in the hands of higher authority' reported the ORB. Undoubtedly, these pilots were completely unaware that one of the seven designated potential threats to the Thor sites identified in the security arrangements was that represented by civilian aircraft![51]

The very nature and novelty of Project Emily meant that the Thor bases attracted a large number of visitors. Feltwell, perhaps not surprisingly as the lead station, had a regular visit schedule but the other stations did not escape. The list of visitors was as varied as the visitors themselves. Inevitably there were senior officers from the

RAF and the USAF. Naturally, Feltwell attracted a number of VIP visitors during the early days. AOCinC Bomber Command, Sir Harry Broadhurst, visited the Missile Squadron – still at that stage called A Flight – on 18 March 1959 and was shown around the site by Sqn Ldr Stanley Baldock DFM, OC of the Flight. A week later Duncan Sandys, accompanied by DCAS, Sir Geoffrey Tuttle, Commanding General 7AD, Major-General William H. Blanchard, President of Douglas Aircraft Company, Donald W. Douglas, AOC No.3 Group, AVM Kenneth Cross and SASO No.3 Group, Air Commodore William Coles, visited both the Headquarters and A Flight, being escorted by the Station Commander.[52] Assistant Secretary to the USAF, the Hon. Phillip B. Taylor, accompanied by Four-Star General Samuel E. Anderson, Commanding General of the Air Matériel Command, visited Hemswell on 8 September 1959. Later in the month General Thomas S. Power, Commanding General of SAC, visited, accompanied by AVM Thomas Parselle, SASO HQ Bomber Command, and Maj. Gen. Edwin B. Broadhurst, Chief of Staff SAC and a future Commander of 7AD. In July 1961 No.77 (SM) Squadron recorded in its ORB, 'whilst the number of visiting personnel reached astronomical proportions at times, the Duty Site Commander usually managed to remain in control of the situation'.

Members of the Joint Atomic Energy Commission visited Driffield on 28 November 1960. The party included Acting Chairman Chet Holifield, First Secretary to the American Embassy Mr William C. Trueheart, who had served with the AEC from 1947–1949, and Major-General Charles B. Westover of 7AD, along with seventeen others. Further visitors included French generals, no doubt keen to see what they had missed out on. General Dellus, Director of the Air Establishment at Toulouse, accompanied by six French officers, visited Feltwell on 4 November 1960. General Paul Stehlin, Chief of Staff of the French Air Force, and later, controversially, to be a strong advocate of US military equipment, accompanied by the AOCinC Bomber Command and AOC No.1 Group, visited Coleby Grange on 31 July 1961 and witnessed an Exercise RESPOND. Feltwell received a visit from the Democratic Senator for New York, Samuel S. Stratton, on 27 November 1961. Reflecting the fact that Thor was not the only IRBM deployed in the NATO arena, there was a visit to Tuddenham on 12 October 1962 by USAF representatives from the Jupiter Missile Force.[53] Royalty was not forgotten. When Princess Margaret visited RAF Finningley, a Thor was taken from Hemswell to the V-Bomber base for display.

There was also the ever-present threat of the unofficial visitors from the Campaign for Nuclear Disarmament (CND) or the Direct Action Committee Against Nuclear War. CND had been established in 1958 and had held its first Aldermaston march in the Easter of that year in appalling weather, which had decimated the ranks of the marchers by the second day. Typical was the activities at North Pickenham. CND had been:

> ...very active from the time the site was being built and they continued to trouble us thereafter. They were quite clever in their attempts to enter our compound. For instance, some of the placards they carried were made of wood and on their backs were 'rungs' so they could be used as scaling ladders when put against our fences.[54]

There was invariably advance warning of anti-nuclear demonstrations; indeed, they were often advertised in the local papers to encourage support. After the prospect of a particularly large demonstration at North Pickenham the CO was advised by the Police to avoid vehicles coming on site. His response was to call in two Flights and extra food.[55] All too often, particularly if the weather was bad, nothing happened. CND were also directing their activities against the V-Bomber bases and were taking a particular interest in RAF Watton, where they believed silos for Blue Streak were being constructed. Despite being expected, no-one turned up. Protests were handled in conjunction with the Civil Police and, generally speaking, were relatively peaceful, being limited to mainly verbal contributions from the protesters, although deliberate damage to property was at least debated in committee. Leading activist and field organiser of the Direct Action Committee, Pat Arrowsmith, left a lasting impression during a protest at Mepal. She and a group of fellow protesters attempted to enter the base but were firmly escorted back outside. However, in so doing, Arrowsmith slipped and fell into some freshly laid concrete adjacent to the Guardroom, leaving an impression of her buttocks in the hardening concrete. Breighton was being actively picketed during July 1959, but a demonstration planned for the 5th of the month failed to materialise and this was not untypical, particularly if the weather was inclement. One Thor NCO remembers that when demonstrators attempted to gain access to the sites, the men were summarily ejected but the women were usually 'well looked after' before being returned to the world outside the fence.

The Church recognised its duty of pastoral stewardship to the bases. North Pickenham, for instance, received a visit in February 1961 from the Lord Bishop of Norwich, the Rt Revd William Fleming, accompanied by the local vicar, the Revd D.C. Green. It is indicative of the level of interest that Thor attracted that this had been just one of eighteen visits hosted by this single remote site in that month alone.

The nominal 'full up' RAF personnel strength of each squadron was around seventy, comprising six officers (CO and five LCOs), five airmen (aircrew) and fifty-nine airmen (Ground).[56] In addition there were five US Authentication Officers (AOs).[57] The senior of these AOs at each site became the Site Commander and supervised the four other US officers. An American was always on site with the RAF crews but rarely, if ever, got involved in RAF exercises or daily routines. Their primary duty was to man their own 'alert phone' in the separate 'key carrier' room. Also, they had nothing to contribute to RAF operations and so they tacitly recognised that they would only 'be in the way', although they were always welcome socially in the Launch Control Trailer. It appears that they neither asked, nor were invited, to participate in RAF crew daily activities.[58] The LCO held the UK launch key which initiated the launch procedures, but only when the AO had activated his US War/Peace key could the warhead be armed. This was the nature of the two-key system. Inevitably rumours of shortcuts in the process circulated. As the launch keys operated the same switch, theoretically one person could launch a missile if he had both keys, or as happened on one occasion during a practice launch procedure when the US officer failed to turn up, a screwdriver could suffice for his key.[59] The launch key switches were triple-wired. When activated, one wire was severed and a connection made between the other two to create the circuit. During an official US Congressional visit to a Thor site, an RAF LCO, displaying perhaps questionable judgement in the circumstances, demonstrated that the launch key for one of the launch pads would also operate as the War/Peace key for one of the other pads. Furthermore, by wetting his finger and pressing War/Peace keyhole, he could change the display from 'Peace' to 'War'. An

No.218 (SM) Squadron accidentally leaned on the US keyhole and armed the missile. Needless to say, immediate steps were taken to rectify these shortcomings. However, banging hard on the side of the Launch Control Trailer (LCT) would not initiate an automatic launch sequence despite beliefs to the contrary – this and a number of similar rumours all had to be tested. Later, US ICBM procedure demanded that the two switch keys were more than an arms-span apart and had to be operated simultaneously so that no one person could initiate a launch, and also that a second 'vote' from another launch team had also to be received so that no one team could launch a missile on its own.

The available manpower allowed for a shift system comprising five Launch Crews, each commanded by a Launch Control Officer and each one designated a flight. Although broadly similar, shift patterns tended to vary slightly from station to station taking into account training needs and periods of leave. Shortage of personnel was a recurrent problem. Air Mshl Sir Kenneth Cross, who had been appointed AOCinC Bomber Command on 20 May 1959, required Thor to operate on what was essentially a war footing – twenty-four hours a day, 365 days a year – and the shift rotas had to provide for this. The Strategic Missile Force – Readiness Policy, dated 25 July 1960, determined that the squadrons were to 'maintain a capability to react within tactical warning at all times'. Initially the requirement was to have 60 per cent of the missiles available at all times, with the hope that this could be raised to 75 per cent as experience with the missiles developed. Routine maintenance schedules had to be allowed for in maintaining this level of readiness, as had the phasing-in of any modifications required. Even at 60 per cent, or thirty-six missiles, the Thors represented a more potent strike force than the fourteen V-Bombers kept at an equivalent state of readiness.

This requirement, though fully understood by Bomber Command, was not fully understood or even recognised by the Air Ministry (who operated a somewhat more relaxed eight-hour working day with sixteen hours on stand-down). It was the latter that was largely responsible for allocating the budgets to provide adequate manning levels. However, Air Mshl Sir Harry Broadhurst, AOCinC Bomber Command at the start of Project Emily, and, from the evidence, not a wholehearted supporter of Thor, had indicated support for a reduced manning level in a letter to VCAS on 10 March 1959 on the subject of the state of readiness required of the missiles. 'It does not,' he wrote:

> ...automatically follow that all establishments either at the site, or along the chain of command, need to be manned to the same criteria, unless it is also desired to maintain an operational readiness at 15 minutes. ... Manpower savings can be made if the requirement for 'operational readiness' as opposed to 'technical serviceability' is relaxed to the 24 hour warning concept that governs the state of readiness of the rest of my Command.[60] This would mean that economies would be possible principally in launch/control personnel on the sites, but even more important, it would avoid the otherwise inevitable ...s in establishment all along the chain of command.

' point of view, of course, but it was the squadron crews who had ⋅tions that resulted from inadequate staffing levels. No.102 (SM) ⋅r January 1961 notes that personnel were having to work a fifty- ⋅ding travelling times, and were having to forego leave. 'Factors such as this do little to improve morale' was the rueful comment.[61] In May it was further noted that 'The continued reduction in strength renders it increasingly difficult to permit members of the Squadron to participate in organised sports activities'. No.220 (SM) Squadron noted in April 1961 that '8th April saw the end of 12 hour watches for the LCCOs. This had been in operation since 30th January owing to sickness and detachment of LCCOs.' Twelve-hour shifts generally became the undesirable norm when a crew was sent to the US for a Combat Training Launch. Much was the relief when the CTL Team returned and normal shifts were once again operated. 'The remaining four flights now revert thankfully to 8 hour shifts.'[62] Sqn Ldr Ken Hayes was even more acerbic when he assumed command of No.77 (SM) Squadron, one in a series of promotions resulting from the Ludford Magna incident (see below). He identified three major problems: acute shortage of trained LCOs, shortage of launch crews, for which he believed the only solution was a sixth crew per squadron, and the lack of an adjutant. 'Far too much of the Squadron Commander's time is taken up by routine administration and supervision of matters of secondary importance,' he wrote, before going on to commend his predecessor, as follows: 'It says much for the previous CO that, with these difficulties, he was able to hand over an efficient operational squadron'.[63]

Each squadron was under the command of a General Duties Branch squadron leader. Although he was Thor trained, his duties were mainly administrative and he was not part of the Launch Control Team. The nominal strength of each Launch Crew was seven. In overall charge was the Launch Control Officer (LCO), a flight lieutenant or flying officer, also drawn from the GD Branch. Unusually at the time, GD officers assigned to the Thor Programme retained their entitled flying pay without having to maintain their currency, although some took advantage of facilities offered by nearby flying stations in order to keep their hands in. The LCO was supported by a warrant officer Launch Control Console Operator (LCCO), also sometimes referred to as the Launch Monitor Console Operator (LMCO) and, even less formally, as the Missile Control Operator or just the Console Operator. The original USAF staffing profile of one-per-missile was not adopted by the RAF, possibly because it would have taken yet more personnel away from the V-Force, although LCOs suggest that one LCCO per shift was entirely adequate. Interestingly, although there was no intention of operating with three LCCOs per shift, the original nominal role of No.77 (SM) Squadron shows fifteen LCCOs and the original three-per-shift was operated for a very short time,[64] possibly merely to provide an initial core of trained LCCOs for the satellite sites as they came on-stream. The LCOs, often helped by the Squadron Commander, were also responsible for maintaining the Long and Short Range Electrotheodolites used to set the guidance of the missiles.

The operational status of each missile was the responsibility of a Missile Maintenance Technician (MMT) or 'mechtech'. Since the RAF had little previous experience of missiles to go on, these men were drawn from various trade groups. Usually present on a three-per-shift basis, one for each missile, they were backed up by a Master Systems Analyst Technician (MSAT) who could be deployed by van from the Wing HQ at the parent site as required. The MMTs were very much a part of the launch team and were effectively the 'pad controllers'. They were on site at all times and assisted with the countdown procedures. In particular, since the LCT had no windows, the MMTs acted as the 'eyes' of the LCO, providing him with visual confirmation of the countdown as it proceeded.

Although he was not directly involved in the launch procedure, another essential member of the team at each three-missile site was a Sergeant or Corporal Thor Electrical Worker (TEW)[65] who maintained the diesel generators which backed up the power supply drawn from the National Grid. His presence on site was essential during practice countdowns when he ensured that the generators started automatically and as required. To overcome shortages of manpower it was not unusual to find personnel cross-trained in other duties and the TEW, for instance, who was largely redundant once his generators had come online, could be found at the LCCO's position. The cook and policemen would also assist with certain launch duties and the dog handler might be found in the Long Range Theodolite Building. No. 142 (SM) Squadron at Coleby Grange noted: 'Due to the imminent return to flying duties of a large percentage of the Launch Consol (*sic*) Operators it has been found necessary to cross train the Missile Maintenance Technicians'.[66] The limited numbers of personnel meant that any periods of sickness could cause problems. A shortage of cooks at North Pickenham in May 1961, unfortunately coinciding with Exercise MAYSHOT IV,[67] saw the meals for the night shift being prepared by the police and firemen assisted by the TEW and an LCO. This was noted in the ORB as being a 'grave inconvenience'. One of the more unusual instances of dual duties concerned one of the National Servicemen who was employed as a Dental Orderly in the Hemswell SSQ. Trained as a Rolls-Royce engineer, he was often called in by the Technical Wing to offer his advice and expertise on engineering and missile modification programme problems.[68]

Unusually, the squadrons adopted the US system of seniority, based on individual qualification, rather than rank. As a result, a well-qualified Corporal could find himself directing a Flight Sergeant. Although this ran counter to traditional RAF practice, a clear precedent had been established during the Second World War, especially within Bomber Command, where commissioned crew members had frequently been subordinated to NCO captains while in the air. As in a bomber crew, rank was of little significance when launching a missile; it was expertise and professionalism that counted and, where it cropped up, the juxtaposition of rank seems to have been accepted without too much resentment. Morale amongst the Missile Fitters took a knock in November 1959[69] when a new trade structure for Missile Trades was introduced, a result of which many lost out financially. No.142 (SM) Squadron's diarist observed that 'a review and a firm statement of policy would do much to stabilise feelings on this subject.'[70]

Close protection was provided by the RAF Police in teams of four, equipped with a Land Rover and, from March 1960, a radio, a much needed and by then very necessary requirement, as CND and other nascent anti-nuclear groups became increasingly active around the launch sites. Each team also had a Police dog handler deployed, mainly for the night shifts, from the main bases where further RAF Police guarded the sensitive buildings. There was a duty fire picket on twenty-four-hour standby. Each site had at least one reservoir for water for firefighting. The reservoir was later plumbed into each launch pad to provide a semi-automatic firefighting capability, although the particularly severe winter of 1961/62 revealed a tendency to freeze up at some sites. The plumbed-in arrangements had been introduced as part of a programme designed to deal with the implications of a serious fire, most likely from igniting fuel, and the consequent potential for radioactive fall out.

Training and Squadron Operations

As well as general security duties, which encompassed keeping a watchful eye on the activities of CND activists around the bases, the RAF Police also provided a covert force to test the security of the launch compounds at all twenty sites. Some of these incursions were conducted with, and countered by, an enthusiasm above and beyond the call of duty! It was not unknown for the intruders to strike at the most inconvenient times, such as during a VIP inspection, a shift change or a countdown. That said, no attempts were made to gain access to any of the US facilities where a 'shoot first, ask questions later' policy was believed to operate. The original security fence was supposedly impenetrable but this was soon disproved by determined attempts to scale it. No.142 (SM) Squadron at Coleby Grange reported a typical incident in its ORB for January 1961: 'No 3 Police District scaled the wire fence and entered the site but all were captured within fi[v]e minutes. The check team was seen in the sterile area. However lack of a landrover slowed down the apprehension of the intruders'. Coils of Dannert wire were then added to the top of the fences and also at a height of 5-6ft from the ground, and this solution appeared to work. Covert access was thereafter usually achieved by pretending to be a representative of a government agency or a utility company or by hiding inside vehicles going into the complex.

Any suspicious vehicles were checked out as a matter of course. At Harrington a local huntsman was surprised to find his parked vehicle the subject of attention when he returned from riding. He had habitually parked his vehicle there but willingly accepted that things had now changed. Other 'suspicious' characters often turned out to be former USAAF personnel nostalgically revisiting the bases where they had been stationed during the war and were somewhat intrigued by the new use to which they had been put. Youthful curiosity was no protection against the long arm of the law. A local Bardney lad climbed a tree in Scotgrove Wood, which was only 1,000 metres from the missile site, whence he proceeded to view the site with the aid of a pair of binoculars. It was not long before he was spotted and he spent a day in the Guardroom for his troubles.[71] Although successful penetrations did take place they were almost always impeded before access to the LEs (the ultimate goal) was achieved. A rigorous system of identity passes operated for all personnel officially on site, whereas access to the LE area itself was restricted to specific personnel, which excluded those involved in non-technical or administrative duties, including the cooks, clerks and Guidance Systems Analysts (GSA).

Up to thirty Police dogs were held centrally at each of the four main bases where proper kennel facilities were available. There were no such provisions at the remote sites, where dogs were generally only present during the night shifts. As with manpower, dogs could also be in short supply, through sickness, for instance, or because of other commitments, such as being required to display their skills in the RAF Police Dog Demonstration Team at the Royal Tournament or elsewhere.

Each Wing HQ had a Station Sick Quarters (SSQ) to care for the welfare of the personnel. In the case of Hemswell, this had sixteen beds and an operating theatre with a staff of eleven providing both medical and dental facilities. Generally, the SSQs were fairly quiet although there were epidemics of measles and chicken pox and flu, but in March 1963 Hemswell had to cope with a case of typhoid – contracted in the Zermatt epidemic. With the, albeit remote, possibility of some form of nuclear incident, the medical section was issued with protective kit. This consisted of gas capes, standard RAF thick overalls, goggles and heavy cleated boots, which would only seem to have provided the most basic degree of protection. There was also a Decontamination Centre. Regular duties included providing a stand-by crash ambulance for flight-line activities (the ambulance radios were not compatible with Air Traffic Control wavelengths) and regularly patching up DAC staff who had suffered motor accidents, most of them in the VW Beetles that seemed to be the *de rigueur* mode of transport for the Americans.[72]

Allowance had to be made to incorporate within the crew shift pattern the necessary training requirements and leave allocation. SOPs indicated that every effort should be made to allow at least some of the personnel to enjoy Bank Holidays – considered by many to be one of the times when the Soviet Union was most likely to attack! However, it was noted that a generous attempt by Bomber Command to allow personnel to enjoy the 1960 Easter break was unlikely to be repeated as Thor became fully operational.[73]

The ORBs routinely reflected the squadron's responsibilities and activities as: administration, operations/exercises, training, maintenance, security and visits, some of which sounded a little low key, considering that Thor was in the front line of Britain's defence. In the early days there was the challenge of a new venture but as time passed, and the daily routine became more established, the risk of boredom setting in became a factor. There was a great deal of initial enthusiasm about the job, particularly among the NCOs, especially as a posting to Thor offered the attraction of travel to the United States. The Sandys White Paper of 1957 had revealed the extent to which the UK intended to rely on missiles in the future. The advent of Thor, and Bloodhound, represented a new, cutting edge and somewhat awesome technology and, not unnaturally, many believed that it had to be a good career move to be involved right from the start. Sadly, their expectations would not be realised. To provide variety to the job, the medical staff from the Wing HQs provided first-aid courses at the various squadron sites. The early US arrivals also benefited from first-aid courses and this allowed at least one of the National Service medical staff to acquire his driving licence so that he could drive to the satellite sites in the luxury of a Standard Vanguard staff car to give the necessary instruction.[74] Sqn Ldr Henry Probert MBE from HQ Bomber Command visited the Wing HQs regularly to assess educational needs and opportunities. Various clubs were also formed to keep the personnel occupied. These varied from art, radio, photographic and model aircraft to motoring and golf. In the case of Hemswell, one of the US staff had been a Hollywood film director and enthusiastically formed an Anglo/US drama group, the Hemswell Dramatic Society.[75] Their final ambitious production was of the Raymond Dyer's farce 'Wanted – One Body'.[76]

Once the missiles had begun to reach the UK, DAC personnel carried out a complete Functional Demonstration of Reliability (FDR) on each pad. This covered all aspects of the missile's operational profile and included a simulated countdown with a full Double Propellant Flow Test. Each FDR was carried out in the presence of representatives of the Technical and Operations Wings from the main base, the CO of the local squadron and staff from Douglas and AC Spark Plug. After a complete inventory check on site, the complex was formally handed over to the RAF, this procedure being verified by HQ staff from the parent base. Once declared operational, the Thors were maintained on standby. As previously noted, 60 per cent of the missiles were required to be in a 'standby' state. This was slightly below 'readiness', at which a missile could be held at T-14.5 minutes indefinitely. Standby missiles lay horizontal in their shelters with minimum equipment switched on, with the missile at fifteen minutes readiness. The RV was monitored electronically and the guidance unit was powered and kept warm. The gyros floated in 'fluorolube' which had to be kept within the range 140–165°F to prevent damage to the sensitive unit. Regular 'birdchecks'[77] monitored this semi-dormant state. 'Sniffer' tests were also conducted routinely by US personnel monitoring radiation levels using a Type 290A monitor, although the presence of a real, as opposed to a dummy, warhead within the RV was not disclosed.

Other than monitoring the state of the missile, much of the launch crews' time was taken up preparing and conducting practice countdowns, of which there were a variety of differing types, both 'wet' and 'dry'. The purpose of these countdowns was to verify the crews' ability to:

- Prepare the missile for flight.
- Erect and fuel the missile.
- Check the sub-systems on internal power.
- Launch the missile.

The countdown was broken down into five distinct phases. The following notes describe the early procedure – it was later fine-tuned to reduce the countdown time:

Phase 1: (Maximum six minutes). Erection of the guidance platform (this was critical, as it effectively determined the duration of the countdown). Engine centring check. LOX Gravity Flow.
Phase 2: (Maximum five minutes). Shelter retracted by two-speed cable-driven electric winches. Missile raised through 90 degrees to vertical. Engine gimballing check. Can be held at this position for extended period of time.
Phase 3: (Maximum six minutes). Fuel and LOX Fine Flow. Fuel measurement starts. Shelter cleared. Target input checked by the long range eletrotheodolite.
Phase 4: (Maximum two minutes). Fuel and LOX Rapid Flow. This position can be held only for a limited period. The US AO used his War/Peace key to arm the warhead and activate the nose cone battery.
Phase 5: System transfer to internal power. Electronic check. LOX top-up. Engine valves sequencing. Igniters fire. Lift-off.

The maximum times shown in the countdown phases were maximum default times as the whole countdown process was scheduled to last no more than fifteen minutes, which coincided with the readiness state for the V-Force.

As part of their training course, officers were informed that:

...time is the most important element of the countdown. The aim is to launch the missile as swiftly as possible without sacrificing any safety precautions. A full and complete knowledge of the countdown is a basic requirement for the Launch Control Officers, Squadron Commanders and Operations Officers. The LCCO should be able to support his LCO at any time and a knowledge of the countdown is a pre-requisite for this. With knowledge, your duties in the missile force, will be efficiently and expeditiously discharged.

After the 'birds had flown', there was a recovery and make-safe phase for the GSE – although one suspects that the crews may well have been more interested in the imminent arrival of incoming Soviet warheads. As there was little more to do by then, and with their jobs effectively over, it was accepted that personnel would want to return to their families.

A shortcoming of all liquid-fuelled ballistic missiles is the time that it takes to load the fuel and oxidant, which leaves the missile vulnerable to attack before it can be launched. The nature of the liquids is such that the missile can only be left in a raised and fuelled position for a relatively short period of time. Progress was made in reducing the nominal fifteen minutes it would take to launch Thor and the necessary modifications were introduced by Operation Consolidate, which was implemented in early 1961. This saw all sixty LEs and missiles individually converted to improve guidance efficiency and accept a shorter countdown time. The latter was largely achieved by increasing the pressure in the system to speed up the propellant transfer rate to 1,800 gallons per minute, eliminating the initial LOX Fine Flow in Phase 3 and starting the LOX tank pressurisation in Phase 2. This permitted 95 per cent LOX fill and 100 per cent fuel fill to be completed in Phase 3. Transfer to internal power and a full internal systems check now took place in Phase 4. External systems checks were also undertaken while the missile was still horizontal. Finally, a recycle switch was added so that recovery from a malfunction was now possible from the point at which the problem arose.

Addressing a problem rarely experienced in California, but not unknown in the UK, was the question of fog on the LE making it impossible to use the Long Range Theodolite. Another unexpected interruption to LRT operations was when a mouse was found to have nested under the mounting plinth and jammed the theodolite table bearings.[78] An Airframe Azimuth switch was therefore added to the Guidance Console in the LCT as an alternative to the theodolite. Target changes could now be made from the LCT with the missile vertical. After the Operation CONSOLIDATE modifications had been made, each missile was individually given a dry countdown, a single flow RP-1 flow test, a single flow LOX test followed by a dual flow propellant test before being declared operational once again. In 1962 a further modification was tested. Much of the work in support of this modification had been undertaken by the training staff of Feltwell's Operations Wing, led by Sqn Ldr Jim Wild. This would have allowed the missile to be held at a ready state in the shelter at T-five minutes forty seconds, held vertical and unfuelled at T-five minutes fifteen seconds for an extended period of time and a fuelled missile held at T-two minutes for up to two hours. The end of the Thor programme meant that this modification was never fully implemented. The missile earmarked for CTL-13, which had been scheduled for September 1962, had had these modifications incorporated but, in view of the termination of the programme, the launch was cancelled.

As far as the missile itself was concerned, its ballistic path after launch would depend on its target. The missile had a range capability between 300nm and 1,500nm (1,727 statute miles) and this put Moscow within reach. At launch, of the total weight of 110,000lb, 98,500lb was accounted for by fuel and LOX. After lift-off the missile rose vertically for the first twenty seconds of its flight and was slowly rolled through a maximum of 20 degrees to align its axis with its target plane, the directional plane connecting the LE to the target. The missile then moved on to its ballistic trajectory and after a further thirty-five seconds its flight path was inclined at 43 degrees to the horizontal. The main engine burned for just over two and a half minutes to achieve maximum range, correspondingly less if a closer target had been selected. For the first one and three-quarter minutes the auto-pilot was controlled by a pre-set programme. Thereafter, until Main Engine Cut Off (MECO), the auto-pilot received instructions from the AC Spark Plug inertial guidance unit. After MECO the 1,000lb thrust vernier engines fine tuned the trajectory for a further six seconds until they cut off at VECO. The warhead then received an internal pre-arm signal. From then on there was no further opportunity to change the ballistic path to re-entry and thence to the target. The nose cone latch squibs were fired and the retro-rockets were ignited allowing the RV to separate from the spent missile body. The retro-rockets mounted on the airframe of the missile externally between the two tanks were angled such that on firing they acted at 180 degrees away from the centre of gravity of the missile. This would minimise the risk of the spent fuselage interacting with the RV in the event that one retro-rocket failed to fire properly. The RV, now on its own and likely to be oscillating, was aligned and spun by GN2 rockets controlled by gyroscopic sensors. On its inward path, the final arming of the warhead took place. The warhead was protected against the heat of re-entry by the RV's cone-shaped copper heat sink. As well as providing stability, the RV was spun to equalise the temperature over the outer surface.

In terms of accuracy, it is clear from an examination of the radial displacement of the IWST and CTL launches that Thor was not suited to taking out pin-point targets such as airfields or launch sites. Towns, cities or area targets were better suited to its capabilities. The warhead was designed for groundburst or airburst, the latter between 3,000 and 12,000ft, with an accuracy of ±1,000ft.[79] Of the twenty-one launches, two were classed as failures with one incomplete trajectory, and of the remaining eighteen, 56 per cent fell within two miles of the target, only just within the RAF's requirement of 50 per cent. There is no reason to suppose that this would not have been representative of wartime performance and, as a result, it was necessary to provide duplicate coverage of Thor's targets by ensuring that they would be attacked by aircraft as well. Finally, it should be recorded that, although Thor was not specifically assigned to NATO, its targeting was co-ordinated within the overall NATO strike plan.

Table IX: Thor flightpath statistics for a nominal 1,500nm range were as follows:

Event	Time (seconds)	Altitude (nm)	Range (nm)	Velocity (ft/sec)
MECO	156	57.5	71	14,400
VECO	162	68.0	83	14,500
Apogee	562	280.0	775	11,000
Re-entry	945	48.5	1,440	14,600
Impact	1,077	0	1,500	367

The simplest and by far the most employed type of practice countdown was Dry Disabled, when the missile remained inside its shelter. There were more comprehensive Wet Enabled Routine Tests of operational capability known as Operational Ready Exercise Count Downs. The minimum standard set by Bomber Command was two dry countdowns per pad per month. There were generally many more of these each month and they initially covered Phases 1 and 2. Later on they extended to include Phase 3 – a dual flow countdown. Although LOX was loaded onto the missile, RP-1 fuel was by-passed and flowed into a separate mobile F6 tanker parked close to the fuel tank. The F6 tankers could overflow in the event of an excess fuel transfer and were replaced by larger-capacity tankers in 1962. That fuel was never loaded was a safety measure to avoid the possibility, however slight, that a fully fuelled missile might be launched by accident. There were also no facilities in the UK to clean the missile once fuel had been loaded. The most complex countdown was the TRIPLOX, where all three missiles were loaded with LOX simultaneously. This was a complicated procedure which demanded the presence of three launch teams for safety reasons. However, as this disrupted the shift system, the TRIPLOX countdowns were relatively rare, although they usually took only around ninety minutes from start to finish. Countdowns, particularly the Phase 3 ones, could often attract a quota of 'observers'. These exercises usually started at 9.00a.m., were finished by late morning, and were designed to provide the launch crews with a variety of different operating procedures and simulated faults. It took six hours to re-cycle the missile back to a ready state after these tests. A full countdown pad validation check usually lasted two to three days and, using a number of 'black boxes', could rigorously validate the whole system. As well as routine training, the squadrons were integrated within the overall Bomber Command Exercise Plan and could receive 'no-notice' orders to bring the missiles to operational readiness.

Categorisation of the crews' ability and competence – a throwback to the rating of aircrew proficiency – was obviously of paramount importance, particularly as personnel were constantly being posted in and out. Different types of assessment were used depending on the status of the crew members. Each Wing HQ had its own Training Flight/Categorisation Team or Training Crew (TC), which normally visited the different sites to examine crew members during their normal working shift. The Training Crew were initially selected from the most proficient launch crew members, and originally consisted of one quadron leader and two SNCOs. Later this was increased to a team of six. These crews became the 'eyes and ears' of the Wg Cdr Ops and the HQ locations. One of the Feltwell Training Flight, Chf Tech Len Townend, commented that 'it was the best job I ever had in the RAF but the hardest I've worked'. The Command Training Team was based at Feltwell, and in turn this team examined the members of all Training Flights at their individual locations.[80]

The main Bomber Command readiness exercise was the Ex-MAYSHOT series, held annually and in which the Thor force played a full part, which included not only a series of countdowns on the missiles but also included a Passive Defence Exercise component which tested response to a simulated nuclear attack on the site. No.77 (SM) Squadron's ORB[81] gives a typical involvement when it reports for MAYSHOT III, held from 11–13 July 1960:

Bomber Command ordered simultaneous countdowns on the three missiles to the end of Phase 2. Three changes of target were also ordered. A final triple countdown was ordered on 13th July resulting in three simulated launches, thus concluding the Squadron's participation in the Exercise. In all three exercises the equipment performed without malfunction.

Of the same exercise, No.150 (SM) Squadron based at Carnaby noted:

> Launch crews were augmented to two crews per shift on the receipt of the alert. During the period of alert Pads 37 and 39 were counted down successfully to an operational hold at the end of phase 2, on three occasions. Pad 38 was counted down successfully on two of these occasions.[82]

No.142 (SM) Squadron reported on May 1961:

> During the period 10th May to 13th May, 1961 the Squadron participated in Exercise MAYSHOT IV which tests the 12 plans, operating procedures and the efficiency of personnel and equipment. Twenty one erections were carried out during the exercise, the average time from Phase 2 Hold LRT aquired (sic) was under nine minutes.[83]

Four types of 'no-notice' exercises ordered by Bomber Command from December 1960.

Exercise RESPOND: This could be initiated either by Bomber Command or the Wing HQ and was designed to test the readiness of the missiles on standby, the communications systems and the readiness procedures. The missiles were placed in an Exercise Ready state and a countdown to the end of Phase 2 and the capturing of the Long Range Electrotheodolite was completed. Demonstrating that authority was not necessarily without a sense of humour, a RESPOND which took place on 5 November 1961 was initiated with the codeword 'Fawkes'.

Exercise REDOUBLE: This took place twice a year and tested the whole of the Thor force integration within the Bomber Command alert and readiness procedures. The exercise called for all the LEs to be placed in Exercise Ready condition and for the launch crews to be doubled up on site, which meant locating and calling back to the sites off-duty crews. Twelve-hour shifts were operated. It tested those missiles that were in a 'standby' state and the ability to reclaim those missiles in either 'available', Out-A (available in less than six hours) or Out-B (more than six hours) states.

Exercise RECLAIM: This tested the squadron's ability to recover to standby, within the stipulated maximum six-hour period, those missiles classed as 'available'.

Exercise NIGHTCHECK: This was a monthly paper exercise which essentially validated the passage of data, countdown information and target control between Bomber Command, the Wing HQs at the four main bases and the individual squadrons.

These exercises were initiated by HQ Bomber Command. Similar exercises when initiated by the Wing HQs were known as JACK (for RECLAIM) and JILL (for REDOUBLE). Six hours was also the period required to recycle the missile to a standby condition after a countdown to Phase 2.

Bomber Command SOPs dictated that all training countdowns were to be suspended if there was any threat of lightning, an erect missile being an effective lightning conductor, and during periods of stormy weather – this sometimes put pressure on the crews' ability to complete the month's training syllabus.[84]

To ensure the mechanical reliability of a system as complex as Thor, regular servicing was clearly essential and each missile was taken out of service at pre-determined intervals for maintenance known as a 'periodic'. Initially this was done on an individual missile basis at fifteen- and thirty-day intervals, later increased to seventeen and thirty-five days – but this procedure was soon modified and from September 1960 all three of a squadron's missiles were serviced simultaneously, although individual servicing was eventually reinstated. These periodics were not immune to an Ex-REDOUBLE, which meant that the servicing had to be abandoned and the missile restored to its operational condition. Routine scheduled servicing was carried out on site but there was a further requirement for a so-called 'Major Periodic', which involved the missile being taken off its pad and transported to the Wing RIM building where comprehensive facilities existed to service all components of the missile in an air-conditioned environment, separate bays being dedicated to handling the individual parts of the missile.

The ongoing need for logisticical support for the deployed Thor force, including spares back-up, was co-ordinated through the San Bernardino Air Matériel Area (SBAMA) at Norton AFB in California, which provided a maximum delivery time of fifty hours on any required part.

With such a variety of complicated equipment, the system-specific GSE as well as the missiles themselves, it was almost inevitable that there would be problems and this proved to be the case. There were a number of incidents which can be divided into three broad categories: technical problems, pyrotechnic problems and human errors. The most serious incident took place on 7 December 1960 at Ludford Magna (affectionately known, because of the amount of water that accumulated on the site, as 'Mudford Magna' or 'Ludford Magma', and noted as a heavy clay site in the original survey).[85] A double propellant flow countdown was taking place on Pad 28 following a routine periodic. The warhead and igniters had been removed from the missile. The countdown would see the missile filled with LOX. The delivery of fuel would also be tested but the RP-1 would be bypassed into a fuel trailer parked close to the fuel tank, rather than actually being loaded into the missile. This was a standard procedure. As was often the case, particularly with the early countdowns, there were a number of onlookers also present in the LCT. The incident occurred owing to uncertainty regarding the launch switch which had three positions: standby, checkout and maintenance (C&M), and launch. Wet countdowns required the switch to be in the launch position. On the day in question, the countdown progressed normally until the LCO noticed that the status switch was in the 'Checkout Maintenance' position. He therefore stopped the count and sought clarification. No one offered any worthwhile suggestions, however, so he consulted the overseeing authority, a Douglas civilian engineer, whose advice was to resume the countdown.

Training and Squadron Operations 121

Wet countdowns normally ended when the systems checks detected that the vernier engines had not ignited. This inhibited main engine ignition and terminated the countdown. However, in this instance at 1650(Z), with the launch switch in 'C&M', three relays were activated thus indicating to the system, *for maintenance purposes only*, that ignition had taken place. The main LOX valve therefore immediately opened and discharged 7,000 gallons of LOX onto the pad. The LOX first changed from a light blue liquid into a gel which filled the trenches around the LE before forming a dense white cloud as the super-chilled LOX boiled off and vaporised. The danger lay in the fact that if the LOX mixed with any hydrocarbons, oils or grease for instance, a distinct possibility around the LE, it would explode spontaneously with potentially devastating results. A further problem lay in the possibility that the super-chilled liquid cascading over the pad had crystallised the metal launch structure presenting problems in lowering the missile. The concrete pad had cracked. The other two missiles on the site had warheads in place.

Civilian firefighters were summoned from Louth, Grimsby, Market Rasen, Brigg and Grainsby. An RAF fire team from Scampton was also summoned but, somewhat surprisingly, and a matter that was questioned at the subsequent inquiry, the RAF Special Safety Team from Hemswell was not deployed. Three RAF fire tenders suffered damage from the LOX, one having to be abandoned as a matter of urgency, leaving its engine running. The USAF was reportedly 'aghast' at what had happened. Fortunately, the threat of nuclear contamination was avoided because, as a safety measure, wet countdowns did not take place with a nuclear warhead in place. There was little the fire services could do until the LOX had dispersed, whereupon the missile was recovered.

A Board of Inquiry was convened[86] and a number of personnel were redeployed after the incident, a not uncommon practice when mistakes were made. The Hemswell Station Commander was posted to Singapore at very short notice. He was followed into oblivion by the Squadron Commander and the OCs of the Operations and Technical Wings. The replacements were all accorded 'acting' rank, substantive rank being dependent on their ability to get things in order, so a bit of a reign of terror ensued for a while. The matter was raised in Parliamentary Questions on 25 January 1961. Emmanuel Shinwell, MP for Easington, asked what damage had been done and why the Group Captain in command of the base had been posted elsewhere. SoS(A), Mr Julian Amery, replied that:

> ...there was no fire or explosion and only very minor damage. The Board of Inquiry concluded that the primary cause was a failure to carry out the correct procedures for controlling the flow of liquid oxygen. This was considered to reflect on the state of efficiency and training at the station, for which the Station Commander is responsible.

Mr Shinwell pursued the matter further, questioning 'whether this was not, in fact, a rather serious accident?' Mr Amery responded that he had:

> ...not categorise[d] the accident as minor ... the damage was very minor [but] could have led to a serious fire. The House and the country are entitled to know that we maintain the highest standards of efficiency in stations of this kind and when there is any fall-down in efficiency very serious steps have to be taken ... There had been minor

deficiencies – not of an accident character, but of other sorts – in the station before. In the circumstances, the Air Officer Commanding thought that the right decision was to recommend the posting of the officer, and we have no reason to take another view.[87]

Nonetheless, the Wing had already conducted completely satisfactory dual-flow countdowns starting with LE23 at Caistor on 22 November. The reality of the situation was that the Hemswell Wing was possibly no worse than any of the others, just unlucky. The danger of LOX mixing with other substances and leading to an explosion was a constant hazard. The No.226 (SM) Squadron ORB notes:

> Flt Lt W Julian, RAF Driffield Safety Officer, visited the site and gave a most impressive demo of the hazards of mixing Liquid Ox and RP-1 fuel. It is hoped that return visits will be made so that all members of the Sqn will be able to witness this demo.

Accidents could easily happen. At Coleby Grange:

> ...during a pre-periodic check on Pad 27 the MMT retracted the shelter manually and gave permission for a Missile Fitter Hydraulic to raise the missile, without checking that the Short Range Theodolite work stands on the missile side were raised. The umbilical mast struck the stand and damaged the hand rail. This accident was a product of over confidence and carelessness but has served as a reminder that this [is] dangerous.[88]

Empire News picked up and reported an incident at Caistor on 23 September 1960 when the missile erector failed to neutralise after erection, and started to lower the locked missile. Although major damage was avoided by the timely throwing of circuit breakers the missile separated at the boat tail, resulting in a 12in crack in the missile airframe.[89]

The most bizarre incident involving Thor happened at Hemswell. Next to the perimeter fence was a field occupied by a herd of cows:

> During the previous night, something had spooked the cows and, in what must have been a mad rush, they damaged the fencing and one cow blundered into the launch area. After the alarm sounded the cows in the launch area were returned to their lawful place of grazing and the fence stoutly and hurriedly repaired. But not before one cow lightly brushed the Thor, at the time horizontal on its transporter [but] with the shelter retracted, and left an inch long indentation about 1/16in at the deepest point about two thirds of the way along the body of the Thor toward the nose cone.[90]

Douglas technicians were apparently happy that no damage had been done to the structural integrity of the missile.

In all, there were fourteen incidents caused by human error, sixteen technical faults and ten involving pyrotechnics (see Appendix 9). Electrical and hydraulic faults largely accounted for the technical faults. Although safety was a priority, and designed into the system, the very nature of the missile inevitably meant that a high level of training had to be acquired and maintained by the crews to minimise the possibility of serious accidents. There were, for example, three over-ride switches: Shelter, Erector and PTS. The Erector over-ride was very special and not without its dangers. A special Training

Notice was issued to highlight these dangers:

> As can be seen this over-ride button is a potent control and must not be pressed until the Erector is up and locked and checked by the MSC as fully up and locked. To press the point, if the over-ride is pressed before the 'up and locked' position is reached the missile will stop erecting and LOX and fuel loading will commence with the missile only part way erected. Taking this to the extreme, when the 100% fuel point is reached the missile would lower to the horizontal position fully loaded, with the launch pins retracted.[91]

Other external dangers also existed. There was, for instance, what might be deemed a 'near miss' in August 1962 when an F-100 Super Sabre fighter from the 48th Fighter Wing USAFE, based at Lakenheath, crashed into the domestic site at Shepherds Grove, killing a painter and destroying four of the 'tobacco' houses, one of which was occupied by the USAF Site Commander.[92] Inevitably, in dealing with complex heavy equipment, there were some injuries to personnel. Sadly, in January 1961, Cpl 'Jesse' James, one of the MT NCOs at Hemswell, was killed when he was pinned under an overturned forklift truck on which he had been hitching an unofficial lift. He was buried in Hemswell Cemetery with full military honours.[93] Other incidents were usually, and fortunately, not too serious in nature, but No.142 (SM) Squadron at Coleby Grange, along with representatives from the Hemswell Wing, had the sad duty of attending the funeral of Chf Tech. Harry Harris in January 1963. The MSC had been found dead at 2015(Z) on 22 January, having apparently fallen from a lighting pylon on LE27. A coroner's verdict of 'death by misadventure' was recorded. With full military honours, he was laid to rest in North Hykeham Churchyard.[94]

By the nature of the job, relations with the local communities had to be somewhat guarded, but local pubs were often the venue for squadron social events, borne out of many entries in the ORBs reporting highly successful parties. The enterprising landlord of *The Jolly Sailor*[95] pub in Bardney had installed a burger-making machine and the pub was well patronised by the US personnel as a result. The locals traditionally vacated the pub at lunch time in favour of the Americans. But even those who had no faith whatsoever in the political value, or the military effectiveness, of Thor had to admit that the presence of the missiles did add significantly to the local economy, particularly as the deployment developed, thus swelling the numbers in the thinly populated rural areas where most sites were located. Perhaps surprisingly, awareness of being a prime target for Soviet missiles appears to have caused little real concern, as the expectation in a nuclear conflict was that few, if any, would escape the effects.[96] CND attempted to provoke fear and concern among the local population on the grounds that they were almost certainly a prime Soviet target, a typical example being the activities of the left-wing journalist and satirist Malcolm Muggeridge and Pat Arrowsmith, who reported on the state of fear in North Pickenham. Local residents treated it all as rather a joke.[97]

Notes:
1 General Duties, i.e. the 'executive' branch, which was synonymous with commissioned aircrew.
2 TNA. AIR 27/2758: No.113 (SM) Squadron Operations Record Book (ORB/Form 540).
3 The GW course was not meant to give officers the ability to lecture on the subject to their

units but gave a general overview to an understanding of missile technology and capability.
4 At least one group crossed on the French Lines Île de France, once a doyen of the North Atlantic route.
5 Sqn Ldr Ken Hayes (LCO and later OC No.77 (SM) Squadron) remembers that having crossed the Atlantic in leisurely style, they were flown to Tucson in an ageing ex-USAF Curtiss-Wright C-46 Commando of Universal Airways. Eventually the aircraft had to land *en route* to effect engine repairs, and the passengers, after their harrowing flight, sought out a local bar in which to calm their nerves only to find they had landed in a dry county.
6 'We crossed the Atlantic on the *Willem Ruys* [the passenger liner was later renamed the *Achille Lauro* and was made famous by being the subject of a Palestinian Liberation Front hijack in 1985], 'steerage'. If you tripped over the bulkhead you would have finished up with a wedge-shaped head. The water-tight door was aft of our hovel which consisted of two-tier bunks, no storage space, the only hanging facility being hooks on the ends of the bunks. All our cases were under the bottom bunks and we lived out of them, more than 20 of us until we reached Montreal. Our toilet facilities were the ones the crew used. We disembarked and went by train to New York. After a few days we went on to Tucson via Chicago by train – four days.' Correspondence with Snr Tech Bernie Worsfold, 2007.
7 Chf Tech Richard Pratt was given only ten days' notice of his posting to the US. He crossed the Atlantic in, somewhat appropriately, a Douglas Super DC-7C. He worked at that time at RAF Lyneham servicing the Comet 2s and daily carried out test flights on almost silent jet power at 40,000ft. The noise of the piston-engined DC-7C came as a surprise to him at takeoff. After eventually managing to climb to 11,000ft, the aircraft struggled against a headwind and landed at New York Idlewwild Airport some thirteen hours later. He thereafter joined about thirty other RAF personnel and he too remembers a worryingly smoking engine on his Curtis Commando flight to Davis Monthan. Conversations with Richard Pratt, July 2007, August 2008.
8 Sgt Dave Jones crossed the Atlantic on the French liner *Flandres* and later returned home on the RMS *Queen Mary*. After landing in New York he mistook a $100 bill for a $1 bill and gave it to a taxi driver. Arriving nearly penniless in Milwaukee he was given a $40 'on the spot' fine for jaywalking on his first walk into town. After intervention from his Commanding Officer, an apology to the precinct desk Sergeant ensured that the fine was cancelled! Correspondence with Sgt Dave Jones, August 2007.
9 For those personnel who had not fully recovered on their return to the UK, they were confined to camp and taken in civilian clothes to nearby hospital Special Treatment Clinics for further examination.
10 TNA. AIR 20/9791. Letter from AVM Sheen to Air Mshl Sir John Whitley, 30 September 1958. (It is interesting to note that exactly the same complaint regarding the poor quality of the tropical kit on issue was made when the RAF first participated in Exercise RED FLAG in Nevada in 1978 – nothing changes.)
11 Conversation with Chf Tech Richard Pratt, July 2007.
12 *Ibid.* Visits included the Grand Canyon, Los Angeles and New York.
13 TNA. AIR 20/9791. DDOps (BM)/BF469, October 1958.
14 TNA. AIR 20/10557. A.290410/58/DGM.
15 Thor 110 does not feature on the flight manifest and appears to have been used as a facilities check vehicle.
16 TNA. AIR 2/14982, 29 September 1959.

Training and Squadron Operations

17 The main purpose of the CTL was to:
Establish confidence in the RAF missiles exposed for a long period in the field.
Establish confidence in the complete readiness of the launch crews.
Establish confidence in the maintenance procedures used by the RAF.
Derive training benefits.
Assist in maintaining the morale of RAF personnel employed in the Thor Force.

18 The number of personnel involved was quite significant. For the 'Welcome 10' launch, an advance party of five was joined by a launch contingent of forty-eight, leaving a rear party of two to clear up after the launch had taken place.

19 The Discoverer scientific research programme was used as a cover name for the joint CIA/USAF Corona photographic reconnaissance satellites. A two-stage Thor-Agena rocket was used. The photo capsules were ejected from the spacecraft and returned to earth.

20 Although classed as a successful launch, incorrect settings in the guidance system caused a 93nm overshoot. TNA 'Thor' Project – 13th Progress Report, 2 June 1959, contained in File DEFE 13/121.

21 Wynn, Humphrey, *RAF Nuclear Deterrent Forces*, P.349.

22 TNA. AIR 20/10325. Note by VCAS, 18 December 1959.

23 Air Mshl (later Air Chf Mshl) Sir Kenneth ('Bing') Cross KCB CBE DSO DFC was AOCinC Bomber Command during the Thor deployment He was one of only forty-five survivors from the sinking of HMS *Glorious*, returning from Norway in May 1940. Described by one officer as a 'miserable sod', Cross knew little about Thor, preferring instead the more traditional power of the V-Bombers but was ultimately supportive of extending the Thor deployment.

24 Correspondence with Air Chf Mshl Sir Brian K. Burnett GCB, DFC, AFC, April 2007.

25 *Santa Maria Times*, Saturday 1 October 1960.

26 'The Officers and NCOs of the Launch Crews and manning the Ops Room are mostly aircrew serving a tour of duty in the GW force. A large proportion of the technicians are NCOs with very considerable experience in aircraft maintenance, specially chosen for ability and make an extremely favourable impression on the USAF.' The RAF's Thor Strategic Missile. Information Division, Air Ministry. TNA. G.19449/SJW/2/60/220.

27 TNA. No.106 (SM) Squadron ORB. '[The launch was] meant to be no-notice, but USAF preparations gave it away.'

28 Conversation with Sqn Ldr Colin Burch.

29 For example, the mileage for all operations within the Hemswell Wing recorded in May 1962 was 115,541 accident-free miles.

30 TNA. AIR 20/9791, 6 November 1958.

31 Conversation with Chf Tech Bill Roseby.

32 Conversation with Chf Tech Len Townend.

33 *The Ermine Link*, Issue No.11, summer 2002.

34 At RAF Harrington Sqn Ldr Burch's successor was unaccompanied and offered the house to one of the LCOs.

35 Telephone conversation with Sqn Ldr (retd) Frank Leatherdale, 24 April 2007.

36 TNA. No.226 (SM) Squadron ORB: in October 1961 – 'The two Squadron pigs had to leave us!!! Net gain £7-1-0. Four more pigs aged 8 weeks have been purchased'; and

in March 1962 – 'The Squadron pigs were sold but as the pork market at the moment is bad, the expected vast profits were not forthcoming, however, a good profit was made, and the next Squadron party will benefit by the addition of the odd barrel or two'.
37 TNA No.142 (SM) Squadron ORB, March 1960.
38 *Ibid*, April 1960.
39 There are still ducks at Caistor, the duck sheds now having expanded to take in the former launch pads.
40 TNA. No.142 (SM) Squadron ORB, January 1960.
41 *Ibid*, June 1960.
42 RAF Museum. No.226 (SM) Squadron ORB, November 1959.
43 TNA. No.142 (SM) Squadron ORB, January 1963.
44 TNA. No.107 (SM) Squadron ORB, January 1963.
45 *Ibid*, February 1963.
46 North Luffenham had its own Snow Clearance Plans drawn up to combat the elements. AIR 28/1496 App 18. NL/S.816/AIR, 16 December 1960.
47 TNA. No130 (SM) Squadron ORB, June 1960.
48 TNA. No220 (SM) Squadron ORB, April 1961.
49 TNA. No223 (SM) Squadron ORB, July 1960.
50 TNA. No254 (SM) Squadron ORB, November 1960.
51 TNA. AIR 20/10081. Agreement Concerning the Physical Security of the Thor Missile Units in the United Kingdom. Annex IV, p.1.
52 *Rocket Review*. Vol.1, No.1, RAF Feltwell, April 1959.
53 Lt Col. T.W. Tedrow, Maj. G. Weitlands, Capt. G.M. Mathis, T/Sgt N.B. Boggs.
54 Correspondence with Sqn Ldr (retd) Frank Leatherdale, May 2007.
55 *Ibid*.
56 No.226 (SM) Squadron ORB gives the following squadron strength of seventy at disbandment:

Operational Staff	Supporting Staff
OC x 1	Cook x 5
LCO x 5	MSAT x1
LCCO x 5	GSA x 1
MMT x 15	TEW x 1
TEW x 5	Clerk x 1

Fireman x 5
Police x 19
Dog handlers x 6

57 TNA. AIR 2/14981. The Thor Technical Agreement outlines the role of the US Authentication Officers as follows: 'One USAF representative will be on duty in each squadron launch control station at all times after each squadron becomes capable of launching a weapon operationally. He will be in addition to the normal RAF launch crew. The USAF representative's duty will be to receive the US authentication launch order through US channels of communication. If the countdown has been started and the RAF authentication order has been received and the USAF authentication order has not been received, the USAF representative will, by use of a keying mechanism, introduce a tactical hold of the missile countdown. This tactical hold will be released by the USAF representative upon receipt of the US authentication order.'
58 Email correspondence with Col. (Retd) Ken Moll USAF, March 2007.

59 *The Times*, 23 September 1974. Letter by Donald Hofford, RAF (Retd). 'He never did turn up, but the situation was saved by the sang froid of the RAF officer whose adroit use of a screw-driver in the other keyhole enabled the simulated launch to take place.'
60 The V-Bombers operated on an eighteen-hour, two-shift basis.
61 TNA. No.102 (SM) Squadron ORB, January 1960.
62 RAF Museum. No.226 (SM) Squadron ORB, May 1960.
63 TNA. No.77 (SM) Squadron ORB. Also conversation with Sqn Ldr (Retd) Ken Hayes.
64 Confirmed in correspondence with Chf Tech Len Townend.
65 In US parlance an EPPO (Electrical Power Production Operator), and sometimes referred to simply as the PPO.
66 TNA. No.142 (SM) Sqadron ORB, Oct 1959.
67 Exercise MAYSHOT was the IRBM component of the annual Exercise MAYFLIGHT series. The exercises were designed to test Bomber Command alert and readiness procedures. Since the Thors were already at constant alert and readiness at T-15, the only aspect that could be introduced was the time taken to augment the crews. As MAYSHOT was a pre-warned exercise, it was not generally seen by the squadrons as a realistic test of augmentation procedures.
68 Conversation with David O'Flanagan, September 2007,
69 The new advanced trades were published in A.276/1959 and were designed to cover the servicing of both ballistic and air-to-surface missiles. They were in the Instrument Engineering Trade Group as follows, and inevitably were known as 'misfits':

Missile fitter (system)   Msl. Fitt (S)
Missile fitter (control)   Msl. Fitt (C)
Missile fitter (guidance)   Msl. Fitt (G)
Missile fitter (propulsion) Msl. Fitt (P)
Missile test equipment fitter M.T.E. Fitt

It was noted that for the time being airwomen would not be employed on these duties.
70 TNA. No.142 (SM) Squadron ORB, July 1960.
71 Conversation with Tony Green, March 2007.
72 Conversation with David O'Flanagan, September 2007.
73 RAF Museum. No.226 (SM) Squadron ORB. 'The Squadron was permitted by Bomber Command to work with slightly reduced crews over the Easter period. This probably is the last time there can be any concession for Public Holidays, as it is anticipated that the squadron will shortly be at the highest level of operational capability. Security and training have been tightened up accordingly.'
74 Conversation with John Lowther, September 2007. After doing an hour at his job in the dispensary, he would often spend the rest of the day driving around the satellite locations. This satisfactorily occupied him during his eighteen months' National Service spent at Hemswell.
75 *Ibid*.
76 TNA. AIR 28/1504, November 1962.
77 Defined in the No.77 (SM) Squadron ORB as 'maintaining a watch over the missile guidance section gyro heaters' but defined by others as a more general monitoring of the missile's state.
78 RAF Museum. No.226 (SM) Squadron ORB, October 1960.
79 TNA. AIR 20/10620. Thor Operational Performance Specifications. 7AD C-7584.
80 Correspondence with Chf Tech Len Townend.

81 TNA. No.77 (SM) Squadron ORB, July 1960.
82 TNA. No.150 (SM) Squadron ORB, July 1960.
83 TNA. No.142 (SM) Squadron ORB, May 1961.
84 TNA. No.223 (SM) Squadron ORB, October 1960.
85 See also *The Independent*, 7 October 1999.
86 Wg Cdr W.A. Thynne, Sqn Ldr L.A. Baldchin and Flt Lt G. Cairns constituted the Board Members.
87 Hansard, 25 January 1961. Cols 143-145.
88 TNA. No.142 (SM) Squadron ORB, April 1960.
89 TNA. AIR 20/10620.
90 *The Ermine Link*, Issue No.14, winter 2003.
91 Correspondence with Chf Tech Len Townend.
92 Correspondence with Capt. (Retd) Doug Ray USAF, November 2006.
93 *The Ermine Link*, Issue No.13, summer 2003.
94 The widow's grief was further added to when on lowering the coffin into the grave, which had been cut out of frozen ground, the thick RAF ropes used jammed against the sides of the grave after the coffin had descended only about one foot. There followed a very protracted lowering of the coffin to its final resting place. Conversation with Chf Tech Richard Pratt who was one of the funeral party, August 2008.
95 Now renamed *The Gypsy Queen*.
96 Conversation with Tony Green, March 2007.
97 Conversation with Mrs Sheila Warner, April 2007.

CHAPTER SEVEN
THE CUBAN CRISIS AND THE END OF PROJECT EMILY

On 1 May 1962 US Secretary of Defense Robert McNamara[1] informed the UK Minister of Defence Peter Thorneycroft that US support for Thor would not be extended after the five-year agreement period, which finished on 31 October 1964. The deployment of the Atlas, Titan and Minuteman ICBMs in the safe haven of the US homeland had rendered both Thor and Jupiter largely obsolescent. The only military advantage of the IRBMs in Europe was the extra targets that the Soviets had to provide for. Thor had no UK successor following the cancellation of Blue Streak, so for those who had seen Project Emily as a way of contributing knowledge to the home-grown missile it had been a waste of effort. There was little enthusiasm to take on the full burden of funding a missile in which the US was fast losing interest as a strategic weapon and unofficially believed it would be obsolete by 1965/66.[2] Furthermore, even in 1960 it was known that there was a 'sizeable gap between the end of the US support period and the disappearance of Thor from Plan M'[3] – the RAF Squadron Patterns Plan. This had superseded Plan L.[4] The RAF would have to shoulder the costs. Plan O showed an ORBAT of sixty missiles on 1 April 1964 but none by 1 April 1965.

In 1961 the Air Council had positively considered the question of extending the five-year Thor Deployment. The wording of the Thor Agreement indicated that it would 'remain in force for not less than five years but may thereafter be terminated by either Government upon six months notice'.[5] The Air Ministry had advised Sandys that:

> Thor can plainly never be a satisfactory second-strike weapon. Nevertheless, 60 megaton weapons at 8-10 minutes readiness[6] are a factor an enemy could never wholly ignore. Their existence would complicate his task and add some measure to his doubts about the outcome of aggressive moves against the West. ... A short extension of Thor's life – from 1964 to perhaps 1966 or 1967 – could then give us at relatively low cost a deterrent supplement of which we might be very glad during the period covering the conversion of the Vulcan for the carriage of Skybolt.[7,8]

This view was largely supported by the Cabinet Defence Committee who, in July 1962, had considered a proposal to reduce the Thor force over a three-year period beginning in 1963. It recognised that manpower was needed for the Skybolt programme, and the Thor experience would mean that candidates would be sought from these personnel. They also noted the need for transparency, as there had been much criticism that the 1960 decision to cancel orders for the Handley Page Victor Bomber had used the parliamentary recess to obfuscate the decision.[9] Consideration had also been given to 'going it alone' and supporting Thor directly from British industry. Gp Capt R.F. Harman (DD Ops(BM)) had noted in December 1958, 'Messrs. Rolls Royce are already producing the same type of engine as is used in Thor, and Messrs. De Havilland are doing work on our own ballistic missile airframe'.[10] In fact a serious approach had already been made to the US Government to:

> ...supply Thor missiles without strings and to make available design information that would enable us to make our own warheads. [It had been ascertained early in 1957 that the UK effectively 'owned' the missiles and could, by implication, develop their own warhead but this could only be used to strike targets in co-ordination with NATO plans.[11]] This would make it possible for us to abandon Blue Streak and to concentrate our efforts, in co-operation with the United States and perhaps also with Continental Europe on the development of a more advanced missile of the Polaris type using solid propellant.[12]

This idea did enjoy a temporary currency and initial advances to Washington were 'noted' by Mansfield D. Sprague, the US Assistant SecDef on 18 August.[13] The matter was one of the agenda items at a series of high-level defence meetings at the Pentagon and State Department between 22–25 September 1958 attended by Sandys.[14] However, the State Department indicated that Secretary of State John Foster Dulles was not ready to express a view at the moment. The UK contingent was brought up to date on Thor development, including a proposal to increase Thor's range to 2,200 miles by a new warhead which reduced the all-up weight by 1,000lb. A proposal for a missile called Thorad to replace Thor was the subject of a presentation by DAC personnel to the Air Ministry on 20 February 1962. This missile was the Long-Tank Thrust-Augmented Thor, also known as the LTTAT, and embodied an elongated tank to increase the fuel load. The missile would have had an increased range of 400nm, but there would be an add-on cost to the UK of £3 million.[15] DAC had also confirmed that Thor could be modified to allow it to be stored underground but it would still have to be launched from the surface. However, events and attitudes were subject to flux and views on the future of Thor were already consolidating. The previous November SoS(A) had written to Minister of Defence Harold Watkinson:

> In your minute of 23rd October you proposed to examine with the USAF the implication of an extension of the Thor agreement. I doubt whether there is any merit in Thor after 1964 unless the US Government wants to keep it here. I am therefore arranging for Sir George Mills[16] to seek the view of the US Department of Defense. The discussions with the USAF should wait until we have them'.[17]

The reply stated, 'When you have the facts we should need to consider very carefully whether it is worth while adding £5 million a year to the cost of defence for a weapon which is not fully under our control and whose limitations are well known'.

This clearly reflected a change of heart about the missile system, fearing perhaps that it would compromise efforts to contain fiscal and manpower budgets. Mills' inquiries proved to be inconclusive. 'Unofficial opinion in HQ USAF suggests that the Joint Chiefs of Staff would like the UK to continue with Thor providing that we do so at our? (sic) expense.'[18] This was a view unlikely to have much appeal to a Treasury seeking to find economies in the Defence budget.

Opposition opinion on Thor had been clearly defined from the start and was expressed by Geoffrey de Freitas on 5 March 1958 when he questioned in Parliament, 'is it not a fact that everywhere outside this Government, Thor is regarded as a highly inefficient missile, and is not it ridiculous to waste £10 million on bringing it over here?'.[19] Emphasising, perhaps, that there had been a strong political element to Project Emily from the start, was the fact that Macmillan had always been a supporter of the missile. Indeed, when he understood that there had been difficulties during the test firings, he commented that 'it would be unfortunate if this weapon was not operational at the time when it was planned to deploy it in the United Kingdom' (i.e. at the end of 1958).[20]

Manpower was never far from the top of the agenda for Thor. In early 1962 efforts were made to reduce the Police contingents. Air Mshl Cross wrote pithily to DCAS, Air Mshl Sir Ronald Lees, 'I feel strongly that manpower is being wasted. Guarding should be based on the actual threat and not on an arbitrary arrangement under American law which, when framed, had little knowledge of local conditions'.[21]

In fact, Thor's most challenging time was still to come. This was to be during the Cuban Missile Crisis when, for ten days, the missiles were put on full alert as President Kennedy and Premier Khrushchev brought the two superpowers to the most freezing point of the Cold War.[22]

The first mention of the crisis in the Thor squadron ORBs was on 23 October when, following President Kennedy's TV address to the US nation at 7.00p.m. (EST) on the preceding day, 'maximum security was introduced (at the missile bases) because of the International situation'.[23] However, only after CAS, MRAF Sir Thomas Pike, met with Macmillan at Admiralty House at 11.00a.m. on 27 October did the Chiefs of the Services become fully involved in the increasing drama.[24] From the start Macmillan was clearly very keen to keep the whole matter from escalating. However, informed of the meeting by Pike, AOCinC Bomber Command Air Mshl Cross ordered Alert Condition 3 at 1.00p.m.; this was a unilateral decision which he was empowered to initiate and can be seen as a precaution to ensure that his Command was prepared, rather than an overtly hostile intention. A similar decision had been made by the US JCS to bring SAC to DEFCON 2 on 24 October, a level at which it was to remain until 15 November, although all other US Forces remained at DEFCON 3.[25] Two days earlier General LeMay had instructed SAC to put its B-52 Bomber fleet on full operational alert armed with nuclear weapons. B-47 squadrons were also dispersed. By coincidence, Bomber Command had only recently completed the second MICKY FINN no-notice readiness and dispersal exercise on 20/21 September, in which the Thor squadrons were fully involved and had been brought to Alert 2 status. Following Cross' ordering of Alert Condition 3, the squadrons recorded various times within the next seventy minutes when it was implemented. 'Unobtrusive measures were taken to increase the readiness state; these consisted primarily of increasing security watchfulness and warning back-up crews and servicing personnel to remain on call.'[26] The order also brought the V-Bombers to a high state of readiness but did not initiate the flying-off of the aircraft to the dispersed airfields. On balance this further supports Macmillan's wish to calm the situation, as the dispersal of the bombers would almost certainly have been interpreted as a provocative gesture and Macmillan was very conscious that a provocative act could all too easily lead to escalation. Although Cross was criticised by some for appearing to have exceeded his authority, he does appear at all times to have acted within the specific instructions of Macmillan. He acted completely within his authority in bringing the Thors to Readiness State One-Five, (fifteen minutes to launch), but this was in essence their normal state of readiness albeit that the level of alert now demanded two full crews to be on station at all times. In many ways the scenario was similar to that appertaining during the annual MAYSHOT exercises. Nonetheless, the Thors and the V-Bombers were inextricably linked. VCAS, Air Mshl Sir Edmund Hudleston, had observed that 'when the decision is made not to recall the manned bombers, we must simultaneously commit the Thor force. It is one and the same decision'.[27] Fortunately, the bombers did not even leave the ground although some of the Vulcans had crews sitting ready in the cockpits. No.77 (SM) Squadron's ORB records that 'anti-sabotage measures were taken in accordance with Feltwell Ops. Plan 6/62'. No.240 (SM) Squadron noted in its ORB that 'no specific actions [were] ordered. LE42 was being prepared for Standby on completion of [the] Training Programme. All communications equipment rechecked.'[28] Some sites evidently had the LCA continuously patrolled by an augmented Police force. Needless to say all training attempts to penetrate the sites were suspended. *Ad hoc* arrangements had to be made for extra accommodation and victualling.[29] However the Police augmentation was later relaxed and their normal shifts were re-instated at 1610hrs(Z) on the 29th, the same day that Bomber Command doubled the number of Vulcans on QRA, although these were still at just fifteen minutes' readiness. Key personnel were also recalled and the squadron OCs were on site at all times. One AO[30] remembers that the US personnel were 'all hyped up' but he was surprised that the RAF crews appeared much more relaxed about the situation:

> Actually we were doing pretty much the same as the RAF crew, watching cricket. We ate in shifts so [we had] one AO at the desk. We were in direct contact with the Command Post at Hemswell. I believe they were in contact with the 7th Air Division, who were in direct contact with SAC HQ [codenamed DROP KICK], [but a lot of that] was far up the chain [of command] from where we sat. We were the grunts.

Fifty-nine of the missiles were brought to T-15 readiness. The sixtieth missile was the one on Pad 3 at Feltwell used for training. At 1545hrs(Z) on the 28th, an order was issued to recover this pad to standby. This order was withdrawn six hours later and the pad was returned to Safe Maintenance Condition.[31] Practice countdowns were immediately suspended until further notice, since undertaking a countdown would require the missile to be recovered afterwards and therefore render it unavailable for six hours. No.102 (SM) Squadron was holding an open day for 100 visitors. The visit went ahead with a LOX demonstration and a film of a live launch, but the scheduled countdown demonstration was cancelled in view of the situation. Nonetheless, the visitors were entertained to tea before they left. Exercise RESPOND, initiated by Bomber Command to test communications, was practised on 30 October. With two full crews required to be on site at all times, the civilian Police had helped to bring back off-duty crews. Macmillan's instruction that no overt actions should be taken meant that the plan to recall Bomber Command personnel over BBC Radio could not be implemented.[32] Personnel away from home were required to advise their locations to the Guardroom, but at a time when private telephones were not the norm this meant that in some circumstances Police had to be used to locate and return personnel.[33]

With little to do other than monitor the missiles, there was time to 'think rather a lot' about what may have lain ahead. Gp Capt Roy Boast, Hemswell's Station Commander, remembered that the 'weather was lovely, making my knowledge harder to bear alone with everyone else behaving normally'.[34] The USAF Alert system differed from the RAF's and the Americans were on a higher alert status. AOs wore their War/Peace keys around their necks[35] – they were normally kept in the safe – and had to remain in their office at all times, forbidden to leave it unattended, even for routine calls of nature. They were not armed, content to rely on the security provided by the RAF Police. They had been placed on elevated alert by a fast reaction message from SAC via 3AD following Kennedy's speech. The Americans were somewhat bemused by the relatively calm way in which the British personnel reacted to their own respective elevated alert status.[36] This attitude is reflected by No.226 (SM) Squadron which, despite the tense situation, still managed to proceed unhindered with its annual families' Halloween party. A representative from the Air Ministry visited Feltwell on the 29th to interview two MSCs about resettlement problems. Nor did it seem to stop the OC of No.107 (SM) Squadron from taking leave from 27–30 October, nor the OCs of No.113 (SM) and No.98 (SM) Squadrons from taking leave during the first week of November.[37] The senior Flight Lieutenants assumed command during their absence. No.144 (SM) Squadron at North Luffenham did not even consider the crisis worthy of a mention in its ORB. But US families had made appropriate arrangements for a rapid evacuation if required. Extra currency in both dollars and sterling had been issued. One AO's wife who was due to give birth was provided with an emergency birthing kit by another AO's wife who was a nurse.[38]

With the passage of time, memories vary about what happened during those days. Most remember it as being largely uneventful, as is suggested by the ORBs, and the suspension of countdowns put the training schedule behind as a result – a matter of some inconvenience for those whose duty it was to keep the training fully up to date. RAF monthly returns did not seem to allow for the possibility of actual operations intervening! Those at the Main Base squadrons were more aware of a frisson of measured activity. The squadron ORBs do not add much detail:

> The tension caused by the Cuba situation decreased on the 5th November, [when Bomber Command reverted to Alert Condition 4 at 0940hrs(Z), but SAC remained at DEFCON 2 for a further ten days], thereby concluding a period of fourteen days during which the Squadron maintained a very high standard of immediate readiness and serviceability of its missiles.[39]

How much was known by the local populations is equally unclear, although many took the view that the Soviets could hardly attack the Thor sites without being detected and so their targets would therefore only be cities and other important infrastructures[40] – perhaps an optimistic view. In the end, Macmillan seemed prepared to use the Thors but only in a de-escalatory role.[41] He had indicated to Kennedy his willingness to immobilise the Thors to facilitate a solution to the crisis or as a way of making the removal of the Turkish Jupiters easier.[42]

Possibly as a result of this period of 'real' alert status, an order was issued advising that, from 5 November, RESPOND exercises would no longer be initiated by an Alert Condition 2 announcement.[43] The OC of No.220 (SM) Squadron, Sqn Ldr R. Henderson, at North Pickenham recorded, 'I was very pleased with the quick and enthusiastic reactions of the service and civilian members of my squadron during the initiation of the Alert 3 programme. The Operational Plan and the augmentation of duty personnel were achieved within one and a half hours of the receipt of the alert'.[44] Just a couple of weeks earlier, on 16 October, the squadron had carried out its first Operational Launch Exercise. This was the 'same as [the] Dual Propellant Flow carried out previously. However it resembles an actual launch in as much as only one missile Servicing Chief is present on the emplacement whilst the countdown is in progress'.[45] The relative ease with which the missiles could be brought to readiness compared with the V-Bombers impressed AOC No.3 Group AVM (later Air Chf Mshl Sir) Brian Burnett. The V-Bombers did achieve their target readiness times 'after many QRA practices, but it was so much easier with Thor and this and its successful penetration prospects were the great advantages of Thor'[46].

It is interesting to consider that had a launch order been given, what percentage of the Thor force would have been successfully launched? The ORBs for November show that after the return to Alert Condition 4, a number of missiles required the servicing of certain components, raising the question of their true serviceability during the Cuban crisis. The Thor Operational Performance Specification suggests a 90 per cent reliability at launch.[47] Some senior officers measured the operational efficiency of a squadron by the number of 'white lights' displayed in the Wing Operations room status panel, indicating the missile was in a 'ready' state. ORBs show that at least some squadrons saw the percentage of missiles at readiness as an important measure of their own operational efficiency. In September 1961 Catfoss proudly noted that it had held 'a missile on Standby longer than any other Driffield site'.[48] Some saw the best way of achieving this was to leave the missiles well alone and not to look for faults, but this of course could tend to disguise their true state of readiness.[49]

The crisis was resolved by a secret agreement between Kennedy and Khrushchev by which the Soviet missiles would be withdrawn with the US removing the Jupiters from Turkey as a *quid pro quo*. There were those who sought to link the withdrawal of Thor as part of the Jupiter deal – and it was possibly convenient for some not to deny this – but of course it was already in hand before the Cuban crisis arose. The Jupiter draw-down (Operation POT-PIE) was not in fact to be confirmed by Kennedy until 24 January 1963. Yet the efficiency that the Thor squadron had demonstrated during the crisis was at least recognised, as on 1 November the Chiefs of Staff were asked to make a rapid examination of the implications of a slower run-down of the missiles.[50] However the 1963/64 Defence budget anticipated a requirement for substantially increased expenditure in support of new Defence requirements and the argument for prolonging Thor was unattractive. Barely had the Soviet ships turned back from Cuba than Roy Mason, MP for Barnsley, and the Labour Party spokesman on Home Affairs, Defence and the Post Office had tabled a question for SoS(A) on when he anticipated starting to dismantle the Thor sites. AUS(A), R.C. Kent, warned that there would be considerable political difficulties to be faced if Thor was going to be retained beyond the already planned date both at home and possibly in America, too.[51] It was clear that the Americans would support only warhead costs after the five-year agreement terminated.

The Bomber Command Strategic Missile School closed on 30 November 1962. Since it had officially opened in May 1961 it had seen 699 students, had trained 187 LCOs and 327 personnel had undertaken technical courses – all without any incidents or accidents.[52] The Categorisation Flight, too, closed its doors at the end of the year. Although Air Mshl Cross had been very pleased with the way in which the Thor force had been mobilised – he was less happy with the arrangement for the rest of Bomber Command – there was little or no support for Thor outside the ranks of the RAF. VCAS, Air Mshl Hudleston, had been advised by a note from the Chiefs of Staff Committee that 'The Thor Force may prove to be militarily ineffective unless the enemy, through error, fails to destroy the weapon system'.[53] As early as 1960, AUS(A) had commented, 'I should have thought that after five years Thor would be so much of a dead duck in an operational sense that we should want to get rid of it'.[54] This had been followed up in 1962 by a letter to VCAS that 'by general consensus of opinion, Thor will become so vulnerable during the next year or two that nobody outside the Air Ministry is prepared to regard it as a serious factor in future discussions about the size of the deterrent'.[55] In Parliamentary Questions on 17 May 1961, John Cronin, MP for Loughborough, asked SoS(A) 'what steps he [was] taking to render the Thor missile sites less vulnerable to missile attack'. Julian Amery gave a splendidly terse reply, 'None Sir'.[56] Two months later, SoS(A) warned the MoD that 'The 1962 costings show that the present Defence programme, limited though it is, will require large increases in expenditure in 1963/4 and in subsequent years. We must do everything possible to contain this increase by removing from the programme anything we can do without'.[57] The Americans had also indicated that they were short of Thors, which were playing an increasingly important part in their space programme, and had asked if, on termination of the programme, some spare missiles could be quickly returned to the US. DCAS had been advised by SecAF Eugene Zuckert,[58] during a visit by the former to the US, that ten missiles were needed fairly urgently, but this was eventually to result in the discrete return of eleven missiles ahead of schedule. In fact, Zuckert may well have been under the impression that there were spare training rounds in the UK which could be sacrificed.[59] This was, of course, not the case, and there were usually only sixty-four missiles in the UK to support the front line of sixty. The RAF was not keen to take out missiles operational on LEs but there was not this number of spare missiles available, and so the eleven missiles were made up as follows:

Two spare missiles (one each from Driffield and North Luffenham).
Three from Breighton.
Three from Catfoss.
One from Carnaby.
Two from Driffield.

The missiles were airlifted back to the US between 9 October 1962 and 5 April 1963.[60]

The public announcement that the Thors would be stood down with the termination of the programme had been made in a somewhat low-key manner during Question Time in the House of Commons on 1 August 1962, a day after the Cabinet Defence Committee had agreed to the run down. In answer to a request for information on the future of the force by Patrick Gordon Walker, Labour MP for Smethwick, Minister of Defence Peter Thorneycroft advised that, 'We have decided that the arrangements under which Thor missiles are retained in this country shall be brought to an end during the course of the next year'. Cross, although aware of the ending of the Thor deployment, had been given no prior warning of the timing of the announcement and responded the following day to VCAS, AVM Sir Wallace Kyle, complaining that the announcement 'came as a complete surprise to me and the 4,000 officers and men of the Thor Missile Force'. He continued, 'Surely a force that carried out a Government policy so loyally deserves better treatment in hearing the news of its demise, than is contained in the statement by the Minister of Defence'.[61] Cross received a fulsome reply from SoS(A), Hugh Fraser:

> The Government's decision announced yesterday by the Minister of Defence, to bring to an end during the course of the next couple of years the arrangement under which Thor missiles are stationed in this country, foreshadows the close of a memorable chapter in the history of Bomber Command.
>
> I should like to take this opportunity of expressing the Air Council's appreciation of the very efficient manner in which this system has been maintained and operated by your Command on behalf of the Royal Air Force. The Air Council are also deeply appreciative of the assistance given by members of the United States Air Force who have been associated with the Royal Air Force in this operation and who must share the credit for your achievement.
>
> Thor was the first strategic ballistic missile system deployed in the free world. You may well be proud that you pioneered the introduction of these weapons into military service. The high state of readiness at which the Thor force has been maintained, the record of serviceability sustained and the success achieved with Combat Training Launches reflects the greatest credit to all concerned.

The announcement was received with mixed feelings and natural concern by the squadrons. The next Combat Training Launch, CTL-13, due to launch on 8 October, was scrubbed and the Engineering Wings noted that a missile upgrade codenamed 'Kathleen Guide' would be cancelled. There was no direct replacement for Thor and there was therefore an uncertain future for those with specialist missile skills, although many of the personnel had been earmarked by Bomber Command to be involved with the Skybolt air-launched ballistic missile (ALBM) programme to be carried by the V-Bombers. Sadly, this was another career cul-de-sac as the Skybolt program, which was experiencing an uneasy development, was about to be cancelled by the Americans.

Maintaining operational proficiency after the announcement of the stand-down of the Thor Force also presented problems. No.226 (SM) Squadron recorded in October 1962, the very month of the Cuban Missile Crisis:

> It was necessary to relieve two MSCs of missile duties as a result of their incompetence during a categorised dual exercise. After undergoing a two week period of intensive training with the Training Flight, Driffield, they were examined by the Categorisation

The Cuban Crisis and the End of Project Emily

Flight and passed as competent; subsequently rejoining the Squadron for normal watch-keeping duties on 1 December. The failure of these two MSCs to obtain a category was due in no small part to their attitude. This pin-points the possibility of spreading of a 'couldn't care less' attitude with regards to the renewal of categories now that we have entered the phasing-out of the Thor Force and will have to be watched carefully.

The original official timeline for the draw-down of the twenty bases was to be by wing, starting with the Driffield Wing on 1 April 1963 and proceeding at forty-five-day intervals with Hemswell (15 May), Feltwell (1 July) and finally North Luffenham (15 August). However, with the request for early return of missiles it was decided to draw-down Breighton first and use LE 40 as a pilot project for the other sites and to test Bomber Command's Thor Phase-out Plan, a concise four-page set of instructions issued in October 1962.[62] At 0800(Z) on 1 December 1962, missile (No.43) on 'Launch Emplacement 40 was taken out of Standby Status and dismantling commenced prior to shipment back to the United States'.[63] The missile was brought to a safe maintenance condition with all pyrotechnics removed before being taken back to Driffield the following day for return to the US. The process for the missile essentially replicated the procedures for returning missiles selected for the CTLs. Thereafter the LE itself was stripped of its equipment 'in absolutely foul weather'.[64] All fuel and LOX was decanted from the storage tanks. The generator trailers were prepared for shipment. The ancillary equipment in the shelters was removed before the prefabricated structures were dismantled. Finally, at 1300(Z) on 20 December, Launch Emplacement 40 'ceased to exist ... all equipment having been removed from the emplacement except the Liquid Oxygen tank. The dismantling having taken 13 days'.[65] Separate arrangements were implemented for the warheads but these would be off-site within two weeks of the initial dates and the AOs would depart as soon thereafter as was practical. No.82 (SM) Squadron recorded a wry comment on the job of the AOs. 'They completed a boring, thankless task with cheerfulness and conscientiousness that was an example to all. Merely holding the second key and being on the end of a telephone allowed them to complete several Educational courses.'[66] Nevertheless, many AOs thoroughly enjoyed their time in Britain and more than one sought a subsequent posting in the UK. However, their knowledge was needed in the USAF ballistic missile force in the US and a return to America was almost inevitable. The squadrons were to remain fully operational until 2359hrs on their appointed day but '[t]he site began to change its character and a lot of the friendliness and warmth went from the daily round'.[67]

The Feltwell Wing recorded 1,043 tons sent to Burtonwood for shipping to the US – 49,934lb were airlifted from Lakenheath, there were 102 trailerised items and 65 tons of general scrap was generated.[68]

Some were philosophical about the situation, even adding a heading 'Morale' in their ORB:

> Although most of the Squadron are disappointed that such a good reliable weapon is being dismantled, since most of the technicians helped to erect the pads in the first place and have been here all the time, they feel that a change from continued shifts would be a good thing. Five years, including States training, is long enough in this work. There is

no doubt that they are tackling the task of dismantling with the same vigour as when the pads were erected. They are determined to see the job through but probably are less inclined in future to volunteer for Missiles should the occasion arize.[69]

The last Douglas Thor IRBM was airlifted back to the United States on 27 September 1963.[70]

No.220 (SM) Squadron at North Pickenham, who made the claim, technically correct, in its ORB to be the first fully operational Thor unit in the Western Alliance, decided that the site would be smart and tidy to the end. In April 'all trailers, storage tanks and equipment inside the shelters were painted. The Police Land Rover was dismantled, cleaned, assembled and painted throughout'.[71]

Before their stand down procedures started, both No.223 (SM) and No.240 (SM) Squadrons held 'Families Days' on 9 June 1963 and 20 October 1962 respectively. This was to show the families, who had suffered their fair share of the inconvenience caused at times by altered shift requirements, what their husbands had been doing for the last four years. 'The weather, for once, was perfect' recorded No.223 (SM) Squadron's ORB where, after a demonstration countdown, the families were given a tour of one of the LEs before being given tea in the crew mess facility.

At the Disbandment Dinner Dance for No.113 (SM) Squadron held at Lakenheath on Tuesday 2 July 1963, Major R.E. Wolf USAF, Deputy Commander of Detachment 7, 99MMS, said that he 'regarded the past four years as wartime. Cold Wartime maybe but wartime nonetheless. The missile squadrons had played as valuable a part in the war of maintenance of peace as they had done during earlier wars'. With his fellow officers he was 'proud to have served side by side with the RAF Squadrons in an experiment in co-operation that was without parallel'.

And so ended the RAF's somewhat brief experience of operating land-based strategic ballistic missiles. It had started with limited interest in the project until the launch of Sputnik 1 changed the perception of Soviet capability and thereby the threat posed to the West. Even allowing for this, the Chiefs of Staff had discussed the IRBM at their meeting on 29 January 1958. DCOS, Lt Gen. R.W. McLeod, advised Sandys that the Chiefs were 'very concerned that we may find ourselves committed to an unsatisfactory weapon'.[72] The AOCinC Bomber Command, Air Mshl Sir Harry Broadhurst, under whose command Thor first operated, appeared little more enthusiastic about the weapon expressing no doubt an honest opinion but perhaps displaying too much candour when he described Thor in a letter to VCAS as 'a weapon of doubtful operational value which, in any case, can never be used until after our deterrent policy has failed, and we have been hit ourselves'.[73] Cross, Broadhurst's successor, was somewhat more circumspect in his Order of the Day on the announcement of the stand-down of the Thor squadrons (see below), but he knew little about Thor and had to be briefed on a one-to-one basis by the OC of No.77 (SM) Squadron – remembered as a somewhat daunting task for a mere squadron leader![74] Cross did support the continuation of Thor, but was this to promote Bomber Command's striking power in the face of the increasing vulnerability of the V-Bombers rather than a belief in the weapon in its own right? The nature of its two-key control meant that it was unlikely to be used as a first strike weapon. There was some recognition for those who had served. Sqn Ldr Stanley Baldock DFM, the first OC of No.77 (SM) Squadron and subsequently promoted to Wing Commander (Operations) at Hemswell, received the

MBE for his work on the initial phase of Project Emily, but for most the Thor experience had not enhanced their career prospects and their names did not seem to feature prominently in the post-Thor RAF.

Generally speaking, there was little ceremony during the squadrons' final days. In some cases the OC took the final shift. Perhaps displaying a certain 'late in the day' enthusiasm for Thor, Cross proposed a special facility being granted to the BBC or ITV to record the final site closure on 20 August 1963, in which he hoped for an opportunity to pay public tribute to the Thor personnel. The Air Staff had already decided in September of the previous year that a suggested Thor documentary would not be made and that the run-down would take place with minimum fuss. The advice from ACAS(Ops), AVM Denis Smallwood, to CAS was a little brusque: 'It is my view that Thor was effectively buried at the RAF Hemswell press facility and it would probably be unwise to resurrect the subject again at this late stage as such action might well invite unnecessary post mortem into the Thor programme.'[75] Some personnel had already departed to their new postings and somewhat *ad hoc* arrangements in some cases had to be made for a final squadron get-together. No.220 (SM) Squadron held a special function on 12 July, two days after the Ensign was lowered for the last time, to allow personnel to get together for the final time. It was attended by Lt Col. H.E. Ross USAF, OC Detachment 7, 99MMS.[76] They had also given an altar front and a squadron crest to North Pickenham village church. It was dedicated by the Venerable (AVM) F.W. Cooks CB QHC MA, the RAF Chaplain-in-Chief. St Andrews Church at Cavenham also benefited from a No.107 (SM) Squadron crest and an inscribed silver plate presented to the Rector, the Revd W.S. Stannard, during the Sunday service on 19 May. More formal disbandment parties were held at the Wing HQs, such as the NAAFI Horseshoe Club at North Luffenham. No.240 (SM) Squadron had held the first disbandment party at the Starlight Club at Driffield on 4 January. It was judged a success based on the erratic tracks in the snow noted at 0300(Z).[77]

The rapid progress of missile development in the US had made Thor redundant. It was visible and, therefore, vulnerable. The potential vulnerability of the IRBMs to rifle fire was demonstrated when a stray Turkish bullet (negligently discharged) severely damaged a Jupiter engine.[78] *RAF Flying Review* had sought to highlight this problem in its article published at the start of the deployment, commenting:

> In this country we suffer the handicap of having no vast land masses in which to disperse our rocket sites. They are all concentrated in a small corner of England – and experience shows that no permanent installations in a limited area can ever be said to be completely invulnerable. The possibility of sabotage, of fifth-column activities directed to nullifying the deterrent at a crucial moment, is a very real one when so much is at stake. For this reason it is comforting to know that at present only one-seventh of the total strength of Bomber Command is committed to ballistic missiles. There are still nearly nineteen thousand officers and men whose task is to keep our second deterrent at full readiness. It may well be that the mobility, accuracy and devastating power of our V-bombers will in the end prove a more effective deterrent than these slim white cylinders embedded on the 235,000 cubic yards of concrete.[79]

This statement of essentially unequivocal support for the manned bomber had many supporters within the ranks of the RAF willingly blinkered against seeing the underlying vulnerability of the V-Bombers themselves in the face of ever more sophisticated Soviet air defence. Nonetheless, Thor was also slow in preparation compared with the promising results of the new solid-fuelled rockets. Although there was a modification in the pipeline to reduce the countdown time yet further, this modification was obviously not implemented.

Most of the sites were now surplus to requirements and were sold off mainly for agricultural or industrial use. By the early twenty-first century only Feltwell and North Luffenham were still in military use. The former, still as RAF Feltwell, is used by the USAF 422nd Air Base Group, and the latter has been taken over by the Army and renamed St George's Barracks, and when visited in 2005 was occupied by the Kings Own Royal Border Regiment.

Table X: Thor sites' current use.

STATION	CURRENT USE (2007)
Feltwell	RAF Feltwell. Occupied by the USAF
Shepherds Grove	Agricultural/industrial estate
Tuddenham	Gravel pit
Mepal	Power station. Agricultural equipment auction site
North Pickenham	Turkey farm. Go-kart track
Hemswell	Agricultural/industrial estate
Caistor	Duck farm
Coleby Grange	Pig farm
Bardney	Agricultural. Poultry farm
Ludford Magna	Agricultural
Driffield	Industrial estate
Catfoss	Agricultural. Light industrial
Carnaby	Industrial estate. Agricultural
Breighton	Agricultural. Timber merchants
Full Sutton	Airfield. Prison. Agricultural/industrial estate
North Luffenham	Army. St George's Barracks
Polebrook	Agricultural
Harrington	Agricultural
Melton Mowbray	Agricultural. Light industrial
Folkingham	Agricultural

Sqn Ldr H.G. Horton, CO of No.107 (SM) Squadron, wrote to his squadron personnel:

> On the occasion of the disbanding of our Squadron I want to thank all of you who have served under me for your loyal support. In my opinion I have had the privilege of commanding one of the finest group of men ever assembled to form an RAF unit. The quality of personnel in all the Squadrons of the Feltwell Thor Complex is similar but by winning the Feltwell Launch Squadron Efficiency Competition you have confirmed my

belief that you are the best Squadron at Feltwell. I am proud to have served with you and sorry to say goodbye.[80]

Major-General Charles M. Eisenhart USAF who had succeeded Major-General Broadhurst as Commander of 7AD, summarised Project Emily as follows:

> The current phase of the Thor IRBM weapon system will terminate a reliable missile capability which has proved an extremely essential contribution to a force positive during a critical period of advanced weapon development. It will also bring to an end a highly successful joint military operation.[81]

On 19 August 1963 CAS wrote to Cross:

> The passing of the Thor Force will mark the end of a unique episode in our service history, and I could not let the occasion pass without sending this note of appreciation to all past and present members of the Force.
>
> When Thor came into service we knew that we would be faced with many new and complex technical and administrative problems and we fully expected that one of the greatest problems would be the task of maintaining morale of the officers and men allocated to the missile sites. In the event, the problems were met and solved with a degree of enthusiasm, skill and resourcefulness which was in the finest traditions of Bomber Command and the Royal Air Force.
>
> The high morale which was a feature of the Force from its inception has never flagged, and Thor's fine record of serviceability and state of readiness over the years is a remarkable tribute to the loyalty and sense of duty of all the personnel who played a part.
>
> They will be able to look back with pride on a most valuable contribution to out deterrent forces, and I would like to extend warm congratulations and sincere thanks on behalf of the Royal Air Force to all concerned.[82]

In hindsight Project Emily can be seen as a political expedient rather than a military requirement, although there was a stronger strategic rationale than the Jupiter deployment, even though advocates of the Jupiter missiles would point out that they caused the Soviet more concern than Thor did. Henry Kissinger described it as an 'added advantage rather than a military neccessity'.[83] Perhaps there was an ever-present doubt about where the Americans really stood and it was this very doubt that nurtured the recurring desire for an independent UK deterrent. No-one knew with certainty, if the moment came, how the dual key arrangement would really work. Would the dual decision process take too long? If the Americans had decided on making a pre-emptive strike on the Soviet Union would the UK have been brought into the planning process? The arguments against this on security grounds alone seem weak. Once the ICBM squadrons were formed and Polaris went to sea, the strategic balance had changed. Initially, Thor did have its supporters but they diminished as time went on, and latterly were relatively few and difficult to find outside the ranks of the two air forces. There was inevitable comparison with the V-Bombers. In the

V-Bombers' favour was the tremendous flexibility of operations, but the cost of holding the aircraft at very short readiness was prohibitive. It was a comparatively simple matter to hold the Thors at short readiness but the missile force lacked flexibility.[84] SAC was ultimately unenthusiastic in overall terms, particularly once their ICBM squadrons became operational, although SACEUR saw it as an asset to the NATO arsenal. The RAF, faced with fiscal restraint, preferred to default to a support for their V-Bombers even though these magnificent leviathans were facing their own obsolescence. It was the improving Soviet air defence capability that had led to the need for the ICBM. The bombers were forced to adopt low-level tactics. Hopes that Skybolt would reduce their vulnerability were dashed when the US summarily cancelled this missile. Consequently, it was to be the Royal Navy, with its Polaris A3-T missile system, that would assume the United Kingdom's nuclear deterrent role from midnight on 30 June 1969.

On 2 August 1962, Air Mshl Cross had written an Order of the Day to all Thor squadrons and stations:

> The decision to phase out the Thor Force of Bomber Command in no way detracts from the vital role which the force has played in the past and the significant part it will continue to play in the future, until the very last missile is withdrawn.
>
> Thor was the first strategic missile system operational in the West. At a time when the threat to this country came almost entirely from manned aircraft, you were the most formidable part of the defence of the United Kingdom, and the Western Alliance.
>
> You in Thor force have maintained a constant vigil day and night for almost four years. You have maintained a higher state of readiness in peacetime than has ever been achieved before in the history of the Armed Forces of the Crown. I am well aware of the sacrifices, so willingly accepted, that this constant readiness has imposed on the officers and men of the force.
>
> I am content that History will recognise your devoted service in the cause of peace. I know that I can rely on you for the same devotion during the rundown phase, as you have shown since the birth of the force in 1958.[85]

There seems little more to add.

Notes:
1 Robert Strange McNamara (1916–2009). McNamara was a successful business executive with an impressive record at the Ford Motor Company before being invited by President Kennedy to become the eighth US Secretary of Defense, a post he held from 1961–1968.
2 Wynn, Humphrey, *RAF Nuclear Deterrent Forces*, Fn.1, page 358.
3 TNA. AIR 2/14982. DUSI 1395, 4 February 1960.
4 W.F.2(58). Dated 9 June 1958.
5 Cmnd 366. 'Supply of Ballistic Missiles by the United States to the United Kingdom', p.3, paragraph 10.
6 This refers to a modification then being tested which would improve the response time.
7 The Douglas GAM-87A Skybolt, a two-stage solid-fuelled air-launched missile, originated

The Cuban Crisis and the End of Project Emily

in the late 1950s and was seen as an alternative way of basing the USAF ICBM force 'in the sky' as opposed to fixed identifiable silo locations. Its development proved troublesome and the programme was cancelled on 19 December 1962, somewhat perversely on the same day that a fully successful flight was finally achieved. Britain was invited to continue with the program on their own – two missiles were to be carried on pylons below the wings of the Vulcan B2s – but the uncertainties over the possible costs of this option were considered prohibitive.

8 TNA. DEFE 13/123. Letter from Air Ministry to Minister of Defence, 23 October 1961.
9 TNA. AIR 8/2307. Cabinet Defence Committee, 31 July 1962.
10 TNA. AIR 2/14947. f.143A. Loose Minute C.102741/58, 31 December 1958.
11 TNA. DEFE 13/593. f E1. Confirmed by Secretary of State John Foster Dulles, apparently on 29 January 1957 (but 29 March 1957, post-Bermuda, would somehow seem a more likely date). It is the author's belief that details of a Blue Streak-derived warhead for Thor lie within file ES/1659 retained by the AWRE at Aldermaston. Should this file ever be released, future researchers may like to verify this aspect of Thor's history.
12 TNA. DEFE 13/194. f E2. Memo from Sir Richard Powell to Minster of Defence to brief Prime Minister. RRP/664/58, 6 August 1958.
13 TNA. DEFE 13/194. f E5.
14 TNA. DEFE 13/194. f E18. Sandys was accompanied by Sir Richard Powell, Sir Frederick Brundrett, Sir Harold Caccia (Ambassador to Washington), Admiral S.J. Denny (Head of the BJSM in Washington) and D.W. Ward. The US was represented by SecDef Neil H. McElroy, SecAF Force Donald A. Quarles, General Nathan F. Twining, Chairman of the Joint Chiefs of Staff and Asst SecDef Mansfield D. Sprague.
15 TNA. AIR 8/2307. Letter VCAS to SoS. AM file:VCAS.1328.
16 Air Chief Marshal Sir George Holroyd Mills (1902–1971), Chairman of the British Joint Services Mission (BJSM) in Washington. Was AOCinC Bomber Command from 1953–1955.
17 TNA. DEFE 13/123 Letter from SoS(A) to Minister of Defence, 22 November 1961.
18 TNA. AIR 8/2307. Signal from RAF Staff Washington, AVM Reginald Emson to VCAS, 17 February 1962.
19 Hansard, Wed 5 March 1958. Col 1115.
20 TNA. DEFE 13/394. f.E8. Extract from Record of Discussion between President Eisenhower and the Prime Minister.
21 TNA. AIR 20/11371. BC/TS.89367/ONC.
22 It is perhaps worth noting that on 4 June 1962 the USAF had unsuccessfully attempted to launch a Thor with a live nuclear warhead from Launch Complex LE1 at Johnston Atoll. Codenamed BLUEGILL, the launch was part of the FISHBOWL series of nuclear tests using Thor missiles as launchers.
23 TNA. No.104 (SM) Squadron ORB, October 1962.
24 TNA. DEFE 32/7, 27 October 1962.
25 DEFCON 5: Normal peacetime readiness
DEFCON 4: Normal, increased intelligence and strengthened security measures
DEFCON 3: Increase in force readiness above normal readiness
DEFCON 2: Further increase in force readiness, but less than maximum readiness
DEFCON 1: Maximum force readiness
(From the website of the Federation of American Scientists.)
The raising of SAC to DEFCON 2 was the only time during the Cold War that this state of readiness was called for by any of the US Armed Forces.
26 TNA AIR 28/1504. Hemswell ORB, October 1962.

27 TNA. Letter from VCAS to CinCBC, 11 August 1959. Contained in AIR 20/10325.
28 TNA. No.240 (SM) Squadron ORB, October 1962.
29 TNA. No.107 (SM) Squadron ORB, October 1962.
30 Correspondence with 1Lt (later Lt Col.) Tom Hafner USAF, 2006.
31 TNA. No.77 (SM) Squadron ORB, October 1962.
32 Referred to by MRAF Sir Michael Beetham in the discussion period during the Royal Air Force Historical Society's seminar on RAF Nuclear Weapons, fully reported in the RAFHS Journal No.26, p.47.
33 Sgt Bill Roseby, based at RAF Mepal, was visiting a relative near Ely with his wife. A Police Sergeant knocked at the door and requested he return to Mepal immediately.
34 'The Ermine Link', *Journal of the RAF Hemswell Association.* Issue No.19. p.29.
35 Hafner, *Ibid.*
36 Correspondence with Major (later Col.) Doug Ray USAF. 2006.
37 TNA. No.113 (SM) and No.98 (SM) Squadrons ORBs, November 1962.
38 Hafner. *Ibid.*
39 TNA. No.106 Squadron ORB, November 1962.
40 Correspondence with Peter Rich, June 2007.
41 Twigge, Stephen and Scott, Len, *The Other Other Missiles of October: The Thor IRBMs and the Cuban Missile Crisis.*
42 Nash, Philip, *The Other Missiles of October,* p.140.
43 TNA. No.106 Squadron ORB, November 1962.
44 TNA. No.220 (SM) Squadron ORB, October 1962.
45 *Ibid.*
46 Correspondence with ACM Sir Brian K. Burnett GCB, DFC, AFC. April 2007.
47 TNA. AIR 20/10620. 7AD C-7584.
48 TNA. No.226 (SM) Squadron ORB, September 1961.
49 Discussion with Sqn Ldr Ken Hayes, October 2006.
50 TNA. AIR 8/2307. Loose Minute from E.F.C. Stanford, Head of S.6 to PS SoS. BF.1746/S.6.
51 TNA. AIR 20/11371. Note by VCAS for the Chiefs of Staff Committee, October 1962.
52 TNA. AIR 28/1501, November 1962.
53 TNA. Letter from R.C. Kent. DUSI/1395, 12 February 1960.
54 TNA. AIR 8/2307. Loose Minute from E.F.C. Stanford, Head of S.6 to PS SoS. BF.1746/S.6.
55 TNA. AIR 20/11371. Letter from AUS(A) to VCAS, 9 March 1962. AM File: AUS(A) 6955.
56 Hansard. 17 May 1961, Col1366.
57 TNA. AIR 20/11371. Letter SoS(A) to MoD. 23 May 1962.
58 Eugene (Gene) M. Zuckert (1911–2000) was the seventh US Secretary of the Air Force.
59 TNA. AIR 8/2307. Draft memo CAS.2937. Not sent.
60 TNA. No.220 (SM) Squadron ORB, October 1962.
61 TNA. AIR 20/11371. Letter from Air Mshl Cross to AVM Kyle, 2 August 1962.
62 Wynn. *Ibid.* p.361.
63 *Ibid.* p.361.
64 TNA. AIR 27/3003. No.240 (SM) Squadron ORB, December 1962.
65 *Ibid.*
66 TNA. AIR 27/2954. No.82 (SM) Squadron ORB, July 1963.
67 The Royal Air Force Museum. No.226 (SM) Squadron F540.

68 TNA. AIR 28/1501. Feltwell ORB.
69 TNA. AIR 27/2954. No.82 (SM) Squadron ORB, July 1963.
70 Wynn. *Ibid.* p.362.
71 TNA. No.220 (SM) Squadron ORB.
72 TNA. DEFE 13/594 f.E6
73 TNA. Letter from AOCinC Bomber Command to VCAS, 10 March 1959. BC/S.91560/CinC contained in AIR 20/10325.
74 Conversation with Sqn Ldr Ken Hayes, October 2006.
75 TNA. AIR 8/2307. Loose Minute ACAS(Ops) to CAS, 7 July 1963. AM File: F.90/10/Ops.8088.
76 TNA. No.220 (SM) Sqadron ORB, July 1963.
77 TNA. AIR 27/3003. No.240 (SM) Squadron ORB, January 1963.
78 Nash. *Ibid.* p.102.
79 *RAF Flying Review*. Vol.XV, No.8.
80 TNA. No.107 (SM) Squadron ORB, July 1963. The Trophy for the Efficiency Competition referred to took the form of a silver 5in THOR missile on a 5IN black wooden plinth. It had been presented to the squadron in June by ACM Sir Brian Burnett, OC No.1 Group. It was retained in the squadron silver. The missile unscrewed into two parts and inside was a vellum scroll bearing the names of all the squadron personnel as at the date of the presentation.
81 TNA. AIR 27/2954. No.82 (SM) Squadron ORB, July 1963.
82 TNA. AIR 8/2307. f.909/7.
83 Armacost, Michael H., *The Politics of Weapons Innovation: The Thor-Jupiter Controversy*, p.208.
84 TNA. AIR 2/14908. Letter from AOCinC Bomber Command to DCAS, 12 December 1958.
85 The SSBN HMS *Resolution* had left the Clyde Submarine Base at Faslane on 14 June en route to starting the first Royal Navy Polaris Patrol.
86 Appendix to No.226 (SM) Squadron F540, August 1962.

APPENDIX 1

From file DCAS 1383/58: Air Mshl Tuttle to SoS, 1 April 1958.

This chart shows the total number of city targets that could be reached by missiles of ranges 1,000nm to 2,000+nm. Moscow (range 1,350nm) was considered an essential target. The very significant increase in target coverage between 1,300nm and 1,400nm is evident. At a 1,500nm range, just under half the desired targets could be reached but these represented 60 per cent of the most important targets.

Available Range (nautical miles)	Total City Target Coverage	Twenty Most Important Targets	Forty Most Important Targets	Sixty Most Important Targets
1,000	7 (6%)	3 (15%)	6 (15%)	7 (12%)
1,100	12 (9%)	4 (20%)	7 (18%)	9 (15%)
1,200	17 (13%)	5 (25%)	9 (23%)	14 (23%)
1,300	25 (19%)	6 (30%)	11 (28%)	20 (33%)
1,400	46 (35%)	10 (50%)	17 (43%)	31 (50%)
1,500	64 (49%)	12 (60%)	23 (58%)	40 (60%)
1,600	72 (55%)	13 (65%)	26 (65%)	45 (75%)
1,700	77 (58%)	14 (70%)	28 (72%)	47 (78%)
1,800	79 (60%)	16 (80%)	30 (75%)	49 (82%)
1,900	85 (65%)	17 (85%)	32 (80%)	52 (87%)
2,000	91 (70%)	18 (90%)	37 (92%)	57 (95%)
2,000+	131 (100%)	20 (100%)	40 (100%)	60 (100%)

APPENDIX 2

RAF Thor* Launches at Vandenberg AFB.

Serial	Pad	Date	Codename	Comments
T151	75-1-1	16 December 1958	Tune Up	First Operational Thor Launch – Success. USAF Crew
T161	75-2-8	16 April 1959	Lions Roar	IWST-1. First RAF launch – Success

Appendices

T191	75-2-7	16 June 1959	Rifle Shot	IWST-2. Safety pins not removed from vernier engines so there was no signal to initiate pitch. RSO destruct at T+105 secs
T175	75-1-1	3 August 1959	Bean Ball	IWST-3. Success
T190	75-2-6	14 August 1959	Short Skip	IWST-4. Failure due to inadvertent fuel depletion
T228	75-1-2	17 September 1959	Grease Gun	IWST-5. Partial success – Warhead off target
T239	75-2-8	6 October 1959	Foreign Travel	CTL-1. Feltwell Wing. Success
T220	75-1-1	21 October 1959	Stand Fast	IWST-6. Success
T181	75-1-2	12 November 1959	Beach Buggy	IWST-7. Success
T265	75-1-1	2 December 1959	Hard Right	CTL-2. Hemswell Wing. Success
T185	75-1-2	15 December 1959	Tall Girl	IWST-8. Success
T215	75-1-2	21 January 1960	Red Caboose	IWST-9. Success – Last IWST
T272	75-2-8	2 March 1960	Center Board	CTL-3. Feltwell Wing. Success
T233	75-2-7	22 June 1960	Clan Chattan	CTL-4. Driffield Wing. Success First missile from UK Stock. No.102 (SM) Squadron.
T186	75-2-8	11 October 1960	Left Rudder	CTL-5. Hemswell Wing. Success
T267	75-2-8	13 Dec 1960	Acton Town	CTL-6. North Luffenham Wing. Success †
T243	75-2-7	30 March 1961	Shepherds Bush	CTL-7. Driffield Wing. Success First FAST countdown. No.98 (SM) Squadron.
T276	75-2-7	20 June 1961††	White Bishop	CTL-8. North Luffenham Wing. Success
T165	LE-7	6 September 1961	Skye Boat	CTL-9. Feltwell Wing. Success
T214	LE-8	6 December 1961	Pipers Delight	CTL-10. Hemswell Wing. Success
T229	LE-7	19 March 1962	Black Knife	CTL-11. Driffield Wing. Failure. RSO destruct at T+26 secs. No.102 (SM) Squadron.
T269	LE-8	19 June 1962	Blazing Cinders	CTL-12. North Luffenham Wing. Success
T 211		8 October 1962		Cancelled following announcement of draw-down of Thor programme

* All the Thors were designated DM-18 (single-stage launch vehicle).
† The Thor used for this launch was an RAF missile that had been inadvertently fuelled in the horizontal position and could not therefore be used as a live round.
†† From this date all CTLs were undertaken solely by RAF personnel.
Note: A launch scheduled for 22 May 1959 was cancelled three seconds before ignition.
Launch dates can sometimes vary by a day depending on whether UK or US time is used.

APPENDIX 3

SENIOR RAF/7AD APPOINTMENTS DURING THE THOR ERA

THE AIR COUNCIL
Chief of the Air Staff (CAS)   Date of Appointment
Air Chief Marshal Sir Dermot Boyle   1 January 1956
Air Chief Marshal Sir Thomas Pike   1 January 1960

Deputy Chief of the Air Staff (DCAS)   Date of Appointment
Air Marshal Sir Geoffrey Tuttle   4 July 1956
Air Marshal Sir Charles Elworthy   15 November 1959
Air Marshal Sir Ronald Lees   18 July 1960
Air Marshal Sir Christopher Hartley   5 June 1963

Vice Chief of the Air Staff (VCAS)   Date of Appointment
Air Marshal Sir Edmund Hudleston★   16 September 1957
Air Marshal Sir Wallace Kyle   2 March 1962

RAF BOMBER COMMAND
AOCinC   Date of Appointment
Air Marshal Sir Harry Broadhurst   22 January 1956
Air Marshal Sir Kenneth Cross   20 May 1959

No.1 Group
AOCs   Date of Appointment
Air Vice-Marshal G.A. Walker   3 October 1956
Air Vice-Marshal J.G. Davis   14 June 1959
Air Vice-Marshal P.H. Dunn   1 December 1961

No.3 Group
AOCs   Date of Appointment
Air Vice-Marshal K.B.B. Cross   2 February 1956
Air Vice-Marshal M.H. Dwyer   4 May 1959
Air Vice-Marshal B.K. Burnett   9 October 1961

★ Air Chief Marshal from 1 January 1961.
For Individual Squadron Commands, see: Wynn, *RAF Nuclear Deterrent Forces*, p. 569.

SEVENTH AIR DIVISION UNITED STATES AIR FORCE

Commanders   Date of Appointment
Major-General William H. Blanchard   25 February 1957
Major-General Charles B. Westover   19 January 1960
Major-General Edwin B. Broadhurst   1 August 1961
Major-General Charles M. Eisenhart   18 September 1962

APPENDIX 4

Missile Comparisons

	A-4 V-2	JUPITER SM-78	THOR SM-75	BLUE STREAK	ATLAS-D
Type	MRBM	IRBM	IRBM	MRBM	ICBM
Country	Germany	US	US	UK	US
Main Contractor	German Army	Chrysler	Douglas	de Havilland	Convair
Length	44.7'	58' 0"	64' 10"	61' 6"	75' 1"
Diameter	51.5'	8' 9"	8' 0"	9' 0"	10' 0"
Launch Weight	28,200lb	103,000lb	109,330lb	199,000lb	255,000lb
Empty Weight	8,000lb	12,590lb	13,500lb		11,895lb
Thrust	60,690lbf	150,000lbf	150,000lbf	150,000lbf	422,800lbf
Engine	Model 39	Rocketdyne MB-3	Rocketdyne MB-3	Rolls Royce RZ2	Rocketdyne LR105, LR89 & LR101
Guidance	Gyro-scopic	All inertial	All inertial	All inertial	All inertial
Re-entry Vehicle	N/A	Goodyear	Mk 2		Mk 4
Warhead	Conventional	W-49, 1.44MT	W-49, 1.44MT	Red Snow, 420KT?	W-38, 4MT
Warhead Weight	1,650lb	3,500lb	3,500lb		3,080lb
Range	200m	1,500nm	1,500nm	2,500nm	7,500nm
Apogee	52m	380m	300m		790m
Accuracy	Variable	2nm	2nm		2nm

APPENDIX 5

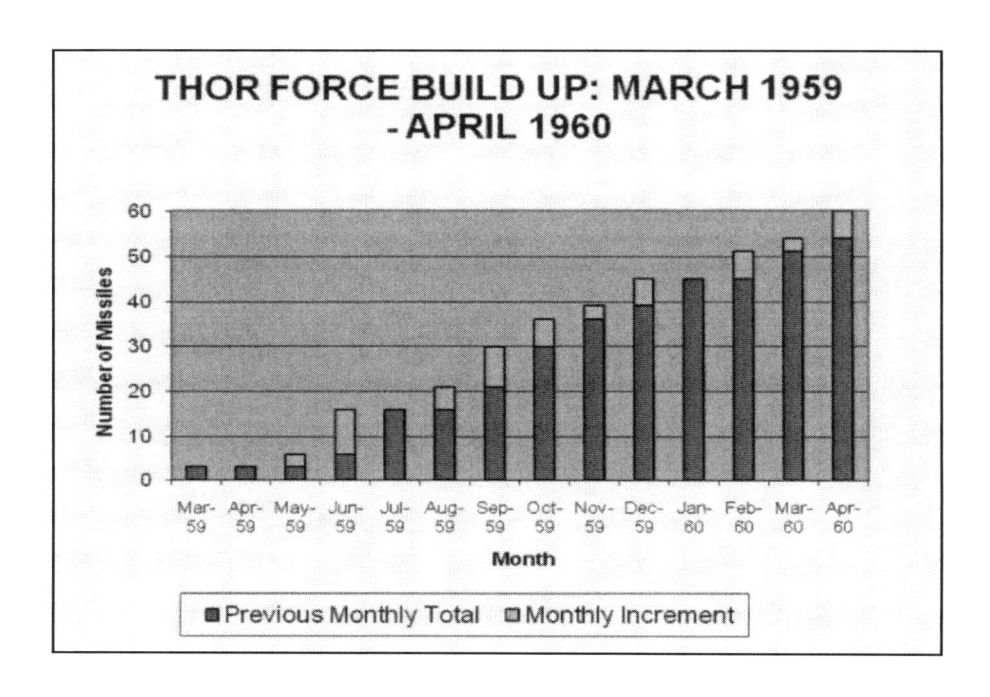

THOR FORCE BUILD UP: MARCH 1959 - APRIL 1960

APPENDIX 6

The Thor bases and squadrons

Site	Squadron	From	To	NGR
FELTWELL	No.77 (SM) Squadron	1 September 58	10 July 63	TL7189
Shepherds Grove	No.82 (SM) Squadron	22 July 59	10 July 63	TL9972
Tuddenham	No.107 (SM) Squadron	22 July 59	10 July 63	TL7671
Mepal	No.113 (SM) Squadron	22 July 59	10 July 63	TL4379

Appendices

North Pickenham	No 220(SM) Sqn	22 July 59	10 July 63	TF8506
Airhead: Lakenheath				
HEMSWELL	No.97 (SM) Squadron	1 December 58	24 May 63	SK9490
Caistor	No.269 (SM) Squadron	22 July 59	24 May 63	TA0802
Ludford Magna	No.104 (SM) Squadron	22 July 59	24 May 63	TF2088
Coleby Grange	No.142 (SM) Squadron	22 July 59	24 May 63	TF0060
Bardney	No.106 (SM) Squadron	22 July 59	24 May 63	TF1471
Airhead: Scampton				
DRIFFIELD	No.98 (SM) Squadron	1 August 59	18 April 63	SE9956
Full Sutton	No.102 (SM) Squadron	1 August 59	27 April 63	SE7454
Carnaby	No.150 (SM) Squadron	1 August 59	9 April 63	TA1464
Catfoss	No.226 (SM) Squadron	1 August 59	9 March 63	TA1348
Breighton	No.240 (SM) Squadron	1 August 59	8 January 63	SE7134
Airhead: Leconfield				
NORTH LUFFENHAM	No.144 (SM) Squadron	1 December 59	23 August 63	SK9404
Polebrook	No.130 (SM) Squadron	1 December 59	23 August 63	TL0986
Folkingham	No.223 (SM) Squadron	1 December 59	23 August 63	TF0430
Harrington	No.218 (SM) Squadron	1 December 59	23 August 63	SP7777
Melton Mowbray	No.254 (SM) Squadron	1 December 59	23 August 63	SK4715
Airhead: Cottesmore				

APPENDIX 7

The UK Thors

Missile Serial	Date of Launch	Type of Launch	Comments
161	16 April 1959	IWST1	Range 1,420nm, no pitch
191	16 June 1959	IWST2	
175	3 August 1959	IWST3	
190	14 August 1959	IWST4	
228	17 September 1959	IWST5	
239	6 October 1959	CTL1	
220	21 October 1959	IWST6	
181	12 November 1959	IWST7	
265	1 December 1959	CTL2	
185	14 December 1959	IWST8	Failure – CEA malfunction
215	21 January 1960	IWST9	
272	2 March 1960	CTL3	
233	22 June 1960	CTL4	
186	11 October 1960	CTL5	
267	13 December 1960	CTL6	
243	29 March 1961	CTL7	
276	21 June 1961	CTL8	
165	6 September 1961	CTL9	
214	5 December 1961	CTL10	
229	19 March 1962	CTL11	Failure of pitch programme
269	18 June 1962	CTL12	

Other operational missiles:

First Missile delivered: No.139

147	150	152	153	155	157	159	166	167
169	171	172	173	180	182	183	188	195
196	197	201	205	207	209	210	211	213
224	225	227	236	240	242	247	248	260
251	252	260	266	268	273	274	275	277
278	279	280	282	284	285	287	288	289
290	291	292	294	299	304	306		

APPENDIX 8

NO.4 G.D. BALLISTIC MISSILE COURSE SYLLABUS (20 April–8 May 1959)

Introduction (five hours).
  Introduction to the Course.
  Introduction to Ballistic Missile Operations.
  Introduction to the Ballistic Missile.
    A typical missile and its sub-assemblies; the airframe, propulsion bay;
    tank section and fuel, feed systems, guidance bay, nose cone and
    warhead, control systems.
  Films
    The A.4 Rocket.
    Introduction to the Thor Weapons System.
  Demonstration Room
    Inspection of missiles and discussion.
Ballistic Trajectories (three hours).
    The theory of the optimum vacuum ballistic trajectory.
Actual trajectories; choice of cut-off point, climb angle and velocity at cut-off and climb path.
High, medium and low trajectories.
  Error Theory (three hours)
    Elements of probability, independent and mutually exclusive elements
    Statistics, The Gaussian distribution.
  The combination of errors. Linear and radial errors. Significance of probability level.
  Airframe and Aerodynamics (four hours).
    Aerodynamics.
Definitions. Differences between sub-sonic and supersonic flow. Significance of the speed of sound. The Mach cone and shock waves.
  Compressive and expansive corners. Prandtl-Meyer expansion. Control effects and problems. Aerofoil sections and planforms.
      Hypersonic aerodynamics and slip flow. Superaerodynamics.
    Airframes.
      The effect of various parameters on the missile weight and structure
      Methods of construction of rigid and pressurised structures.
  Propulsion (eleven hours).
    Rocket propulsion.
  Rocket propulsion theory. Laws of reaction propulsion. Thermal efficiency. Comparison of various methods of propulsion.
Gas conditions in a nozzle, convergent-divergent nozzles. Stagnation temperature, pressure and Mach number.
Total impulse, specific impulse, expansion ratio, critical pressure ratio, effective efflux velocity.
  Cooling problems.
Rocket Fuels.
Liquid fuels including handling risks.
Solid fuel and typical solid fuel motors.
Assessment of the advantages and disadvantages of liquid and solid fuels. Fuel feed systems.
Visit to RAE Westcott.
A typical liquid fuel rocket and its design problems.
Rocket motor testing practice.

Demonstrations.
Guidance (eleven hours).
Radar Guidance.
Introduction to ballistic missile guidance problems.
Stable platforms and Schuler tuning.
Corrections, components and errors.
Pure inertial systems.
Monitored inertial systems.
Inertial Guidance.
Application of inertial guidance to ballistic missiles.
The stable platform; choice of axes and reference frames and their effect on platform design and component requirements.
Pre-computed guidance computers.
Setting up problems.
Error analysis.
Nose Cone and Warhead (eleven hours).
Nose Cone.
   Object and roles in life. General re-entry problems. Aerodynamic heating.
   Surface temperatures and rates of heat input, possible methods of dealing with these.
   Effects of temperature on material strengths, assessment of suitable materials for use as heat sink and eroding heads.
   Construction of nose cones, present and future methods. Advantages and disadvantages of heat sink and eroding heads.
The Enemy's Defence Problem.
Warhead.
   Evolution of Nuclear Weapons. Part I Theory, Part II Weapons.
   Nuclear Weapons Effects.
   Target Coverage and Weapons Effects.
Arming and Fusing.
   Arming theory, methods of pre-launch and post-launch arming. Fusing.
Control (six hours).
Servo Theory.
   Outline of the theory and use of servo-mechanisms.
Control Systems.
   Methods of control during the boost phase, with particular reference to jet vanes and swivelling combustion chambers.
   Separation problems.
   Methods of control during the ballistic and re-entry phase, with particular reference to pneumatic and bonker systems.
Russian Ballistic Missiles (one hour).
   Russian ballistic missile development. The satellites and their significance.
Thor Weapon System (five hours).
   Introduction to the System.
   USAF Ballistic Missile Organisation.
   Use of Thor by the RAF.
   Forum.
RAF Ballistic Missile Program (two hours).
   Blue Streak: its deployment and future development.
Syndicate Study (five hours).
Administrative Briefing (one hour).
   Administration and other matters in USA.
Conference and Preparation (two hours).
Preparation for final course conference.
Course Conference.

APPENDIX 9

THOR MAJOR INCIDENTS
HUMAN ERROR
23/9/59   Hemswell
700 gallons of fuel loaded into missile tank. Faulty operation of a poorly lubricated valve
1/6/60   Shepherds Grove
Tech tested suspected electrical failure in missile shelter by moving shelter towards erect missile. Electrical fault confirmed and shelter crashed into missile.
15/6/60   Feltwell
Training RV battery activated by faulty operator procedure.
14/10/60   Caistor – Pad 24
Missile erector failed to neutralise after erection and pulled downwards against the locked missile. Faulty adjustment of hydraulic actuator.
14/10/60   Polebrook – Pad 54
Shelter removed manually before workstands were stowed. Extensive damage to workstands, theodolites and collimator. Slight skin damage to missile.
7/12/60   Ludford Magna – Pad 28
7,000 galls LOX released through engine onto pad during propellant flow exercise. Main LOX valve opened because status switch was in wrong position.
23/6/61   Tuddenham
Circuit breaker opened in error. Cut power to guidance system. Damaged gyros.
17/8/61   Harrington – Pad 50
Fuel into missile because storage tank pressurising valve was opened inadvertently.
2/9/61   Tuddenham – Pad 8
Fuel into missile because of faulty non-return valve. Primary cause over-pressurisation of main storage tank.
6/11/61   Melton Mowbray – Pad 56
Trichloroethylene supply hose connected to wrong inlet during Flush and Purge procedure. 30 gallons of hot trichloroethylene forced into missile plumbing. Engine had to be removed and returned to USA.
31/1/62   Shepherds Grove – Pad 6
Driver moved a nitrogen trailer which was still connected to the emplacement pneumatic system.
14/6/62   Caistor – Pad 24
Umbilical plate release cable left connected. Trailing plate tangled with erector which dragged plate from missile during erector lowering.
18/8/62   Carnaby – Pad 38
Launch crew failed to remove pyrotechnics from an operational flight safety switch check. Both retro-rockets and all three RV latch squibs fired. (Missile 150)
31/12/62   Folkingham – Pad 58
Split found in main engine thrust chamber. Probably caused by careless use of screwdriver.

PYROTECHNIC FAILURES
2/4/60   Shepherds Grove – Pad 6
Gas generator igniter found discharged.
9/8/60   Driffield
RV latch squib found discharged. Safety pin broken.
14/8/60   Driffield
Vernier engine igniter found discharged.
18/8/60   Hemswell

Gas generator igniter found discharged.
24/8/60   North Luffenham
Vernier engine igniter found discharged.
28/9/60   Bardney
RV latch squib found discharged.
29/9/60   Hemswell
RV latch squib found discharged.
5/6/61   Driffield
RV latch squib found discharged.
3/7/61   Coleby Grange
RV latch squib found discharged.
20/6/62   Coleby Grange – Pad 27
Lower retro-rocket ignited. Bent connector caused short circuit.

TECHNICAL FAILURES
4/6/59   Feltwell Pad 3
Missile erection commenced inside shelter causing slight damage to RV. Electrical failure.
25/8/59   Feltwell
Missile erection commenced inside shelter. No damage. Electrical failure.
18/2/60   Feltwell
Missile erection commenced inside shelter causing slight damage to RV. Electrical failure.
27/9/60   Shepherds Grove – Pad 5
Chain bucket fell from shelter hoist. Retaining bolt sheared. No damage.
28/1/61   Full Sutton – Pad 43
Hydraulic Pumping Unit started involuntarily and missile erection started inside shelter. No damage.
14/2/61   Hemswell
Umbilical Mast Latch Hook released through interference between pivot and washer.
6/3/61   Carnaby
Heat exchanger on tanker exploded during LOX replen. Caused fierce fire. Prompt action limited damage to H/E.
21/6/61   Catfoss
Sticking regulator caused excessive pneumatic pressure in propellant transfer system which blew off the tops of the fuel and LOX loading valves.
8/12/61   North Pickenham
Short-circuit in a generator van caused a battery to overheat and split.
12/12/61 Driffield – Pad 32
Shelter failed to revert to slow speed during closure and struck free standing wall. Electrical failure.
2/1/62   Full Sutton – Pad 43
Shelter failed to revert to slow speed during closure and struck free standing wall. Electrical failure.
28/2/62   North Pickenham – Pad 15
Shelter failed to revert to slow speed during opening. Electrical failure.
6/3/62   Feltwell – Pad 1
Shelter moved to high speed when being closed manually and struck free-standing wall. Electrical failure.
22/8/62   Tuddenham – Pad 9
Electrical failure caused c/d ex to go beyond the normal hold point. LCO applied manual stop switch.
27/9/62   Tuddenham – Pad 9. 1040Z
The FST pressurisation line failed to the rear of the high pressure pneumatic line which fractured and caused damage to LE plumbing.
7/11/62   Hemswell – RIM
High pressure pneumatic hose failed during tests. Test chamber broke free from its mountings and broke a technician's leg.

BIBLIOGRAPHY

Selected References
Periodicals/Miscellaneous Papers:
Airfield Focus, Nos 32, 47, 48, 54, 59.
Airfield Review, December 2004. pp.170,171.
Airview News: Final Edition, Douglas Aircraft Co. 1960.
Ermine Link, The, Nos 11,13,14,19.
Flight, 5 December 1958.
Flypast, April 2000. pp. 36,37.
Journal of the Royal Air Force Historical Society, Vols 26, 30 and 42.
Meccano Magazine, Vol.XIV No.5, May 1960 pp. 228/9.
Miscellaneous Papers of Wing Commander E.R.G. Haines RAF.
RAF Flying Review, Now: The RAF's Missile Force. Vol.XV No.8.
Rocket Review, Vol.1, No 1. RAF Feltwell April 1959.
Rocketry at Rolls-Royce, Rolls-Royce Limited, Derby. Undated.
Thor-Delta Launches: 1957–2004, compiled by Peter Hunter, Sydney, Australia.

Books:
Armacost, Michael H., *The Politics of Weapons Innovation – The Thor-Jupiter Controversy*, Columbia University Press, New York and London. 1969.
Campbell, Duncan, *The Unsinkable Aircraft Carrier*, Michael Joseph, London. 1984.
Cocroft, Wayne D. and Thomas, Roger J.C., *Cold War*, English Heritage. 2003.
Dobinson, C.S., *Twentieth Century Fortifications in England*. Vol.XI.1. Council for British Archeology. 1998.
Gavin, Lt Col. James., *War and Peace in the Space Age*, Hutchinson & Co., London. 1959.
Gibson, James N., *The Navaho Missile Project*, Schiffer Publishing. 1996.
Gibson, James N., *Nuclear Weapons of the United States. An Illustrated History*, Schiffer Publishing Ltd. 1966.
Hansen, Chuck, *U.S. Nuclear Weapons – The Secret History*, Orion Books, New York. 1988.
Hartt, Julian, *The Mighty Thor*, Duell Sloan and Pearce, New York. 1961.
Lonnquest, John C. and Winkler, David F., *To Defend and Deter: The Legacy of the United States Cold War Missile Program*, USACERL Special Report 97/01. November 1996.
Menaul, Stewart, *Countdown – Britain's Strategic Nuclear Forces*, Robert Hale, London, 1980.
Millis, Walter (editor)., *The Forrestal Diaries*, Viking Press, New York. 1951.
Moyes, Philip, *Bomber Squadrons of the RAF and their Aircraft*, Macdonald & Co. 1964.
Nash, Philip, *The Other Missiles of October*, The University of North Carolina Press. 1997.
Neufeld, Jacob, *The Development of Ballistic Missiles in the United States Air Force 1945–1960*, University Press of the Pacific, Honolulu, Hawaii.
Simmons, Geoff and Abraham, Barry. *Strong Foundations: Driffield's Aerodrome from 1917 to 2000*, Hutton Press Ltd, 2001.
Twigge, Stephen and Scott, Len, *The Other Other Missiles of October: The Thor IRBMs and the Cuban Missile Crisis*, Institute of Historical Research, Electronic Journal of Interational History, Article 3, June 2000.
Wynn, Humphrey, *RAF Nuclear Deterrent Forces*, The Stationery Office, London. 1994.

INDEX

Achille Lauro 124
AC Spark Plug 30, 41, 100, 114, 117
Aeroflot 88
Aeroplane, The 94, 98
Aircraft
  B-36 Peacemaker 17
  B-47 Stratojet 17
  B-52 Stratofortress 17
  B-58 Hustler 17, 37
  C-124 Globemaster II 29, 40
  C-133 Cargomaster 29, 65
  C-46 Commando 100, 124
  C-47 79
  CF-105 Arrow 67
  F-100 Super Sabre 123
  F-106 Delta Dart 45
  Halifax 14
  Lancaster 14
  Proctor 107
  Stirling 14
  Super DC-7C 124
  Tu-16 Badger 97
  Tu-104 Camel 88, 97
  Valiant 69, 70
  Victor 69, 70, 129
  Vulcan 36, 59, 69, 70, 129, 132, 143
Amery, J. 121, 135
Arrowsmith, P. 109, 123

Bannister, K.D. 72
Barnwell Manor 62
BBC 107, 132, 139
Bermuda Conference 46, 47, 50, 143
Bishop, F. 52
Blackburn Aircraft Co 61
Boeing 37
Boyesen, J. 52
Broadbent, E. 53, 69, 96
BROKEN ARROW 95
Bromberg, J.L. 28
Brown, G.A. 53
Burke, Admiral A.A. 20

Caccia, Sir H. 51, 54, 143
Cameron, Maj Gen A.M. 15
Chetwynd, G. 55
Combat Training Launch (CTL) 10, 96, 101–103, 111, 116, 117, 124, 136, 137, 147, 152
Convair Division of General Dynamics 17, 23, 27, 35, 37, 45, 149
Cooke AFB 50, 51, 99
CND 6, 10, 56, 82, 94, 108, 109, 112, 113, 123

Daily Express, The 87, 89, 94
Daily Mail, The 79
Daily Telegraph, The 53, 85
Daily Worker, The 52
de Freitas, G. 55, 131

de Gaulle, President C. 70
de Havilland 47, 97, 130, 149
de Zulueta, P. 97
Direct Action Committee Against Nuclear War 82, 08, 109
D-Notice 52, 87–90, 94, 96
Dornberger, Gen W.R. 13–16
Douglas Aircraft Company 10, 27–29, 40, 42, 46, 48, 51, 52, 54, 65, 71, 77, 79, 80, 87, 93, 94, 99–102, 105, 108, 114, 120
Douglas, D.Jr 28, 93, 108
Duke of Gloucester 62
Dulles, J.F. 130, 143

Eastern Daily Press, The 85
Eden, Prime Minister A. 46
Eisenhower, President D.D. 20, 24, 25, 27, 36–38, 45, 47, 50, 51, 53, 67, 68, 143
Empire News 122
Ermine Link, The 125, 128, 141
Exercises
  JACK 119
  JILL 119
  MICKY FINN 131
  MAYSHOT 112, 118, 119, 127, 132
  MAYFLIGHT 127
  NIGHTCHECK 119
  TRIPLOX 118
  RECLAIM 119
  REDOUBLE 119, 120
  RESPOND 108, 119, 132, 133

Fleming, Rt Rev W. 109
Flight 84, 94, 98
FORTNUM 95
Fraser, H. 136
Fuchs, K. 18, 35, 68

Gardiner-Hill, Capt R.C. 63
Gardner, T. 25, 26, 37
Gates, T.S. 96, 101
General Motors 30, 36
Glenn L Martin 22, 27, 28, 37, 39, 99
Green, A. 127, 128
Green, Rev D.C. 109
Godfrey, H 85
Guest Keen Iron & Steel Ltd 74

Hanson, D. 85
Harrison, J. 55
Head, A. 46
Hemswell Dramatic Society 114
Henderson, C. 22
Holifield, C. 108
Hudson, P.J. 97
Hughes, E. 53

IBRAHIM II 9
Isle de France 124
Independent, The 127
Integrated Weapons System Training (IWST) 10, 96, 101, 102, 117, 146, 147, 152

Kent, R.C. 96, 134, 144
Key West Agreement 18
Killian, J.R.Jr 20, 26, 37
Korean War 18, 24, 40, 44
Korolev, S.P. 31, 33, 38
Khrushchev, Premier N.S. 32, 44, 131, 134

Los Alamos Scientific Laboratory 10, 18, 35, 68
Lloyd, S. 88
Lynford Hall 79, 85

MacMahon Act 55
Macmillan, Prime Minister H. 9, 46, 47, 52, 53, 67, 68, 87–89, 93–95, 131–133
McNamara, R.S. 129, 142
MARCO 95
Maydon, S 53
McElroy, N.H. 31, 38, 52, 54, 69, 143
McLeod, Lt Gen R.W. 138
Medaris, Maj-Gen J.B. 21
Missiles/Launchers
  A9/A10 15, 33
  Atlas 12, 23–29, 36, 37, 44, 46, 83, 95, 129, 149
  Bloodhound/SAGW 12, 59, 63, 70, 114
  Blue Streak 12, 37, 47, 48, 59, 60, 68, 109, 129, 130, 143, 149, 154
  Corporal 35, 45, 67, 112
  JB-2 Loon 17
  Jupiter 9, 12, 20, 21, 23, 26, 27–30, 36, 41, 44, 45, 46, 48, 51, 52, 59, 60, 70, 83, 108, 129, 133, 134, 139, 141, 145, 149
  Matador 22, 39, 40, 44, 51, 99
  Mace 30
  Minuteman 12, 24, 37, 129
  Navaho 19, 25, 29, 34, 36
  Polaris 22, 34, 130, 141, 142, 145
  Redstone 18–22, 31
  Regulus II 30
  Skybolt 15, 129, 136, 142
  SS-3 Shyster 32
  Thorad 130
  Titan 12, 24, 26, 28, 37, 42, 129
  V-1 14, 17, 34
  V-2/A-4 13–17, 19, 23, 30, 32, 33, 40, 43, 67, 149
  Vanguard 22, 34, 41, 44
Molson. H. 59, 70

Index

Moscow 74, 88, 116, 146
Muggeridge, M. 124

NATO 6, 23, 24, 32, 39, 47, 52, 60, 70, 108, 117, 130, 142
New York Times, The 37, 54
Nordhausen 14, 15, 18, 33, 35
Norton AFB 82, 120

Oberth, Dr H. 20
Omaha (SAC HQ) 80, 103
Operations
  BACKFIRE 15, 16, 33, 34
  CONSOLIDATE 116
  OVERCAST 15
  PAPERCLIP 15
  PINGUIN 32
  POT-PIE 134
Orr-Ewing, C.I. 88

Peace News 52
Peenemünde 13, 14, 19, 32, 33, 71
Perkins Ltd 62
Pincher, C. 87, 94
Powell, R. 51, 52, 69, 70, 97, 143
Princess Margaret 108
Project-E 91, 92
Project EMILY 107, 110, 129, 131, 138, 141

Quarles, D.A. 31, 45, 48, 50, 51, 54, 97, 143
Ramo-Wooldridge Corporation 29, 37, 44

RAF Flying Review 9, 89, 97, 98, 139, 145
RAF Groups
  No. 1 Group 56, 64, 65, 69, 80, 108, 145, 148
  No. 3 Group 56, 65, 69, 80, 90, 103, 108, 134
RAF Personnel
  Baldchin, Sqn Ldr L.A. 127
  Baldock, Sqn Ldr S.O. 108, 138
  Beetham, MRAF Sir M.J. 144
  Boast, Gp Capt R. 133
  Broadhurst, Air Mshl Sir H. 61, 69, 91, 105, 108, 110, 138, 148
  Bufton, AVM S.O. 96
  Burch, Sqn Ldr C.E. 125
  Burnett, AVM B.K. 103, 125, 134, 144, 145, 148
  Cairns, Flt Lt G. 127
  Cross, AVM K.B.B. 69, 103, 108, 110, 125, 131, 135, 136, 138, 139, 141, 142, 144, 148
  Coles, Air Cmdre W. 108
  Cooks, The Ven (AVM) F.W. 139

  Coulson, Sqn Ldr P.G. 102
  Dawson, ACM Sir W. 62, 105
  Emson, AVM R. 143
  Finlayson, Wg Cdr P.J. 101, 103
  Frogley, Gp Capt R.T. 102
  Gibson, Sqn Ldr G.P. 70, 71
  Glover, MPlt A.E. 102
  Haines, Wg Cdr E.R.G. 97

  Harris, Chf Tech H. 123
  Harman, Gp Capt R.F. 130
  Hayes, Sqn Ldr K. 111, 124, 126, 144, 145
  Henderson, Sqn Ldr R. 134
  Hudleston, Air Mshl Sir E. 132, 135, 148
  Horton, Sqn Ldr H.G. 140
  James, Cpl J. 123
  Jones, Sgt D. 85, 124
  Julian, Flt Lt W. 122
  Knight, Wg Cdr T. 71, 85, 100
  Kyle, AVM Sir W. 136, 144, 148
  Leatherdale. Sqn Ldr F.R. 105, 125, 126
  Lees, Air Mshl Sir R. 131, 148
  Melvin, Air Cdre J.D. 71
  Mills, ACM Sir G.H. 130, 143
  O'Flanagan, D. 72, 127
  Parselle, AVM T. 108
  Pike, MRAF Sir T.G. 131, 148
  Pratt, Chf Tech R. 124, 128
  Pretty, AVM W. 91, 97
  Probert, Sqn Ldr H.A. 114
  Rankin, Gp Capt L. 71
  Rich, Sgt P. 85, 144
  Roseby, Chf Tech W. 125, 144
  Searby, Air Cdre J.H. 61, 70, 91
  Sheen, AVM W. 100, 124
  Slater, Gp Capt K.R.C. 100
  Sloan, MPlt M.H. 102
  Smallwood, AVM D. 139
  Sword, Flt Lt W.E. 105
  Townend, Chf Tech L. 118, 125, 127, 128
  Tuttle, Air Mshl Sir G. 91, 97, 102, 108, 146
  Thynne, Wg Cdr W.A. 127
  Wherry, Wg Cdr G.H. 71
  Worsfold, Snr Tech B. 124
  Wild, Sqn Ldr J. 116
RAF Squadrons
  No.77(SM) 55, 64, 69, 87, 108, 111, 118, 126, 127, 132, 138, 144, 150
  No.82(SM) 137, 144, 145, 150
  No.83 (Pathfinder) 71
  No.97(SM) 97, 151
  No.98(SM) 76, 102, 133, 144, 147, 151
  No.102(SM) 106, 110, 126, 132, 147, 151
  No.104(SM) 64, 105, 143, 151
  No.106 70
  No.106(SM) 107, 125, 144, 145, 150
  No.107(SM) 126, 133, 139, 140, 144, 145, 150
  No.113(SM) 123, 133, 138, 144, 150
  No.130(SM) 151
  No.142(SM) 77, 106, 112, 113, 119, 123, 125-128, 151
  No.144(SM) 133, 151
  No.148 70
  No.150(SM) 119, 127, 151
  No.218(SM) 105, 110, 151
  No.220(SM) 106, 111, 33, 138, 139, 144, 145

  No.223(SM) 127, 138, 151
  No.226(SM) 106, 122, 125-127, 133, 136, 144, 145, 151
  No.240(SM) 132, 138, 139, 144, 145, 151
  No.242 OCU 62
  No.254(SM) 151
  No.269(SM) 151
  No.617 71
RAF Stations
  Bardney 49, 57, 61- 63, 71, 113, 123, 140, 151, 156
  Breighton 61, 63, 73, 109, 135, 137, 140, 151
  Brize Norton 55
  Caistor 57, 61, 63, 103, 106, 122, 125, 140, 151, 155
  Carnaby 49, 56, 61, 63, 73, 119, 135, 140, 151, 155, 156
  Catfoss 56, 61, 63, 73, 106, 134, 135, 140, 151, 156
  Church Fenton 61
  Coleby Grange 61, 63, 77, 106, 108, 112, 113, 122, 123, 140, 151, 156
  Cottesmore 65, 107, 151
  Desborough 62, 63
  Digby 61
  Dishforth 49, 50, 57, 58, 62, 63
  Driffield 49, 56-58, 61, 63, 65, 72, 73, 76, 79, 89, 94, 102, 104, 105, 108, 122, 134-137, 139, 140, 147, 151, 156
  East Kirkby 57
  East Moor 61
  Feltwell 12, 49, 56, 57, 60, 63-66, 70, 71, 76-80, 85, 89-94, 99, 104, 107, 108, 116, 118, 126, 132, 133, 137, 140, 145, 150, 155, 156
  Finningley 69, 108
  Folkingham 2, 63, 73, 107, 140, 151, 155
  Full Sutton 49, 57, 61, 63, 73, 106, 140, 151, 156
  Harrington 62, 63, 73, 104-106, 113, 125, 140, 151, 155
  Hemswell 49, 56-58, 60, 61, 63-65, 72, 77, 79, 85, 97, 105, 108, 112-114, 118, 121-123, 125, 127, 132, 133, 137-140, 143, 144, 147, 151, 156, 157
  Holme-on-Spalding Moor 49, 57, 61
  Honington 49, 56, 60, 77
  Hornsea 49
  Kelstern 61
  Kirmington 49
  Kimbolton 62, 63
  Lakenheath 43, 49, 65, 72, 79, 81-83, 87, 89, 91, 95, 123, 137, 138, 151
  Leeming 49, 57, 58, 61
  Leconfield 57, 58, 61, 65, 151
  Lindholme 69
  Ludford Magna 49, 57, 61, 63, 105, 111, 120, 140, 151, 155
  Marham 49, 56, 60, 77, 81
  Market Harborough 62
  Marston Moor 49, 57, 61

Melton Mowbray 2, 63, 73, 107, 140, 151, 155
Methwold 49, 57, 71, 79
Mepal 61, 63–66, 77, 85, 89, 105, 109, 140, 144, 150
Mildenhall 56, 57, 65, 72, 77
Neasham 49
North Luffenham 62, 63–65, 73, 79, 80, 94, 101, 103, 106, 126, 133, 139, 140, 147, 151, 156
Northolt 79, 101
North Pickenham 60, 63, 65, 77, 80, 82, 105–109, 112, 123, 134, 135, 137–140, 151, 156
North Witham 62
Pocklington 61
Polebrook 62, 63, 73, 107, 140, 151, 155
Riccall 57, 61, 63
Scampton 49, 65, 121, 151
Scorton 57, 61
Shepherds Grove 60, 63–65, 77, 89, 93, 123, 140, 150, 155, 156
Sherburn-in-Elmet 49, 57, 61
Spadeadam 59, 68, 70
Stradishall 49
Sturgate 57, 79, 105
Tuddenham 60, 63–65, 77, 105, 106, 108, 140, 150, 155, 157
Turweston 70
Waddington 57–59
Waterbeach 77, 56, 60, 77, 81, 109
Watton 49
Witchford 49, 56, 60, 61, 66
Wombleton 61
Wyton 77
Rayborn, Rear Admiral W.F. 22
Redstone Arsenal 18, 21, 36
RIM Building 77, 80, 81, 90, 91
RMS *Queen Mary* 124
Robertson, R.B. 26
Rocket Review 79, 85, 126
Rolls-Royce Ltd 47, 112, 130, 149
Rokossovskii, Gen K. 14
Ross, Lt-Col H.E. 139
Rowland, J. 28
Rubery, Owen & Co. Ltd 62
Rumbel, K. 22

SACEUR 11, 60, 67, 70, 92, 142
Sacramento – DAC Facility 101
Sandys, D. 46–48, 51–54, 56, 59, 62, 68–70, 80, 83, 88, 89, 93–95, 97, 108, 114, 129, 130, 138, 143
San Bernardino AFB 82, 120
Santa Maria Times 103, 125
Santa Monica 40, 54, 79, 82, 93, 101
Shinwell E. 121
Sir A McAlpine & Son Ltd 78
Soviet nuclear weapons
  RDS-1 18
  RDS-6 18
Spadeadam
Sprague, M.D. 130, 143

Sputnik-1 31, 38, 41, 51, 138
Stanford E.F.C. 144
Strategic Air Command (SAC) 6, 11, 17, 18, 20, 21, 23, 24, 26, 35, 43, 47, 49–51, 53, 55, 56, 61. 69, 72, 80, 81, 92, 101, 103, 108, 131–133, 142, 143
Strategic Missile Force – Readiness Policy 110
Stratton, S.S. 108
Stehlin, Gen P. 108
Suez Campaign 39, 43, 46, 70
Sunday Times, The, 93
Tactical Air Command (TAC) 11, 23, 26
TASS 52
Taylor, P.B. 108
Teapot Committee 25, 32
Thiel, Dr A.K. 29, 40
Thomson, Rear Admiral G.P. 88
Thor IRBM
  Arrival in UK 87–91
  Contract with Douglas 28
  First launch 40
  Launch Phases 115, 116, 118, 119
  Launch programme 44, 103
  Media and Press 27, 33, 43, 52, 53, 64, 83, 87 93, 96, 97, 101, 107, 139
  Origin of Name 28
  Run-down of bases 137–140

  Survey of UK launch sites 57–63, 71, 74, 75, 85, 88
  Thor Hauls 65, 72, 75, 81, 82
  Thor Phase Out Plan 137
  Thor Project 10th Progress Report 94
  Thor Project 13th Progress Report 125
  Thor Project 14th Progress Report 71
  Training Programme 29, 43, 50, 53, 54, 65, 89, 90, 93–96, 99, 100–107, 116
  Warhead 30, 40, 41, 43, 45, 55, 74, 76, 77, 82, 83, 90–95, 99, 103, 104, 106, 109, 115, 117, 120, 121, 130, 134, 137, 143, 147, 149
  Warhead – UK developed 83, 130, 143
  White Paper 52, 114
Thomas, H.M. 28
Thorneycroft, P. 129, 135
The Times 38, 126
Truax, R. 29
Trueheart, W.C. 108
Truman, H.S. 24

USAF Personnel
  Anderson, Gen S.E. 108
  Blanchard, Maj-Gen W.H. 91, 97, 101, 102, 108, 148
  Boggs, T/Sgt N.B. 126
  Broadhurst, Maj-Gen E.B. 108, 141, 148

Cole, Col G.P. 101
Eisenhart, Maj-Gen C.M. 141, 148
Hafner, Lt-Col G. 144
LeMay, Gen C.E. 17, 20, 35, 131
Mathis, Capt G.M. 126
Moll, Col K.L. 126
Power, Gen T.S. 27
Ray, Capt D. 128, 144
Schriever, Brig-Gen B.A. 24–27, 29, 36, 46
Smith, Lt Col W.D. 28
Tedrow, Lt-Col T.W. 126
Twining, Gen N.F. 143
Vandenberg, Gen H.S. 68
Wallace, Maj J. 54, 90
Weitlands, Maj G. 126
Westover, Maj-Gen C.B. 108, 148
White, Gen T.D. 41
Wolf, Maj R.E. 138
Zink, Col H. 53, 81
USAF Units
  1 Air Division 68
  1 Missile Division 50, 68, 101
  1607 MATS Wing 65
  3901 Combat Support Group 82
  392 Air Base Group 52
  392 Missile Training Squadron 51, 99
  422 Air Base Group 140
  48 Fighter Wing 123
  6591 Support Squadron 51
  672 Ballistic Missile Squadron 53, 81, 85
  7 Air Division 91, 102, 132, 148
  701 Tactical Missile Wing 39
  705 Strategic Missile Wing 65
  99 Munitions Maintenance Squadron 74, 76, 138, 139
USS *Midway* 17, 34

Vandenberg AFB 10, 42, 43, 51, 75, 99–103, 146
V-Bombers 21, 23, 24, 26, 29, 30, 33, 36, 44
Von Braun, W. 13–21, 23, 24, 26, 29, 30, 33, 36, 44
Von Braun, M. 14
Von Neumann, J. 25, 32, 37

Walker, P.G. 135
Ward, D.W. 52, 143
Ward, G. 48, 53, 55, 62, 69, 94
Warner, S. 128
Watkinson, H. 94, 97, 130
Willem Ruys 124
Wilson, C.E. 20, 22, 24, 27, 28, 31, 36, 46–48, 50, 68
Wright Air Development Center 11, 23

Yellow Sun 92

Zilliacus, K. 94
Zuckert, E.M. 135, 144

Printed in Great Britain
by Amazon